Professional
Live Communications Server

Fred,
Thanks for attending
the event today!

Stay in touch!

–Joe
10-4-2006

Professional
Live Communications Server

Joe Schurman

Randy Thomas

Bob Christian

Wiley Publishing, Inc.

Professional Live Communications Server

Published by
Wiley Publishing, Inc.
10475 Crosspoint Boulevard
Indianapolis, IN 46256
www.wiley.com

ISBN-13: 978-0-471-77321-4
ISBN-10: 0-471-77321-2

Manufactured in the United States of America

10 9 8 7 6 5 4 3 2 1

1MA/RT/QW/QW/IN

For general information on our other products and services or to obtain technical support, please contact our Customer Care Department within the U.S. at (800) 762-2974, outside the U.S. at (317) 572-3993 or fax (317) 572-4002.

Wiley also publishes its books in a variety of electronic formats. Some content that appears in print may not be available in electronic books.

Library of Congress Cataloging-in-Publication Data:

Professional Live Communications Server / by Joe Schurman ... [et al.].
   p. cm.
   Includes index.
   ISBN-13: 978-0-471-77321-4 (paper/website)
   ISBN-10: 0-471-77321-2 (paper/website)
   1. Microsoft Office live communications server. 2. Client/server computing. I. Schurman, Joe, 1977-
QA76.9.C55P753 2006
005.2'768—dc22

                2006011850

I would like to dedicate this book to my wife, Christy, and our kids, Paige, Bailey, and Davis, who have been so patient with me throughout this whole process. I have traveled most of the world during the writing of this book and they have been so awesome, even during my really busy days, and I couldn't be happier to have them in my life.

— Joe Schurman

About the Authors

Joe Schurman

Joe Schurman is the co-founder of Connected Innovation and is a member of the Microsoft Unified Communications Readiness team for Microsoft. As a Microsoft Most Valuable Professional for Live Communications Server, Joe is deployed globally to provide training for Microsoft employees, partners, and customers in each region of the world. Joe has authored several whitepapers, has developed many Live Communications Server 2005 SP1 readiness kits, provides global speaking engagements, sales and technical training world tours, Microsoft TechNet webcasts, and has developed the Microsoft Live Communications Server 2005 SP1 certification program, due out later this year. Joe's articles and comments have been featured in *Pocket PC Magazine, Waggener Edstrom, AMR Research, Wainhouse Research,* and several other publications. Joe is also a black belt in Chinese Kung Fu as well as a United States National Kung Fu judge.

Randy Thomas

Randy Thomas started his IT career as a support person for a company in Houston, and then was blessed enough to get an opportunity to become a consultant for a content management company during the tech boom. He traveled around the world for them for a long time, thanks to an incredibly understanding spouse and children. He thanks his wife, Abbie, and two daughters, Samantha and Emma, for being so gracious while he was always gone. After moving to Washington, D.C., he was granted some very nice government projects building CM and Portal solutions with high security. He had pretty much lost all passion for the IT industry until the day he started working with Live Communications Server and all that goes with it. He then began traveling around the world speaking about and training people on Live Communications Server and unified communications. Randy also spends a lot of time on the newsgroup sites where he tries to help as many people in the community as possible. Currently, he lives in The Woodlands, Texas, where baby number 3 is on the way.

Credits

Executive Editor
Chris Webb

Development Editor
Sydney Jones

Production Editor
William A. Barton

Copy Editor
Luann Rouff

Editorial Manager
Mary Beth Wakefield

Production Manager
Tim Tate

Vice President and Executive Group Publisher
Richard Swadley

Vice President and Publisher
Joseph B. Wikert

Project Coordinator
Michael Kruzil

Graphics and Production Specialists
Jonelle Burns
Denny Hager
Jake Mansfield
Barbara Moore
Shelley Norris
Lynsey Osborn
Heather Ryan

Quality Control Technician
Brian H. Walls

Media Development Specialists
Angela Denny
Kit Malone
Travis Silvers

Proofreading and Indexing
Techbooks

Contents

Contents

Contents

Contents

Contents

Acknowledgments

I would like to thank a bunch of people who assisted me in the writing of this book. To start, I would like to thank Debbie Davis, who gave me my first job in the IT industry, starting out at Compaq those many years ago. I would like to thank God for giving me the patience and determination to complete what has been one of the most tedious tasks of my entire career. I am forever in His grip! I would like to thank Jerry Smith for believing in me, and Eyal Inbar for the same, as well as helping me keep our delivery dates on time. Thanks, also, to the entire LCS product development team—all are truly stellar individuals. I would like to thank my co-authors, Randy and Bobby, for all of their help. I can't count how many times Randy helped me reviewing the chapters, and aided in the daunting task of all of our product image placements and naming. I would like to thank the Microsoft Unified Communications team, which is directed by Anoop Gupta and Gurdeep Singh Pall, for creating such an awesome product and inspiring so many of us. Microsoft Unified Communications will change the world and I'm glad to be a part of this exciting time. I want to thank the Microsoft gurus whom I have worked with on this book and on other projects. I would also like to thank my MVP leads, Kevin Engman and Mike Sampson, for inspiring me to put forth as much effort to help others as possible. The program has been so good to me and I am forever grateful!

— Joe Schurman

Introduction

The purpose of this book is to provide a real-world understanding of Microsoft Office Live Communications Server 2005 SP1. The book begins by providing an introduction to this technology and the suite of Unified Communications products offered by Microsoft, including a business introduction. Starting with Chapter 4 until the end of the book, we cover the lower level technical details of Live Communications Server and Communicator configuration, and provide notes from the field, which include troubleshooting information and where to find additional resources.

Who This Book Is For

This book is targeted for those who want to understand Microsoft Unified Communications products or are looking for an enterprise collaboration and communications solution, as well as those who need technical information related to Live Communications Server 2005 SP1 that cannot be found in existing technical whitepapers.

What This Book Covers

This book provides an introduction to and overview of Microsoft Unified Communications products, which include Live Communications Server 2005 SP1, Live Meeting 2005, and Communicator 2005. In addition, it offers technical configuration and troubleshooting information for Live Communications Server 2005 SP1 and Communicator 2005. This material covers Live Communications Server 2005 with Service Pack 1 and Communicator 2005 as part of the Microsoft Unified Communications product suite, which has recently been updated to the Microsoft Unified Communications group.

How This Book Is Structured

The chapters have been organized to begin with an introduction and overview of Microsoft Unified Communications products. Subsequent chapters explain how to introduce this technology to the enterprise. The heart of the book covers the technical configuration of Live Communications Server 2005 SP1 and Communicator 2005 for those who are deploying this technology or are reviewing this technology for deployment within their own infrastructure. We end the book by providing troubleshooting information, answers to frequently asked questions, resources, and templates for test plans and design guides.

What You Need to Use This Book

If you would like to follow along with some of the steps outlined in this book, we recommend that you deploy Live Communications Server 2005 SP1 on a physical or virtual server running Microsoft Windows Server 2003. To run Communicator 2005, you will need a physical or virtual PC running Windows XP or Windows Server 2003. To fully test Microsoft Office integration with Communicator 2005, you need to be running Microsoft Office 2003 with Service Pack 2.

Errata

We make every effort to ensure that there are no errors in the text or in the code. However, no one is perfect, and mistakes do occur. If you find an error in one of our books, such as a spelling mistake or faulty piece of code, we would be very grateful for your feedback. By sending in errata you may save another reader hours of frustration and at the same time you will be helping us provide even higher quality information.

To find the errata page for this book, go to www.wrox.com and locate the title using the Search box or one of the title lists. Then, on the book details page, click the Book Errata link. On this page you can view all errata that has been submitted for this book and posted by Wrox editors. A complete book list including links to each book's errata is also available at www.wrox.com/misc-pages/booklist.shtml.

If you don't spot "your" error on the Book Errata page, go to www.wrox.com/contact/techsupport .shtml and complete the form there to send us the error you have found. We'll check the information and, if appropriate, post a message to the book's errata page and fix the problem in subsequent editions of the book.

p2p.wrox.com

For author and peer discussion, join the P2P forums at p2p.wrox.com. The forums are a web-based system for you to post messages relating to Wrox books and related technologies, and to interact with other readers and technology users. The forums offer a subscription feature to e-mail you topics of interest of your choosing when new posts are made to the forums. Wrox authors, editors, other industry experts, and your fellow readers are present on these forums.

At http://p2p.wrox.com you will find a number of different forums that will help you not only as you read this book, but also as you develop your own applications. To join the forums, just follow these steps:

1. Go to p2p.wrox.com and click the Register link.
2. Read the terms of use and click Agree.
3. Complete the required information to join as well as any optional information you wish to provide and click Submit.
4. You will receive an e-mail with information describing how to verify your account and complete the joining process.

You can read messages in the forums without joining P2P but in order to post your own messages, you must join.

Once you join, you can post new messages and respond to messages other users post. You can read messages at any time on the Web. If you would like to have new messages from a particular forum e-mailed to you, click the Subscribe to this Forum icon by the forum name in the forum listing.

For more information about how to use the Wrox P2P, be sure to read the P2P FAQs for answers to questions about how the forum software works as well as many common questions specific to P2P and Wrox books. To read the FAQs, click the FAQ link on any P2P page.

Professional
Live Communications Server

1

Introducing Microsoft Unified Communications

Instant Messaging and integrated voice communications have become an everyday business and a personal necessity. The demand for Instant Messaging alone has increased dramatically over the past several years and is predicted to become the preferred communication solution over e-mail in the near future. Within the past year, billions of instant messages were sent each day, and will certainly increase due to the overwhelming popularity of having direct, real-time access to colleagues, friends, and family at the click of a button. Today's youth, which includes my own children, already communicate with one another via Instant Messaging using popular applications such as Yahoo Messenger, AOL Instant Messenger, and MSN Messenger. These applications have also emerged in small and enterprise businesses as preferred communication tools as a result of the immediate contact they enable. The use of Instant Messaging in the enterprise is changing the perception of Instant Messaging as an entertainment solution to a real-world business-critical application.

Of course, as Instant Messaging becomes more prevalent in the business community, security remains a primary concern. With the new threat of SPIM (Instant Messaging Spam) and Instant Messaging viruses, IM poses great risks to business organizations. Despite these risks, and alongside the need for a secure, unified communications solution, many other challenges face business users today. Based on surveys and polls taken over the past two years, the most common challenges include the following:

❑   Travel

❑   Telecommuting

❑   Distributed teams and global communication

❑   Time-to-market pressures

❑   Access to information and subject matter experts

❑   Cost reduction

Business users today are under serious pressure to provide even greater efficiency in all of their assigned tasks. With new government sanctions for compliance, reduced labor, and the globalization of the workplace with outsourcing, the ability to access information and expertise, while reducing travel and associated costs is extremely difficult. Time-to-market pressure has increased with the pressure applied to companies to provide products and results to validate shareholder investments. The corporate landscape has changed as well with reduced travel, increased telecommuting, and geographic disparity with outsourcing and globalization of the workforce. All of these challenges demand solutions to increase productivity and collaboration, while reducing costs. The Microsoft Unified Communications platform has placed a focus on providing a solution for each of these challenges, leaving time for innovation and ingenuity.

The purpose of this chapter is to provide an overview of the Microsoft Unified Communication platform and to introduce Microsoft Office Live Communications Server 2005 with Service Pack 1, a product that addresses the aforementioned business challenges by providing a unified platform of real-time communication and collaboration solutions. This chapter covers the following Microsoft Unified Communications components:

❑ Live Communications Server 2005 with Service Pack 1

❑ Session Initiation Protocol (SIP)

❑ Transport Layer Security (TLS)

❑ Microsoft Office Communicator 2005

Introducing Microsoft Office Live Communications Server with SP 1

Part of the Microsoft Office System and the Microsoft Unified Communications suite of products, Live Communications Server 2005 SP1 provides enterprise-level security, scalability, and performance by offering a flexible infrastructure and enterprise platform that enables real-time communication and collaboration. The launch of Live Communications Server 2005 SP1 was the answer to numerous customer and industry requested features, including telephony integration and call control features, Instant Messaging threat protection and filtering, and the most exciting feature of them all, Public Instant Messaging Connectivity (PIC). The PIC feature within Live Communications Server now provides the capability to communicate with popular public Instant Messaging applications, including Yahoo Instant Messenger, AOL Instant Messenger, MSN Messenger, and a new client application called Microsoft Office Communicator 2005. With the Communicator 2005 client, a user can now seamlessly communicate with co-workers, business partners, customers, friends, and family with one client application. The purpose of Microsoft's "unified communications" vision is not only to supply customers with a solution that fits their immediate needs, but also to provide a foundation for future development and enhancements. As many companies are starting to implement Instant Messaging and real-time communications technologies within their enterprise infrastructure, Live Communications Server provides a complete solution, and one that is integrated within the Microsoft Office suite of products. Moreover, it provides an application interface to enable communications, presence, and collaboration features to be built into custom applications. By building the Unified Communications products within the Office suite of products, Microsoft was able to provide customers with desired features within products with which they are already familiar. Millions of users start their day with Microsoft Office, including Microsoft Outlook, Excel, PowerPoint, and SharePoint. The Unified Communications vision is to provide interoperability with the Office suite of products to increase productivity, while maintaining desktop familiarity and ease of use. Realizing their original vision only three years later, users can now work within one suite of applications, rather than manage separate and disconnected applications.

Microsoft Office Communicator 2005

Another exciting Unified Communications product is the Live Communications Server client, Microsoft Office Communicator 2005. Microsoft Office Communicator 2005 is the new client for Live Communications Server 2005 SP1. With features that include Instant Messaging, audio/video communication, whiteboarding, application sharing, and conferencing capabilities, the Communicator 2005 client has gained enormous popularity, especially with public Instant Messaging integration and telephony integration. A major feature of the Communicator 2005 client is the capability to integrate with existing telephony services. With the Remote Call Control (RCC) feature, the Communicator 2005 client application controls a Private Branch Exchange (PBX) phone system that provides users with features such as call answering and call forwarding. This feature enables users to make and accept calls, and forward calls to other phone numbers, truly liberating users from their desktop phone. Another telephony integration feature of Communicator 2005 is the Public Switched Telephone Network (PSTN) service. With PSTN integration, individuals can use the Communicator 2005 client to leverage conference calling services and Voice over Internet Protocol (VoIP) conversations.

Microsoft Office Live Meeting 2005

To reduce travel costs and to increase global communication, Microsoft has released an additional Microsoft Unified Communications product: Microsoft Office Live Meeting 2005. With Live Meeting, business users now have the ability to launch products, mobilize meetings and conferences, provide live and on-demand training services, and present new ideas without connection boundaries. Integrated with PSTN services and the capability to record meeting and audio sessions, Live Meeting enables true meeting productivity without the need for travel. Live Meeting enhances the Unified Communications portfolio by providing event services, online business meetings, training, customer support, and presentation capabilities. All of this is made possible with features such as PowerPoint, Office Document, PDF, and other data resource uploading. These features enable users to enjoy vibrant presentation, whiteboarding, and application sharing, including live demonstrations and attendee interaction with surveys, polls, and attendee mood awareness. With Live Meeting, presentations and training sessions can be realized regardless of where the participants are located; each service can be cast remotely with only one requirement: an Internet connection. With Live Meeting attendee interaction functionality, presenters and trainers can obtain instant feedback, and more intelligent pre-meeting or event attendee intelligence through the Live Meeting registration system. Rounding out the Microsoft Unified Communications vision, Live Meeting provides capabilities that meet today's business challenges by enabling cost-effective collaboration and communication by reducing or eliminating the need for travel.

The Business Value of Presence

While mobile communications have brought contacts closer than before, the game of "phone tag" is still being played. Instant Messaging technologies present something that telecommunications companies do not offer regarding the ability to view the status of a given contact. Within Instant Messaging applications, contacts can utilize basic presence settings such as Offline, Online, and Away, but with Microsoft Office Communicator 2005, contacts have enhanced presence status settings with features such as integration with PBX and PSTN services and the Microsoft Office Outlook 2003 Calendar presence and schedule. With the provided integration functionality, the Communicator 2005 client will update status automatically based on the availability of the individual. For example, if individuals are scheduled to be in a meeting per their Outlook 2003 calendar, then their Communicator 2005 client will automatically update to the status of "In a Meeting." Now, an individual's co-workers can see that the contact is signed into the system but is in a meeting and should not be disturbed unless absolutely necessary.

Many organizations are now globally dispersed, with employees working in other countries and in multiple time zones. With presence-enabled applications, co-workers, customers, and business partners can decide to use e-mail instead of Instant Messaging to send a communication, expecting a response whenever the individual is online again. This is part of the Microsoft Unified Communications vision combining Exchange Server and Outlook with Live Communications Server, Communicator 2005, and Live Meeting. Another scenario includes waiting for an individual to become available. With Microsoft Office Communicator 2005, contacts can not only see each other's presence, but also when they will be available again. With the Communicator 2005 "tagging" feature, contacts can tag one another so that when they become available or online, a message is presented to the awaiting contact letting them know that the contact they tagged is now available for communication. The value of presence is so great that Microsoft decided to build presence integration within many products, starting with the Office system as the foundation, by enabling presence within Microsoft Office, Live Meeting, and SharePoint (SharePoint Portal Server and Windows SharePoint Services). To further extend presence integration, Microsoft has provided an application interface for Live Communications Server to enable presence functionality within custom developed applications.

Providing Secure Communications

In many businesses today, Instant Messaging has become the preferred method of interpersonal communication, surpassing e-mail, and it will likely become the preferred method of online communication within the next 5–10 years. Many companies are already heavily dependent upon Instant Messaging applications, specifically within trading organizations and call centers. Most messaging occurs between co-workers, but a recent trend has seen a shift in which partners and customers are reliant on Instant Messaging as well. This dependency has also attracted parties that are interested in leveraging these communications for their own purposes, both benign and malicious. As SPAM has attacked the e-mail community, SPIM, a new form of SPAM, is quickly becoming prevalent in Instant Messaging applications today. Business owners and information technology (IT) decision makers have been faced with securing these communications or banning them completely.

When contemplating which type of Instant Messaging application to deploy, three scenarios present themselves. The first scenario is to enable public Instant Messaging applications provided by companies such as Yahoo, MSN, AOL, and others, which creates a major security breach. The second scenario is to ban Instant Messaging applications altogether, which will result in employee, business partner, and customer dissatisfaction or users who decide to install and use Instant Messaging applications against company policy. The third scenario is to provide users with a client that is secure and manageable. If a company decides to choose the third scenario to deploy a secured and managed Instant Messaging application, limited options are available. Essentially, customers need to decide between Live Communications Server and alternative options such as IBM Sametime. The problem with products like IBM Sametime is that when deployed, users lose the ability to communicate with contacts who are using MSN, Yahoo, or AOL Instant Messaging clients. With Live Communications Server and Communicator 2005, companies can provide their users with a single client that includes connectivity to public Instant Messaging networks and other LCS environments, securely. Live Communications Server dominates the market with this solution, as other applications such as Trillion require users to have an account set up with each public Instant Messaging provider before they can establish communication. With Live Communications Server and Communicator 2005, there is one client and one account, which enables direct access to all the public Instant Messaging networks.

Beyond the rich features and capabilities of the Microsoft Office Communicator 2005 client, Live Communications Server provides multiple layers of security. The first level of security is enabled with the integration of Live Communications Server and Active Directory. LCS uses Active Directory to authenticate users of the Live Communications Server service by validating a user's Active Directory account. Adding another layer of protection, LCS provides Transport Layer Security (TLS) for client connectivity to the Live Communications Server environment, which requires digital certificates to authenticate trusted users and servers within an LCS environment. Implementing certificates within your Live Communications Server environment will ensure a chain of trusted authentication from client to server. Leveraging certificates with Live Communications Server provides encryption for Instant Messaging conversations.

Implementing anti-virus solutions for your Live Communications Server environment is as critical as securing e-mail communications, a lesson learned after many infamous viruses such as the "Melissa" and "I Love You" viruses. With the provided security features included with Live Communications Server 2005 SP1, companies can secure their environment in numerous ways: by disabling URLs within Instant Messaging conversations, by preventing SPIM using the SPIM filter tool, by encrypting communications using Transport Layer Security, by preventing viruses using solutions such as the Microsoft-owned Sybari Antigen product, and by managing the entire environment via Group Policy settings.

Live Communications Server 2005 SP1 Server Roles

Live Communications Server 2005 SP1 is available in two separate versions that vary according to size and type of deployment. Live Communications Server 2005 SP1 Standard Edition is targeted at smaller businesses or single-server implementations, as the Standard Edition only requires one server and includes a scaled-down database using Microsoft MSDE, supporting up to 15,000 users per server. Live Communications Server 2005 SP1 Enterprise Edition provides a scalable and high-performance LCS deployment that includes load balancing, a tiered architecture, and a back-end SQL Server database with cluster support, supporting 20,000 users per server.

Included with the available Standard and Enterprise Edition versions of the software, Live Communications Server provides additional server roles to enable specific features for a Live Communications Server deployment. This section provides an overview of the following server roles that are available, which provide additional features such as IM Archiving, remote access, branch office access, routing, and telephony integration:

- ❑ Live Communications Server Access Proxy
- ❑ Live Communications Server Proxy
- ❑ Live Communications Server Director
- ❑ Live Communications Server Front-End Pool Servers
- ❑ Live Communications Server Back-End SQL Server Database
- ❑ Live Communications Server IM Archiving Server
- ❑ Live Communications Server SIP/PSTN Gateway

Live Communications Server Access Proxy

A Live Communications Server 2005 SP1 Access Proxy Server is used to enable remote access for users connecting to a Live Communications Server environment without the need for a Virtual Private Network (VPN) connection. It is also used for federation with other Live Communications Server environments and to enable integration with the popular Public Instant Messaging Connectivity (PIC) service with Yahoo, MSN, and AOL. Enabling connectivity without the use of a VPN connection has become a new standard for Microsoft enterprise server products, including Microsoft Exchange Server 2003. Remote access is a required feature for enterprise organizations, as it enables the capability to offer collaboration and communication solutions to partners, customers, branch offices, and external resources. Figure 1-1 depicts the Live Communications Server 2005 SP1 Access Proxy server.

As Live Communications Server penetrates the marketplace, LCS-enabled organizations want the capability to connect with other organizations that are also running Live Communications Server within their environment. This connectivity between Live Communications Server environments is called *federation*. Federation enables multiple organizations that have deployed Live Communications Server to communicate with one another directly or through what is called a Live Communications Server *clearing house* solution, such as companies that are members of industry-specific organizations. Both the federated and clearing house connectivity options require the Live Communications Server Access Proxy.

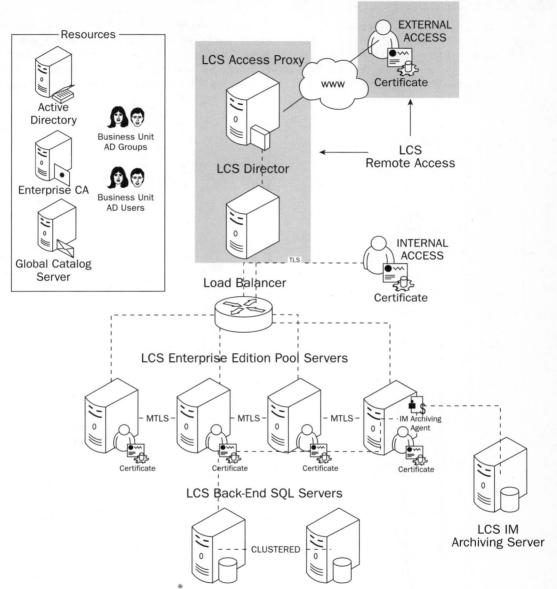

Resources

Active Directory

Business Unit AD Groups

Enterprise CA

Business Unit AD Users

Global Catalog Server

LCS Access Proxy

EXTERNAL ACCESS

www

Certificate

LCS Director

LCS Remote Access

INTERNAL ACCESS

TLS

Certificate

Load Balancer

LCS Enterprise Edition Pool Servers

MTLS — MTLS — MTLS — IM Archiving Agent

Certificate   Certificate   Certificate   Certificate

LCS Back-End SQL Servers

CLUSTERED

LCS IM Archiving Server

Figure 1-1

Live Communications Server Proxy

Applications that provide Instant Messaging and real-time communications are becoming more common than ever. Leveraging the Live Communications Server Proxy, organizations can build real-time applications using the LCS Proxy as an interface between applications that use the Live Communications Server service and the Live Communications Server Enterprise Edition or Standard Edition servers. The Live Communications Server Proxy acts as an application proxy, as depicted in Figure 1-2, enabling data transfer to and from applications that are utilizing the LCS service.

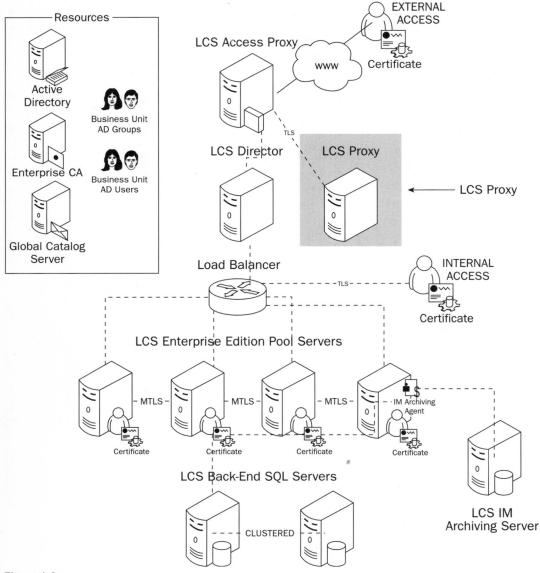

Figure 1-2

The Live Communications Server Proxy provides developers with the capability to write custom real-time applications that leverage the LCS Application Programming Interfaces (APIs). Exposing these components also enables developers to integrate existing Line of Business (LOB) applications to take advantage of the communication, collaboration, and presence features of the Live Communications Server service. For example, integrating LCS with mapping and Geographical Information System (GIS) systems, mobile applications, or even workflow applications provides existing applications with enhanced features.

The Live Communications Server Proxy also provides branch office access to an LCS environment. By using an LCS Proxy, instead of having remote offices all connect through an LCS Access Proxy directly, the LCS Proxy can compress the packets sent from these users to the LCS server environment. The LCS Proxy then sends these client requests to the LCS Access Proxy to route the users to their appropriate LCS server.

Live Communications Server Director

While LCS Access Proxy Servers enable remote connectivity into a Live Communications Server environment, the Live Communications Server Director performs the authentication of the remote user within Active Directory. By design, the Live Communications Server Access Proxy Server does not access the internal directory because an Access Proxy is meant to live on the outside edge of the network. The Director receives the requests from the Access Proxy and then authenticates and transfers each user to a Live Communications Server Standard Edition or Enterprise Edition server.

Figure 1-3 shows a diagram depicting the Live Communications Server Director within a Live Communications Server environment.

Although the Live Communications Server Director is not a required component of a Live Communications Server environment, it is heavily recommended. It helps buffer external communications and handles integration with telephony-based services such as the PBX and PSTN services, which most enterprise and mid-market companies utilize. The Live Communications Server Director provides a layer of abstraction for the Live Communications Server Access Proxy as well so that custom applications that leverage the Live Communications Server APIs do not have direct access into the system. With a Live Communications Server Director deployed, these applications will have a route configured within the Live Communications Server Director console, which allows for better management and control of the internal Live Communications Server environment.

Live Communications Server Front-End Servers

Live Communications Server 2005 SP1 Enterprise Edition is deployed using the concept of a pool of servers. That may be alarming to customers who are already concerned about the amount of required servers to support a Live Communications Server environment, but in order to provide a scalable and highly available solution, the pool architecture enables a Live Communications Server environment with a redundant amount of servers, enabling servers to be removed and replaced in case of system failure or to support growth, i.e., adding more users to the system, easing the pain of enterprise Information Technology administrators. A Live Communications Server pool comprises Live Communications Server pool servers (Front-End) Enterprise Edition Servers and Live Communications Server Back-End SQL Servers. Each Live Communications Server pool can provide service for up to 100,000 users. Each LCS pool server communicates with other servers in the pool to provide highly available user support. This communication occurs over a newly introduced transport called *Mutual Transport Layer Security (MTLS)*, which is an enhanced version of Secured Sockets Layer (SSL) that provides encryption of the communication between users and servers.

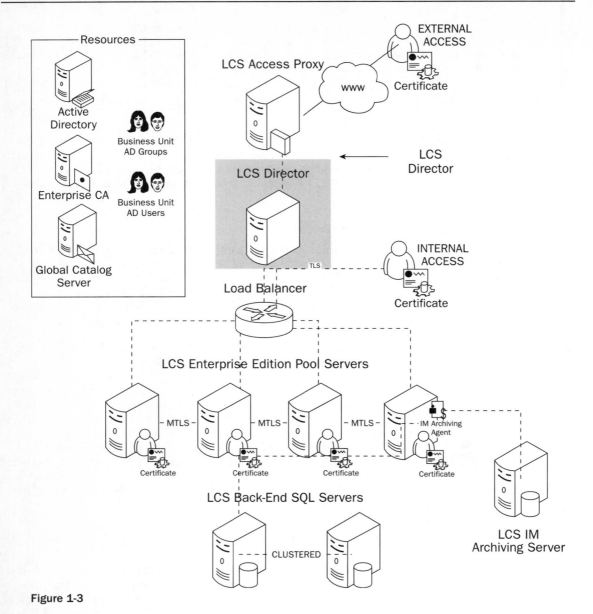

Figure 1-3

Figure 1-4 shows a diagram depicting a Live Communications Server Enterprise Edition pool server within a Live Communications Server environment.

The Live Communications Server Enterprise Edition architecture provides excellent support for organizations that are dispersed globally. Large organizations can deploy Live Communications Server pools in different locations to limit the bandwidth of users communicating overseas or to simply provide a highly scalable and highly available service to its users.

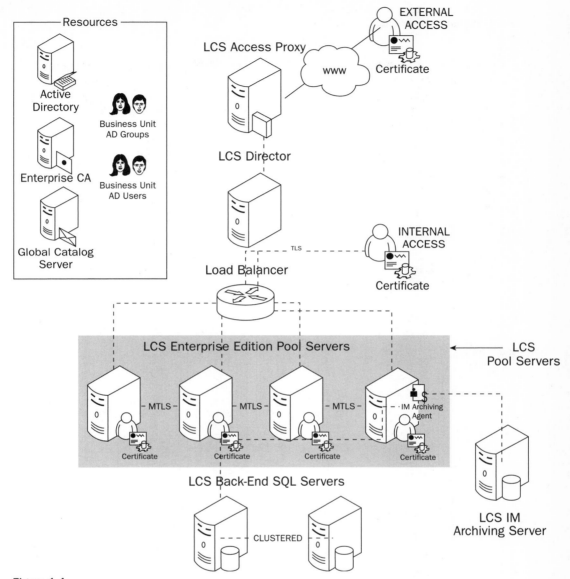

Figure 1-4

Live Communications Server Back-End Servers

The Live Communications Server Back-End Server maintains all of the LCS configuration information as well as LCS user data. This information includes presence information, server configuration data, contact lists, and block and allow settings. The Live Communications Server Back-End Server requires Microsoft SQL Server 2000 with Service Pack 3a at a minimum, and at present Microsoft SQL Server 2005 is currently being tested for full support. Leveraging SQL Server database functionality enables scalability in that SQL Server can be clustered for performance and fail-over purposes. SQL Server databases can also be attached to back-end Storage Area Network (SAN) storage systems for even more storage capacity.

Figure 1-5 shows a diagram depicting the Live Communications Server Back-End Server within a Live Communications Server environment.

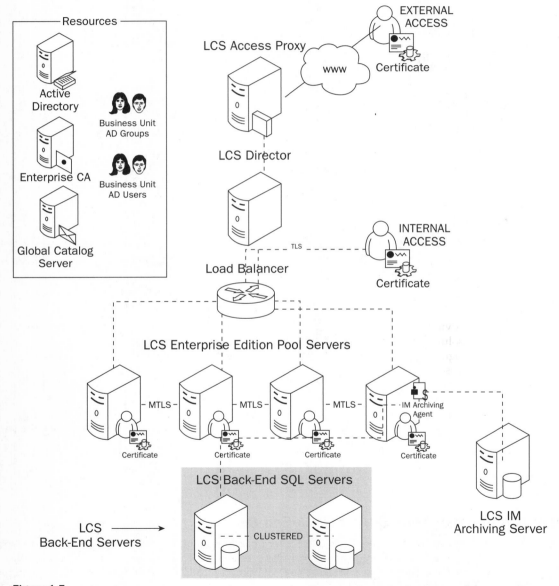

Figure 1-5

Within a Live Communications Server deployment, it is important to place emphasis on back-up and restore services for the Live Communications Server Back-End SQL Servers so that if data is lost on one server, it is available on either the clustered server or back-up tape drive. Regarding the back-up support of a Live Communications Server Back-End server, note that the LCS system is a real-time system, so log shipping and tape backups will not provide a real backup of the system; therefore, they are not supported as part of a Live Communications Server environment. Enabling SQL Server clustering for an LCS environment supports a scenario whereby should one Live Communications Server Back-End Server fail, the Live Communications Server service continues to be operational. Conversely, in an LCS environment with only one Live Communications Server Back-End Server, should that server fail, then all Live Communications Server services terminate immediately.

Live Communications Server IM Archiving

The Live Communications Server IM Archiving Service is an optional service that enables archiving of Instant Messages sent between LCS users. Enabling the IM Archiving Service provides businesses with the capability to archive communications of individual users. The IM Archiving Service is a powerful feature that continues to push the privacy boundaries; nonetheless, it is a necessary service for companies that want to archive communications for security or compliance purposes. The IM Archiving Service, like the Live Communications Server Enterprise Edition Server, requires Microsoft SQL Server 2000 with Service Pack 3a. With SQL Server maintaining archived messages, organizations can build custom reports that provide transcripts of actual messages that have been sent between users of the system, which can be helpful for compliance purposes. For example, for companies that must adhere to compliance policies such as HIPPA and Sarbanes-Oxley, the Live Communications Server IM Archiving Service is a great feature for conversation record retention. In addition, the archived messages can be integrated with existing record retention applications, which maintain existing digital records and messages from other applications such as e-mail and data within an enterprise environment.

Figure 1-6 shows a diagram depicting the Live Communications Server IM Archiving Service within a Live Communications Server environment.

Third-party providers such as IMlogic and Akonix have enhanced the Live Communications Server IM archiving solution by providing more robust and compliance-related features. I recommend the use of the IMlogic IM Manager application for Live Communications Server. This solution provides superior features for IM archiving and compliance. For more information, visit IMlogic's website at www.imlogic.com.

Live Communications Server SIP/PSTN Gateway

Another powerful feature of Live Communications Server 2005 SP1 is the integration of telephony services such as Voice over Internet Protocol (VoIP), Private Branch eXchange (PBX) integration, and Public Switched Telephone Network (PSTN) integration. To enable integration between your Live Communications Server environment and a PSTN service such as Verizon Business or British Telecom, the LCS environment must be configured with a Live Communications Server SIP/PSTN Gateway. The Live Communications Server SIP/PSTN Gateway enables users to place a VoIP call using Microsoft Office Communicator 2005.

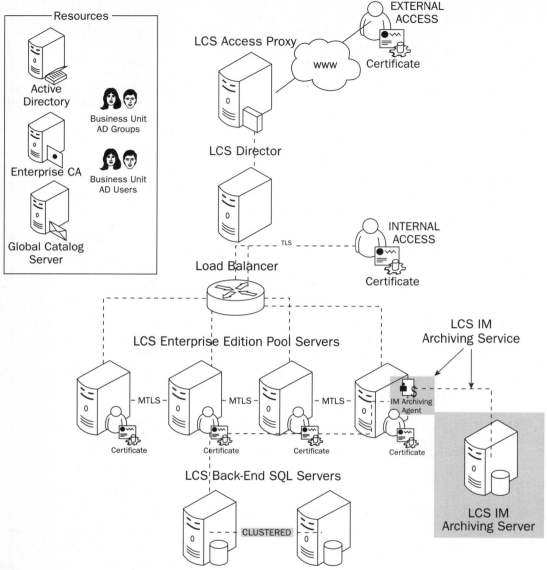

Figure 1-6

Figure 1-7 shows a diagram depicting the Live Communications Server PSTN Gateway within a Live Communications Server environment.

The Live Communications Server PSTN Gateway component is another step in Microsoft's collaborative offerings to enhance the way people communicate within one another without boundaries, making communications more productive. Live Communications Server 2005 SP1 also provides integration with existing PBX systems by providing Remote Call Control (RCC) to control the phone line in order to receive and make calls using the Communicator 2005 client. No longer are you limited to your desk phone: If you are away from the office, you can still receive calls made to your office line directly from the Communicator 2005 client. In addition, once a call is received, you have other telephony features available, such as call transferring so that you can transfer an incoming call to your mobile phone or device of choice.

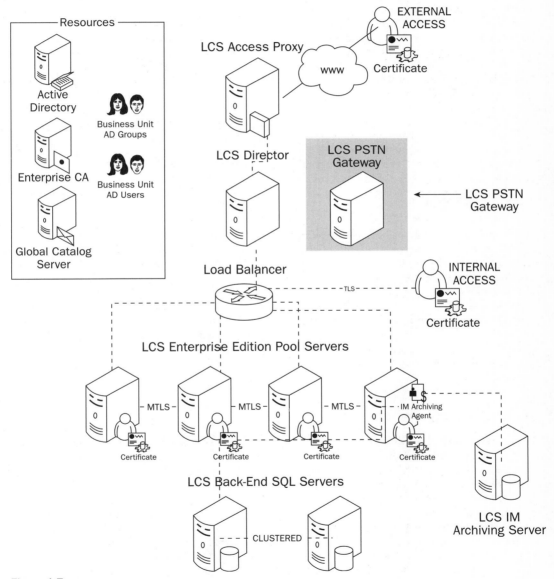

Figure 1-7

Introducing Session Initiation Protocol

Session Initiation Protocol (SIP) is the protocol that Live Communications Server uses to transfer messages between Live Communications Server clients. While this book introduces SIP for its use within Live Communications Server, I recommend that you read the Request for Comment (RFC) 3261, available via the Internet by browsing to www.ietf.org/rfc/rfc3261.txt. To describe SIP in laypersons' terms, SIP messages are initiated by a client application that requests information from a SIP server. SIP manages not only instant messages, but also multimedia communications as a whole. In relation to Live Communications Server, Microsoft Office Communicator 2005 and Windows Messenger both initiate SIP requests to a Live Communications Server, and the Live Communications Server responds to each client by sending and receiving instant messages, invoking collaboration requests that include whiteboard sharing, and invoking video and voice communications. This is why when enterprises are interested in integrating Live Communications Server with their VoIP service, the VoIP routers and phones must be SIP compliant in order to provide a seamless connection.

Session Initiation Protocol is the primary multimedia messaging protocol and it is heavily used not only by Live Communications Server, but also by VoIP, PSTN, and PBX providers, as these solutions are becoming increasingly popular in the commercial and residential markets. You've likely heard the Vonage "Woo Hooo" commercial more than one million times. The point is that telephony services, instant communications, and collaboration are now both here and in demand, and Live Communications Server is the best interface for this technology with the release of Microsoft Office Communicator 2005.

Real-time communications have become a necessity among business and consumer markets. The demand for instant communications between individuals has reached an unprecedented level, communications that include not only Instant Messaging, but integrated video, voice, and collaboration communication. Although many people think of teenagers as the prime users of Instant Messaging and webcams, using popular technologies that include Yahoo Messenger, AOL Instant Messenger, and MSN Messenger, these applications have emerged in the business landscape and are rapidly becoming a preferred tool of communication over e-mail. Why not? You can now reach someone immediately and in return receive an immediate response. As suggested earlier, the main issue involved with enabling these popular applications within a business enterprise today is that public network messaging applications do not provide the level of security that businesses require to protect corporate data and communications.

SIP Architecture

SIP is divided into three different components. A SIP *proxy* receives client requests and then determines where to forward these requests (to other SIP servers). With regard to Live Communications Server, a client using Microsoft Office Communicator 2005 sends a SIP request to an LCS SIP proxy server, which sends the request to a Live Communications Server pool server or Standard Edition server. The Live Communications Server pool server or Standard Edition server then acts as the next component of an SIP server: a SIP *redirect server*. A redirect server receives requests from a SIP proxy or a SIP client directory and then responds to a client as to where the message is to be sent. The final SIP component is an SIP *registrar server*, which receives a SIP client request and then maps that client to a specific SIP uniform resource identifier (URI). The SIP URI is the sign-in name that LCS users will use to sign into the LCS service. It is important that you first outline what the SIP URI for your company or customer will be before deploying LCS, as the SIP URI will be a user's identity for all Microsoft Unified Communications products. Currently, the best practice is to use a client's e-mail address as the SIP URI, such as user1@companyname.com. Properly planning how the company will set SIP URIs for each client will prove useful in later stages of a Live Communications Server deployment and for future use of Microsoft Unified Communications products.

SIP Methods

Session Initiation Protocol uses its own methods to communicate SIP messages between SIP clients and SIP servers. Similar to other Internet protocols, SIP provides a messaging structure. SIP messages include the following methods:

❑ INVITE

❑ ACK

❑ BYE

❑ CANCEL

❑ OPTIONS

❑ REGISTER

❑ SUBSCRIBE

❑ NOTIFY

❑ MESSAGE

❑ INFO

❑ SERVICE

❑ NEGOTIATE

❑ REFER

Each SIP message request requires a method, a SIP URI, and the version of SIP that the message request is using. The following table describes briefly each SIP method.

SIP Method	Method Description
ACK	The ACK and INVITE message are synonymous in that they are sent together by an initiating client. The ACK method verifies that the session has been initiated.
BYE	The BYE method terminates the SIP session. This method would be used by a contact that has finished its session with another contact and is ready to exit the session.
CANCEL	A CANCEL method is used by a client that may have a pending message request that it wants to cancel, terminating the request, but not the session. This would be used if a contact wanted to initiate a collaboration sharing session with another contact and then decided to cancel the request, although both contacts could continue other messaging requests such as Instant Messaging each other.

Table continued on following page

SIP Method	Method Description
INFO	The INFO method is used to notify a SIP client about information regarding the contact or contacts with whom a specific contact is initiating a message. For example, in LCS, when a Microsoft Office Communicator 2005 client is Instant Messaging another user, the INFO method is used to indicate whether the other contact is typing a message. The INFO method is also used with 3PCC gateways that allow you to control and view events for your desktop phone. These INFO messages send commands to the PBX and are used to receive events from the PBX.
INVITE	This method initiates a SIP message, including the identifying information for each SIP client as well as the type of message that is to be exchanged (Instant Message, Collaboration, etc.). The INVITE method initiates all sessions and is the root method for SIP.
MESSAGE	The MESSAGE method is used for SIP Instant Messaging sessions. The MESSAGE method contains the actual text message body that one contact sends to another.
NEGOTIATE	The NEGOTIATE method is used to implement settings such as message compression. When used, this is the first SIP message that servers will exchange after TLS negotiation has completed and before user-level SIP data is exchanged.
NOTIFY	SIP clients receive a NOTIFY method response when a SUBSCRIBE event occurs. An example of the NOTIFY method in LCS is when a Microsoft Office Communicator 2005 client receives a notification that they have been added to a contact list.
OPTIONS	The OPTIONS method is used by a SIP client to determine which features have been enabled by the SIP service or other SIP-compliant devices. Regarding Live Communications Server, the Microsoft Office Communicator 2005 client will verify the options available for a contact to use during messaging sessions.
REFER	The SIP REFER method is more commonly known in the VoIP world for forwarding calls. Within Microsoft Office Communicator 2005, you can forward incoming calls to a mobile phone using the REFER method.
REGISTER	The REGISTER method is used to sign users in using their assigned SIP URI.
SERVICE	SIP uses the SERVICE method to add or search for contacts. The SERVICE method uses Simple Object Access Protocol (SOAP) to carry these data transactions. Remember that the Live Communications Server Back-End Server will receive data when a user adds a contact to his or her contacts list or changes other client settings, so the SERVICE method needs to use a messaging protocol that is transaction-based in order to do this, i.e., SOAP.
SUBSCRIBE	SIP clients use the SUBSCRIBE method to subscribe to specific events, including presence status and contact settings such as the allow and block profiles. It also enables clients to be added to contact lists and groups.

Microsoft Office Communicator 2005 utilizes these SIP methods for client registration and to send messages between clients and servers. Figure 1-8 depicts an example of SIP methods that are used by Microsoft Office Communicator 2005.

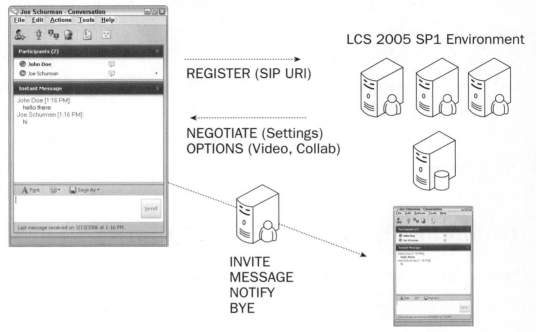

Figure 1-8

SIP Messages

Using the methods described in the previous section, SIP messages are used to communicate requests and responses between SIP clients and SIP servers. The following is an example of a SIP request message:

```
INVITE sip:joes@connectedinnovation.com SIP/2.1
Via: SIP/2.0/UDP workstation1.connectedinnovation.com
Max-Forward: 70
To: "Joe" <sip:joes@connectedinnovation.com>
From: "Dan Willis" <sip:danw@awesome.com>;tag=456
Call-ID: 972-555-5555@192.168.1.102
CSeq: 1 INVITE
Contact: <sip:danw@awesome.com>
Content-Type: application/sdp
Content-Length: 200
```

In this example, Dan Willis is sending an invitation to initiate a messaging session with me. If I want to communicate with Dan, even when it's 2 A.M., I will respond with the following SIP response message:

```
SIP/2.0 200 OK
Via: SIP/2.0/UDP workstation1.connectedinnovation.com
To: "Joe" <sip:joes@connectedinnovation.com>;tag=987
From: "Dan Willis" <sip:danw@awesome.com>;tag=123
Call-ID: 972-555-5555@192.168.1.102
CSeq: 1 INVITE
Contact: <sip:joes@connectedinnovation.com>192.168.1.103
Content-Type: application/sdp
Content-Length: 200
```

As you can see, SIP messages contain the information required for one contact to communicate with another contact, much like our mobile and digital phones use to contact one another — for example, when someone calls you on the phone and you see the Caller ID. Caller ID is one of many settings that are negotiated between callers.

Introducing Transport Layer Security

Transport Layer Security (TLS) is the security protocol that is enabled for use within a Live Communications Server environment to provide encryption and authentication trusts between LCS clients. This book provides an overview of TLS, so I encourage you to read the RFC 2246 for TLS. As the next evolution of SSL, TLS continues to provide an encrypted transport for messaging traffic to be sent and received. Enabling TLS within a Live Communications Server environment, like SSL in a web server environment, requires a Public Key Infrastructure (PKI), which requires certificate configuration and application on both the client and server devices. Live Communications Server requires each server to have a TLS certificate installed, while the root Enterprise Certificate Authority that issued the server certificates must be trusted on the client device, whether it is a laptop, desktop, or mobile device.

Figure 1-9 shows an architecture diagram that depicts how TLS and Mutual Transport Layer Security (MTLS), described in the following section, are used for client-to-server and server-to-server communications within a Live Communications Server environment.

Live Communications Server does not require TLS for client-to-server communication, as it offers TCP as its default communication protocol and uses Active Directory to authenticate users, but it does require MTLS for server-to-server communication, which means if you are deploying a LCS Enterprise Edition pool or multiple LCS servers, you will need to enable MTLS connectivity between servers. Enabling TLS within your Live Communications Server environment will provide the level of security that is required to encrypt and authenticate messages between your Live Communications Server users and servers.

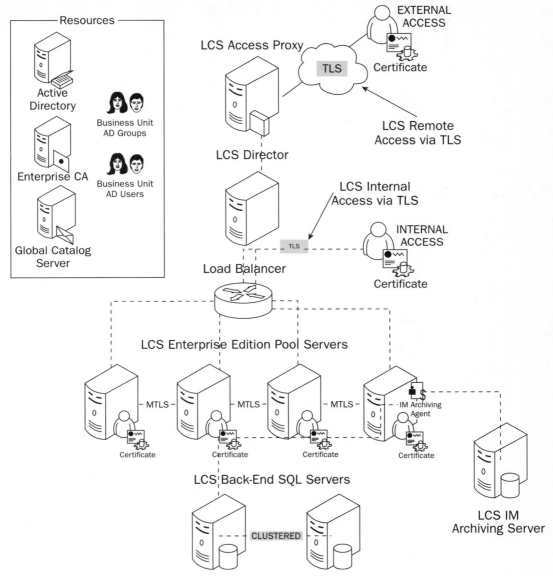

Figure 1-9

MTLS

Live Communications Server also uses Mutual Transport Layer Security (MTLS) to configure a trust between Live Communications Server servers. A server certificate is applied within the Live Communications Server console to enable a MTLS connection from one Live Communications Server to another with an Extended Key Usage (EKU) setting of Server Authentication. MTLS is also used to provide secure connectivity to the public Instant Messaging networks, which include Yahoo, MSN, and AOL.

Introducing Microsoft Office Communicator 2005

Without the Microsoft Office Communicator 2005 client, Live Communications Server would just be a service. The attraction to the Live Communications Server solution is primarily due to the features and functionality present in the Communicator 2005 client, with its capability to enable secure Instant Messaging, communication and telephony integration, as well as the capability it offers to connect with public Instant Messaging contacts through one client application. This section highlights some of the most popular features within Microsoft Office Communicator 2005. For more detailed information, please visit the Microsoft Live Communications Server website via www.microsoft.com/lcs.

Communicator 2005 Features

Microsoft Office Communicator 2005 is packed full of features and functionality beyond Instant Messaging. Based on customer requests and common use of existing Instant Messaging application features, Communicator 2005 provides the following features out of the box:

❑ **Instant Messaging:** Instant Messaging is provided for Communicator 2005 users to contact one another or public Instant Messaging applications such as Yahoo Messenger, AOL Instant Messenger, and MSN Messenger, as shown in Figure 1-10.

❑ **Contact Search:** This feature provides the capability to search for a contact by name, as shown in Figure 1-11. During a contact search, a user enters the name of an individual or group and instantly can view the contact's presence without having to add the resource to their contact list.

❑ **File Transfer:** File transfer, shown in Figure 1-12, is provided to enable quick access to sharing and sending of files between contacts. To enhance your LCS environment, utilize the anti-virus integration capabilities to cleanse files before they are received.

Figure 1-10

Figure 1-11

Figure 1-12

❑ **Mode Type:** With MOC, you can take part in a messaging conversation in one of three modes: handwrite, type, or convert. Tablet PC users now have the option to handwrite their instant messages to contacts, as shown in Figure 1-13.

Figure 1-13

❑ **Conversation Type:** MOC provides the capability to create Instant Messaging, audio/video, or telephony conversations, as shown in Figure 1-14.

Figure 1-14

❑ **Presence:** With MOC, contacts are enabled with presence status, which can be modified individually or by using advanced status with direct integration with Microsoft Office 2003, as shown in Figure 1-15.

❑ **Application Sharing:** MOC provides contacts with the capability to share applications, including the desktop, with one another.

❑ **Whiteboard:** With the MOC Whiteboard feature, contacts can express ideas and thoughts by using a shared whiteboard application, as shown in Figure 1-16.

❑ **Office Integration:** MOC provides direct integration with the Microsoft Office system, with integration into Microsoft Outlook 2003 for calendar presence, and the capability to be started within Office programs such as Microsoft Word, Excel, PowerPoint, and SharePoint Portal Server 2003. More information related to integration with Microsoft Office 2003 is covered in Chapter 3.

❑ **Telephony Integration:** MOC and LCS provide integration into PBX and PSTN services to provide contacts with a truly integrated communications client.

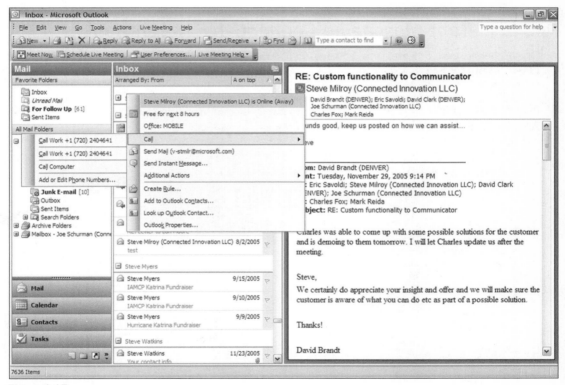

Figure 1-15

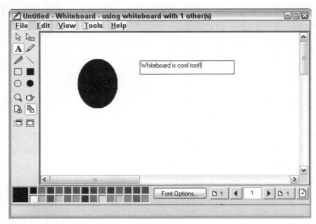

Figure 1-16

Public Instant Messaging Connectivity Integration

One of the most exciting and most anticipated features of Live Communications Server 2005 SP1 is the Public Instant Messaging Connectivity (PIC) service. With PIC, LCS users have the ability to add and contact users of a public network from their Microsoft Office Communicator 2005 client. These conversations are then secured using Mutual Transport Layer Security (MTLS). Figure 1-17 shows a diagram depicting the PIC architecture for external connectivity to public Instant Messaging applications, including Yahoo, AOL, and MSN, over a secured MTLS connection.

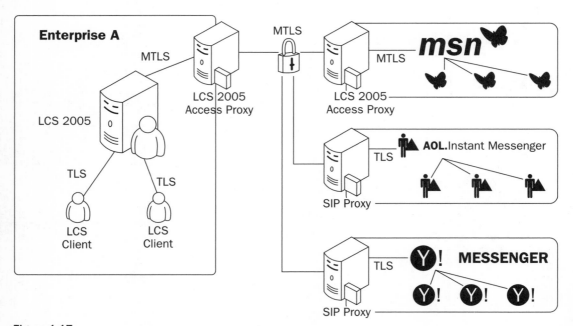

Figure 1-17

Although the diagram depicted in Figure 1-17 showcases integration with the three most popular Instant Messaging applications, the Live Communications Server service can integrate with other provisioned public Instant Messaging services as long as the services provide a proxy that allows Session Initiation Protocol (SIP)–based communications. Once enabled, users have the ability to add PIC contacts to their Microsoft Office Communicator 2005 client and are ready for instant communication, as depicted in Figure 1-18.

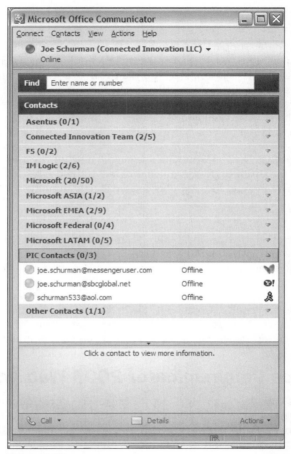

Figure 1-18

Another noteworthy aspect regarding communication between LCS and PIC contacts is that when a contact's status changes in Communicator 2005, it is displayed in whatever way the public Instant Messaging client application is set to display the contact's status. For example, when a contact's presence status is set to "Away" in Communicator 2005, the presence status for this individual is listed as "Stepped Out" in Yahoo Messenger. All in all, the PIC service within LCS enables greater reach without sacrificing the security of enterprise data.

Telephony Integration

Converged communications is becoming a necessity in today's marketplace. With Live Communications Server 2005 with Service Pack 1 and Microsoft Office Communicator 2005, organizations now have the ability to integrate telephony features, Instant Messaging, and Audio/Video communications all within one application. Integration with new and legacy PBX systems and PSTN services is provided as an out-of-the-box feature with minor configuration.

PBX Integration

LCS supports the Computer Supported Telecommunications Applications (CSTA) over SIP protocol, which is accepted by most PBX providers. For legacy PBX applications, LCS requires a third-party solution such as the Genesys GETS service, which translates SIP over CSTA communications to legacy PBX systems. Newer PBX systems will support SIP natively without the need for this SIP/CSTA bridge, but most companies are reluctant to upgrade their PBX systems because they have been in place for decades. Therefore, as a consultant, when deploying LCS for a customer, it is important to have some familiarity with these third-party solution providers (e.g., Genesys, Nortel, Mitel, and others).

When integrating your LCS environment with a legacy or new PBX system, Communicator 2005 is enabled with Remote Call Control (RCC), which provides individuals with the ability to control their desk phone to accept, return, and forward phone calls directly from the application.

PSTN Integration

Where LCS PBX integration provides local calling features within Communicator 2005, PSTN integration with LCS provides connectivity with PSTN services or 1-800 calling services such as MCI. LCS uses the LCS PSTN Gateway to transfer and translate data between the internal LCS environment and the PSTN service to provide seamless integration.

When PSTN integration is enabled, Communicator 2005 enables individuals to create Live Meeting Web conferences and participate in conference calls directly from one client. This combined solution provides ease of use for a Communicator 2005 user and a truly converged communication client application.

Microsoft Office Communicator 2005 Web Access

To provide customers with the capability to deploy Microsoft Office Communicator to almost any desktop, Microsoft released a web-accessible client to LCS with the Microsoft Office (r) Communicator 2005 Web Access (CWA) application. CWA is especially useful for organizations that have tight control over their users' desktop applications, and it can reduce deployment time frames dramatically. CWA provides Instant Messaging and presence features only, and it does not enable the advanced telephony integration and sharing features that are available in the desktop client.

Figure 1-19 depicts the CWA client application.

Microsoft Office Communicator 2005 Mobile

Extending Microsoft Office Communicator 2005 even further, the Microsoft Office Communicator 2005 Mobile client, known by its nickname "CoMo," provides client access to LCS via a mobile device. With CoMo, contacts can take their presence on the road and never skip a beat. CoMo provides contacts with the IM and presence features similar to that of the CWA client so that a contact can take part in IM sessions when needed.

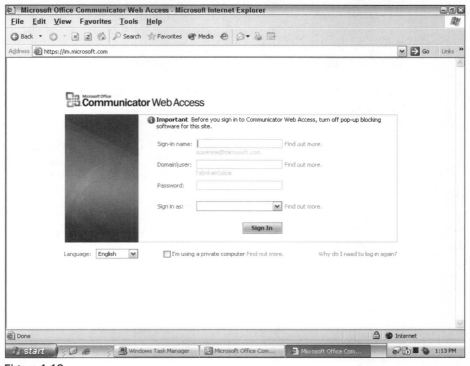

Figure 1-19

What I personally love about the CoMo client is that I have the capability to search for contacts I do not have in my contacts list on my device, including a list of published numbers for each contact. If you are a geek like me, you purchase a new Microsoft Windows Mobile device as soon as the latest one hits the shelves. What is great about CoMo is that I never have to worry about whether or not I have a contact in my mobile contacts list. With IM, presence, and search functionality within CoMo you are in total control.

Summary

The purpose of this chapter was to introduce Microsoft Unified Communications by providing an overview of all of the components that are included in the Unified Communications suite of applications. Chapter 2 discusses how Microsoft Unified Communications fits in the enterprise, as existing applications such as IBM Sametime have dominated the market for some time. Also covered in the next chapter are deployment time frames and what a typical UC project can consist of when deploying Live Communications Server 2005 and Communicator 2005 for enterprise customers.

2

Live Communications Server 2005 SP1 in the Enterprise

When deploying Live Communications Server within an enterprise organization, many details have to be considered during the initial analysis of the deployment. Live Communications Server can be easily installed into a lab environment without any errors, team interaction, or unexpected occurrences. However, when installing LCS within an enterprise network infrastructure, unexpected technical incompatibilities, delays due to team member participation, missing security rights, and other real-world challenges come into play. The purpose of this chapter is to provide guidance through the sales and deployment process of Live Communications Server 2005 SP1 and how to thwart competition in the enterprise Instant Messaging market, which has been dominated by IBM.

Understanding the Live Communications Server Pre-Sales Process

When interfacing with a potential Live Communications Server customer, it is important to deliver as much comprehensive technical and sales-related material as possible to educate the customer about the product and its competition, and to determine the type of deployment that matches the customer's requirements for their organization. Of course, each customer is unique, and the hours estimated within this section do not account for schedule delays.

The following table outlines the activities you should expect when interfacing with a customer who is interested in purchasing and deploying Microsoft Office Live Communications Server 2005 SP1:

Activity	Details	Estimated Schedule
Overview presentation	100–200 level overview Live meeting or on-site meeting LCS features and components Demonstration (client) Pricing (EA licensing discussion)	1 hour
Technical deep dive (by request)	300–400 level Break-out sessions Security Architecture PIC (Public IM Connectivity) integration Client Archiving Demonstration	2 hours
Architecture guide (optional)	LCS architecture guide, including customer name and addressing of required user deployment	8 hours
Consulting services work order	Schedule Deliverables Rate Disclaimers (legal)	8 hours
Total estimated hours	**19 hours**	

Deploying for an Enterprise Customer

This section provides an estimated schedule for the deployment of a typical Microsoft Office Live Communications Server 2005 SP1 environment for an enterprise organization. (Live Communications Server is primarily intended for organizations with 250 or more desktops.) The sample Live Communications Server deployment is intended to illustrate the primary steps required to deploy Live Communications Server; it is not exhaustive.

Use the information outlined within this section as a guide to estimating deployment schedules. The information captured in this section serves only as a baseline for a hypothetical deployment scenario, with the understanding that each customer environment possesses unique business processes and requirements. Therefore, the hours presented here are necessarily estimates. Also note that these estimates assume that the customer has provided the required network permissions or personnel for the deployment of Live Communications Server.

The scenario described in this section is based on an enterprise customer who has decided to deploy Live Communications Server for their entire company. The requirements for this customer include the ability to deploy Live Communications Server 2005 with Service Pack 1 and Communicator 2005 to support up to 150,000 users. The customer also wants the following: secure, remote access to the environment, archiving for reporting and compliance purposes, and Public Instant Messaging Connectivity (PIC) integration. In addition, the solution must be highly scalable. Finally, the customer requires that the environment be monitored by their existing Microsoft Operations Manager service.

Setting Down Requirements

The following table outlines the requirements set forth by the customer within the scenario described in the overview of this section:

Features	Recommended LCS Software	Recommended Configuration
Support for 150,000 users	Live Communications Server 2005 SP1, Enterprise Edition	LCS Servers running on Windows Server 2003, Enterprise Edition
	Live Communications Server 2005 SP1, Enterprise Edition Director to provide further separation of LCS Servers from the external network	Active Directory Domain Controller and Global Catalog Server running on Windows 2000 Server with Service Pack 4 (minimum, preferred Windows Server 2003) located within the Forest root
		Microsoft SQL Server 2000 with Service Pack 3a (minimum)
High availability and fail-over	Live Communications Server, Enterprise Edition Pool	Hardware Load Balancer sitting in front of two LCS Enterprise Edition Pool Servers
		Microsoft SQL Server clustering (active/passive) for LCS Back-End Servers
PIC (Public IM Connectivity) integration	Live Communications Server 2005 SP1, Standard Edition Access Proxy to provide PIC integration	TLS Port 5061 enabled
		TCP Port 5060 enabled
		VeriSign Public Certificate Authority to issue server and client trusted root certificates
		LCS Access Proxy running on Windows Server 2003, Standard Edition configured within a workgroup
Instant Messaging Archiving	Live Communications Server 2005 SP1 IM Archiving Service	Microsoft SQL Server 2000 with Service Pack 3a (minimum)
		Microsoft Message Queue service (MSMQ) running on LCS Front-End Pool Servers
LCS Environment Monitoring	Live Communications Server 2005 SP1 Microsoft Operations Manager Pack	Microsoft Operations Manager 2005

Planning Your Schedule

Based upon the requirements outlined in the previous section, the following table lists the schedule of tasks with estimated hours required to support the deployment scenario presented earlier in this section. The estimated hours listed in the table are based on the assumption that the customer has Microsoft Active Directory deployed. The estimates also assume that the customer either is either willing to grant Enterprise Administrator credentials to the engagement team or provides project sponsors to facilitate changes to DNS, Active Directory, SQL Server, and general Windows Server builds to enable Live Communications Server service within the environment.

Tasks	Details	Timeline Estimate	Consulting Hours
Customer approval/ sign-off	If required, customer signature to approve details to kick off the engagement	40 hours	1 hour
Public IM connectivity provisioning	Completed registration of the Public IM Connectivity Provisioning System	40–160 hours	2 hours
	In addition, a valid purchase order from the large account reseller (LAR) needs to be received by Microsoft Corporation prior to the entry on the provisioning page being successful.		
Equipment order	Ordering of Live Communications Server equipment	120–160 hours (depends on vendor)	1 hour
Ordering digital certificates	Request of digital certificates to apply to LCS Access Proxy and Standard Edition Servers	40 hours	1 hour
	Required certificates:		
	LCS Access Proxy External Edge LCS Access Proxy Internal Edge LCS Enterprise Edition Pool Servers LCS Enterprise Edition Director Server Trusted Root Certificate for Clients		
Configuring equipment	Rack and mounting of servers Operating system load IP address configuration Security baseline (if required)	80 hours	80 hours

Tasks	Details	Timeline Estimate	Consulting Hours
Applying DNS records	Request and implementation of required DNS records to support LCS service	40 hours	40 hours
	Required DNS entries:		
	DNS host record(s) to support LCS service running within the customer's forest/domain DNS Service Records (SRVs) to support client connectivity to the LCS environment by resolving TCP and TLS SIP addresses VIP (Virtual Internet Protocol) address for hardware load balancer		
Active Directory preparation	Running LCS Active Directory Preparation steps:	80 hours	80 hours
	Schema prep Forest prep Domain prep DomainAdd Enabling users		
Hardware load balancer setup	Configuration of the hardware load balancer to meet Microsoft requirements	40 hours	40 hours
SQL Server preparation	SQL Server application installation and configuration for LCS Enterprise Edition Pool Servers, Director Server, and IM Archiving Service	40 hours	40 hours
LCS application install	Installation of Live Communications Server Access Proxy, Enterprise Edition Pool servers, IM Archiving Service and Director servers	40 hours	40 hours
LCS application configuration	Configuring LCS servers:	80 hours	80 hours
	LCS Access Proxy configuration LCS Enterprise Edition Pool and Pool Servers configuration LCS Director Server configuration LCS IM Archiving Service configuration LCS Microsoft Operations Manager configuration Connection Entry Ports Forest settings Server settings Configuring certificates		

Table continued on following page

Tasks	Details	Timeline Estimate	Consulting Hours
SharePoint Portal Server 2003 configuration	Configure SharePoint Portal Server 2003 to enable online presence	1 hour	1 hour
Microsoft Office 2003 configuration	Enable the shared workspace client feature within Microsoft Office 2003	1 hour	1 hour
Office system configuration	Configure the Office System to use Microsoft Office Communicator features**	1 hour	1 hour
Testing	Testing of the LCS environment	80 hours	80 hours
Client deployment	Packaging and distribution of applications to client machines: Windows Messenger 5.1 Microsoft Office Communicator 2005	80 hours	80 hours
Total estimated hours		**1,040 hours**	**610 hours**

**Estimate does not include distribution of the Microsoft Office Service Pack 2, which is required for this task

Scheduling Additional Deliverables

The following table outlines the expected additional deliverables to be completed and distributed to the customer upon project completion, with additional estimated hours:

Deliverable	Consulting Hours
Live Communications Server Design Document	120 hours
Live Communications Server Test Plan	80 hours
Total estimated hours	200 hours

The Live Communications Server Design Document, which is also provided as an example in Appendix B, should include all of the design components that are part of the LCS deployment. These components include an architectural outline drawing of the LCS infrastructure, a listing of records and IP addresses, as well as hardware and software configurations. The purpose of this document is to provide a blueprint of the deployment for review or reference. The Live Communications Server Test Plan, which is provided in Appendix A, is a step-by-step testing document that can be used to test each LCS service after the technology has been deployed. This document is helpful both to certify that your deployment is working correctly and to provide a written proof of success.

Deployment Schedule Summary

The following table summarizes the required configuration of the scenario described in this section, accompanied by the total project timeline and total estimated number of consulting hours to complete the entire deployment:

Required LCS Components	Total Timeline Estimate	Total Consulting Hours
10 Live Communications Servers: 5 LCS 2005 SP1, Enterprise Edition Pool Servers Load Balanced (Hardware Load Balancer) IM Archiving Service 1 LCS 2005 SP1, Access Proxy Server 1 LCS 2005 SP1, Enterprise Edition Director Server 2 Back-End LCS SQL Servers (clustered) 1 Microsoft Operations Manager Server w/ LCS Pack Configured for secure, remote access PIC (Public IM Connectivity) integration Documentation Equipment and certificate requests	1,260 hours	830 hours

The following table outlines the required software and hardware configuration related to the deployment scenario described within this section:

Role	Required Hardware
Active Directory	Domain Controller and Global Catalog running on Windows Server 2003 with Service Pack 1
	Active Directory native mode
	Active Directory GC/DC located on same subnet
	LCS will be deployed within the default AD site
	LCS service accounts will be named with default configuration nomenclature
Permissions	Administrators granted Enterprise Administrator permissions within Active Directory with Schema Admin rights
	Administrators granted SQL DBO permissions for Back-End SQL Server access
	Service accounts will be granted with default privileges or Enterprise Admin rights to simplify configuration

Table continued on following page

Role	Required Hardware
Certificates	Internal Windows Certificate Authority
	Server Authentication EKU certificates for LCS servers (minimum 128-bit encryption)
	LCS certificate friendly names/common names must match name of pool (LCS Enterprise Edition) or server (LCS Standard Edition)
	Client machines must have trusted root CA configured for each desktop
	LCS Pool Servers
	Pool Server CN = POOL.COMPANY.COM
	LCS Standard Edition Server:
	Pool Server CN = SERVER.COMPANY.COM
DNS records	DNS "A" Host Record for SIP.COMPANY.COM
	DNS SRV Records:
	_sipinternaltls._tcp.Company.com _sipinternal._tcp.Company.com _sip._tls.Company.com _sip._tcp.Company.com
LCS Enterprise Edition Pool Servers	LCS 2005 SP1, Enterprise Edition Windows Server 2003, Enterprise Edition with SP1 MSMQ (if archiving is enabled) Windows Script Host version 5.6 Flat File Logging–Level 3 Remote registry service running CPU: Dual Pentium Xeon 3.2 GHz w/HT
	Disks: 2 × 18GB (RAID 1) 2 × 36GB (RAID 1) 15K rpm SCSI 1MB cache Memory: 4GB Network: GBit NIC Examples: DELL PowerEdge 2850 (2U) HP DL380 G4 (2U)

Role	Required Hardware
LCS Back-end SQL Servers	Windows Server 2003, Enterprise Edition with SP1
	SQL Server 2000, Standard Edition (Enterprise Edition if clustering) with Service Pack 4
	Database installed on default instance
	CPU: Quad Pentium Xeon 3.0 GHz w/HT
	Disks:
	2 × 18GB internal drives
	4 × 36GB (RAID 1+0)
	External Ultra320 SCSI Array
	(HP StorageWorks MSA500 G2)
	Disk configuration:
	OS loaded on C:
	Data Log Files = D:\UCSQL\DATA\
	Transaction Log Files = D:\UCSQL\DATA
	Memory: 8GB
	Network: GBit NIC
	Examples:
	DELL PowerEdge 6850 (4U)
	HP DL580 G2 (4U)
LCS Archiving Servers	LCS 2005 SP1, IM Archiving Service
	Will run IM Archiving database on an additional or same LCS Back-End Server
	Windows Server 2003, Standard Edition with SP1
	Microsoft SQL Server 2005 SP1
	CPU: Dual Pentium Xeon 3.2 GHz w/HT
	Disk configuration:
	2 × 18GB (RAID 1)
	2 × 36GB (RAID 1)
	15K rpm SCSI
	1MB cache
	Memory: 4GB
	Network: GBit NIC
	Examples:
	DELL PowerEdge 2850 (2U)
	HP DL380 G4 (2U)

Table continued on following page

Role	Required Hardware
LCS Access Proxy Server	LCS 2005 SP1, Standard Edition Windows Server 2003, Standard Edition with Service Pack 1 Windows Script Host Version 5.6 CPU: Dual Pentium Xeon 3.2 GHz w/HT Disk Configuration: 2×18GB (RAID 1) 15K rpm SCSI 1MB cache Memory: 2GB Network: GBit NIC Examples: DELL PowerEdge 2850 (2U) HP DL380 G4 (2U)
LCS Address Book Server	Address Book Service will run on LCS Pool Servers or Standard Edition Servers IIS 6.0 Virtual Directory pointing to physical shared folder for ABS files Windows Server 2003, Standard Edition with Service Pack 1 Windows Script Host version 5.6 CPU: Dual Pentium Xeon 3.2 GHz w/HT Disk configuration: 2×18 GB (RAID 1) 15K rpm SCSI 1MB cache Memory: 2GB Network: GBit NIC Examples: DELL PowerEdge 2850 (2U) HP DL380 G4 (2U)
Client Machines	Microsoft Office Communicator 2005 CPU: Pentium 1.2 GHz or higher processor Memory: 128MB RAM Disk: 1.5GB free space Monitor: SVGA with 800×600 resolution minimum Video Camera (optional): USB 1.1, 640×480 resolution (e.g., "Logitech QuickCam Pro 4000") Microphone (optional) Bandwidth: 10 MB/s recommended

Special Notes:

Minimum requirement for the LCS back-end database is Microsoft SQL Server 2000 with Service Pack 3a.

If virtual servers are to be used in place of physical equipment, the same virtual hardware (memory, CPU, disk space) recommended in previous sections should be allocated to each instance of LCS.

Building the Team

As easy as this sounds, building the LCS deployment and planning team is probably the most critical element of any LCS deployment whether it is a proof of concept, pilot, or production roll-out. LCS touches many different components of an enterprise network and requires expertise and network permissions for each respective task. It is best to organize your team early with a core LCS team and representatives or champions from additional teams comprised of network administration personnel and business analysts within an organization.

The core team should comprise the following resources:

❏ **Deployment project manager:** The deployment project manager should be the person responsible for the required tasks and action items related to a LCS deployment. The project manager should provide weekly status reports, maintain a list of issues and action items, and be considered the primary point of contact for the project. In most cases, the project manager should also be the liaison between the LCS deployment team and the business sponsors of an organization.

❏ **LCS architect:** The LCS architect should be the overall authority of the LCS deployment design. The architect should provide guidance and direction as a subject matter expert (SME) and provide assistance to the project team when needed. In most cases, the SME is not a full-time consultant, but a guide who ensures the technical correctness of a deployment, as well as the person who answers questions related to the technology specifically. Typically, an LCS architect is utilized on many different LCS deployments at one time.

❏ **Customer IT or business champion (sponsor for the entire project):** The project sponsor, or champion, should serve as a liaison between the business and the technical project team. The sponsor is the person who is ultimately responsible for the success or failure of the deployment. The sponsor should provide assistance to the deployment team in terms of providing facility access, remote desktop access to equipment, badge or security access to a company's deployment environment/infrastructure, as well as provide any company policy training or awareness to the contract deployment team of consultants.

❏ **Customer IT architect:** In some cases, a customer-sponsored IT architect is provided to ensure that the overall architecture for the LCS deployment fits within the company's technical architecture guidelines. The IT architect ensures that standards or approved methods of deployment are used in all or most cases throughout the life cycle of the project.

The extended team should consist of the following resources:

❏ DNS administrators

❏ PKI/Certificate administrators

❏ Active Directory administrators (Enterprise and Domain administrators)

❏ Desktop security administrators

❏ Server security administrators

❏ Client deployment administrators (client software packaging and deployment)

❏ Security baseline administrators (can be both desktop and server)

❏ Group Policy administrators (GPO)

❑ SQL Server database administrators

❑ Telephony administrators (PBX and PSTN)

❑ IT operations and support

❑ Training and communications team

Depending on the size or structure of the company, only three or four resources may perform all of these roles; in the rarest of cases, you have the unbelievable opportunity to work with an internal resource that has Enterprise Administrator credentials on the network. In reality, most enterprise organizations have a resource or representative competent in each area listed, and in most cases all reside in separate geographic regions. In any case, it is important to build the team early to avoid any confusion and time delays, and to anticipate concerns and lay out a strategy to mitigate risks throughout the deployment.

In the preliminary kick-off meetings, a representative from each area should be present. Critical aspects of the project that warrant discussion include Active Directory, network architecture, security, integration, deployment, and client configuration.

Entering the IBM Sametime Domain

When selling or deploying Live Communications Server within an enterprise organization, you'll generally be faced with a competitive analysis between LCS and an existing Instant Messaging solution. Over the past several years, enterprise customers have been heavily invested in IBM for enterprise collaboration technologies, beginning with Lotus Notes for e-mail, Sametime for Instant Messaging, and QuickPlace for online portal collaboration. Due to the recent large investment that Microsoft has made in its UC platform, these customers have decided to invest in UC technology in an effort to provide a better integrated solution for their users, leveraging the dominating Office system suite of products. The information provided within this section includes reasons why enterprise companies have decided to migrate from IBM to Microsoft, especially in the area of Instant Messaging technology.

At a high level, both IBM Sametime and Microsoft Office Communicator provide Instant Messaging functionality which will become the preferred method of electronic communication within the next five years. Both clients provide users with the capability to view another contact's presence and, if available, instantly send and receive messages. The major difference between Sametime and Communicator, outside of many major telephony feature enhancements available with Communicator, is that Communicator is an integrated solution. Sametime is a stand-alone application, whereas Communicator, which can be run via the Web, the desktop, or a mobile device, is integrated within the Office system, including Microsoft Word, Excel, PowerPoint, and SharePoint.

At a high level, the Microsoft Office Communicator client is an enterprise messaging application that provides a unified approach to communications by providing Instant Messaging, voice, presence, video, and telephony integration, using a seamless approach to all of these provided features.

The current IBM Sametime client is a stand-alone messaging application that requires its own directory and offers no voice or video communication. In my professional opinion, the IBM Sametime solution is a sunset technology like that of Windows 95. Even with enhancements it could not compete with Communicator and is not, in my opinion, an enterprise-class application.

IBM Attrition Scenarios

The information in this section has been gathered through my hands-on experience with customers who have decided to move from IBM Sametime to the Microsoft UC platform based on scenarios that factor in cost, functionality, and feature set. The purpose of offering this information here is to provide you with some leverage when caught in a competitive selling situation.

Cost Comparisons

The question of cost as its related to software licenses of IBM Sametime or Microsoft Live Communications Server 2005 SP1 and Office Communicator 2005, surprisingly enough, has not been a primary concern with the enterprise and federal organizations that I have worked with. More often than not, customers have analyzed the technical infrastructure and support costs that are incurred by supporting either application.

The defining factor in infrastructure costs that does tend to tilt customers toward the Microsoft solution is the enormous capacity of users that a Microsoft server can support—up to 15,000 users using the Live Communications Server 2005 SP1 Standard Edition version, and up to 100,000 users per pool using the Enterprise Edition version of the software. As a case study, one enterprise customer I worked with, who was one of the largest IBM customers in the world, had 11 servers running with IBM Lotus Domino supporting 55,000 users. The server count has been reduced to five servers running Microsoft Live Communications Server 2005 SP1 Enterprise Edition, and supports 100,000 users. These costs add up in terms of the physical cost of each server, as well as the cost for supporting each server. The customers I have worked with use outsourced network support and in some cases pay up to $15,000 per month just for patch cable management. Needless to say, these support costs add up and affect the bottom line of the overall cost of the chosen solution.

To attract new customers, Microsoft created "early adopter cost savings programs" for their licenses, which proved to be successful. Along with the features and functionality provided with the Microsoft solution, these price discounts were almost impossible to turn down. As an additional strategy to make the costs for Microsoft UC software licenses even more attractive, Microsoft included the licenses via a customer's existing Enterprise Agreement. This strategy enabled easier transition in terms of initial costs and future upgrade costs. In response, IBM, because of the increased attraction, in some cases began throwing their software at customers in hopes of retaining them, which underscored IBM's understanding that they were losing market presence in this area.

Actual costs have been measured, and in some cases the cost of supporting and deploying the Microsoft UC solution is one-third of the cost of IBM's Sametime environment. This includes license costs. The following table compares the estimated costs to two customers who have migrated from IBM Sametime to Microsoft Live Communications Server:

Customer	IBM Licenses Costs	Microsoft Licenses Costs	Server Consolidation Numbers
Enterprise Commercial	55K licenses at $1.5M	100K licenses at $1M	11 IBM to 5 Microsoft
Enterprise Federal	100K licenses at $3M	100K licenses at $1M	20 IBM to 9 Microsoft

Note: Due to confidentiality agreements, exact dollar amounts and organization names are not displayed.

Features and Functionality

In most cases, functionality was more important than cost for the enterprise customers I worked with who decided to move away from the IBM Sametime client to the Microsoft UC platform. The key capabilities described in this section center around the Communicator client and the integrated UC platform that led to these decisions.

Understanding Microsoft's Integrated Platform

An integrated communication and collaboration platform was the leading reason enterprise customers began moving away from IBM to Microsoft. After all, Microsoft leverages the dominating enterprise Office system, which is installed on hundreds of millions of desktops around the world. The majority of large enterprises have some version of Microsoft Office deployed throughout their enterprise, so the decision to move to technologies in the Office system suite, including SharePoint, Live Communications Server, Live Meeting, and Communicator, is an easy one. Regarding Instant Messaging specifically, Microsoft leverages existing Office applications such as Word, Excel, and PowerPoint by building integrated communication through Communicator, offering users a totally integrated experience on the desktop.

Because Instant Messaging is the most popular communication tool today, giving users the ability to leverage a client within familiar applications was a major advantage for Microsoft in retaining or gaining customers.

In contrast, IBM provides little or no integration with desktop business applications. It would have been wise for IBM to have built integration into Office or even their own portal product, QuickPlace, but the ingenuity was not there, and there is little current evidence that there ever will be integration provided. Even from a directory standpoint, Sametime is stand-alone. The IBM Sametime directory is a silo and is supported separately by Sametime administrators. Microsoft took the same desktop integrated approach with the Live Communications Server directory by leveraging Microsoft Active Directory. This strategy, as with all Microsoft products, capitalizes on the Active Directory infrastructure, which consists of updated user directory information that Microsoft applications can leverage. Even better, it is already maintained and supported.

Access Anytime, Anywhere

Providing users with the capability to access their corporate messaging infrastructure without the requirement of Virtual Private Network (VPN) connectivity has been a strategy with not only the Microsoft UC platform, but also with Exchange e-mail and remote portal access to Microsoft SharePoint. This flexibility gives users "anywhere, anytime" flexibility, enabling system access regardless of location. This strategy has been important to large enterprises that use third-party contractors and engage in secure transactions with business partners that are not members of the internal infrastructure. Giving these parties external access without requiring the use of VPN connectivity, obtaining secure certificates, and so on, is a cost and time saving solution that can affect hundreds and even thousands of users. IBM Sametime provides no remote access solution without the use of a VPN connection.

Integrated Public Instant Messaging Connectivity

Microsoft's Public Instant Messaging Connectivity (PIC) service is an extremely popular solution, and next to the integrated platform scenario, it is the second largest reason for customer attraction to the Microsoft UC platform over IBM. Most enterprises, especially within the financial arena, consist of users who have made Instant Messaging a critical form of business communication with their partners, in addition to internal communications. Before the release of the Microsoft UC platform, most financial traders were using AOL Instant Messenger or Yahoo Messenger to conduct Instant Messaging sessions over a public transport without encryption. With the Microsoft PIC service, these users can utilize the Microsoft Office Communicator client to enable Instant Messaging to the public Instant Messaging providers, which includes AOL, Yahoo, and MSN (refer to Figure 1-8 in Chapter 1) over a secured communication transport.

Not only is PIC integration provided, but the communication is also secured using Transport Layer Security (TLS). The communication transport, or pipe, is encrypted using TLS from the client connecting to the environment, and then further encrypted between the LCS server environment and the public network using Mutual TLS encryption. Now, with Communicator, enterprise organizations can provide access and integration with public Instant Messaging applications and provide the level of security that is needed, whereas in the past these users were communicating private company information over non-secured public lines.

IBM Sametime provides encryption but this is only applied internally without remote access or integration to public Instant Messaging networks. This was, again, a major deciding factor for customers in moving away from the IBM messaging solution.

Understanding the Benefits of Real-Time Security

Securing Instant Messaging has become an increasing concern, and thankfully Microsoft invested in securing the UC platform. A Microsoft UC solution addresses security at the communication layer, or pipe, and at the identifying level by challenging the user for the correct user credentials. The connection between the client and server using the Microsoft UC platform is encrypted using Transport Layer Security (TLS). TLS is the next generation of security over Secured Sockets Layer (SSL), and it follows the same process of implementation—using secured server certificates. When configuring the Microsoft UC environment, a certificate is applied; and when a client connects to the environment, the server certificate checks to see whether the issuing Certificate Authority (CA) root certificate matches the root certificate on the client's local computer certificate store. In order to thwart or spoof a user's identity, a hacker would also have to obtain this root certificate to enable the client to connect. In addition, Microsoft leverages Microsoft Active Directory to challenge the user for logon credentials, which are only available if the user has an Active Directory–enabled account. In all enterprises, Active Directory is highly secured and supported, so the capability to obtain an account in the directory is only accomplished through a detailed approval process. Both levels of security and a configurable Instant Messaging filter, which blocks users from transmitting links or harmful viruses, are provided out of the box. Additional components such as anti-virus protection tools and intrusion detection systems can be added and are highly recommended.

The IBM Sametime solution provides security internally between client and server, but does not provide integration with Active Directory. Instead, it maintains its own separate directory service for Sametime users.

Meeting Compliance Regulations

With the recent implementations of new processes to enable enterprises to meet the compliance regulations of acts that include, but are not limited to, the Sarbanes-Oxley Act, ISO, and many other U.S. and international compliance regulations, finding a compliant Instant Messaging application has become mission critical. The enterprise customers I have worked with and met through compliance and security consortiums have recently switched to the Microsoft UC platform due to Microsoft and Microsoft partner solutions to assist enterprises in providing a compliant messaging platform. The Microsoft UC platform, along with Microsoft partners, provides the highest level of platform compliance, with functionality that includes segregating Instant Messaging user communities and enabling the recording of conversations. For example, most financial trading communities are, by legal definition, not allowed to communicate in any electronic form to other departments within even their own corporations. This solution has been a critical component in deploying the Microsoft UC solution for these customers, and it has proven to be a win with information technology executives of these firms and agencies.

IBM Sametime, in partnership with third-party providers, also provides compliance features, but the overwhelmingly large number of additional Microsoft compliance components continues to attract enterprise customers.

Scalability and Availability

Scalability and availability are critical considerations when deploying any technology service. Providing high-bandwidth applications that have a guaranteed run rate of 99.9% has always been the goal of any technology application. As Instant Messaging becomes more of a critical business application, the reliability of the messaging server and network environment becomes equally as important. Scalability and high availability are features that the Microsoft UC platform has invested in, whereas IBM has not. With the UC platform, the messaging environment can be load-balanced to provide a pool of messaging servers in case one or more servers unexpectedly fails; the remaining servers in the pool continue to run and provide service to users. Load-balancing is a solution that provides more than an additional server or service; it is completely identical to its counterpart. The purpose of load-balancing is to provide more than one identical copy of a service in the event that the primary service is lost. Additional load-balanced servers would then pick up the load of the primary service in real time, providing no loss of service to a consumer. Load-balancing is not a feature of the IBM Sametime solution.

Another feature of the Microsoft UC platform is back-end database clustering. The Microsoft UC user and system configuration is stored in Microsoft SQL Server, so it is important to back up the databases that support the UC system. Clustering is now available, so when a back-end server fails, another back-end server is available to keep the system running. Microsoft has applied this level of high availability to all of its enterprise server applications, which is an infrastructure requirement with businesses today.

Figure 2-1 provides an example of Microsoft's Live Communications Server 2005 SP1 Enterprise Edition scalability and availability design.

Mentioned earlier was the advantage of server consolidation and the capacity of Microsoft UC servers versus that of IBM's. Existing IBM customers who have been used to multiple servers supporting their environments have been awed by the capacity of a given Microsoft LCS server to support users. In some cases, enterprise customers have seen the required server count to support additional users with their existing IBM Sametime solution drop by half when they switched to the Microsoft UC solution. Microsoft provides two editions of its Live Communications Server software, Standard and Enterprise. A Standard Edition server can support up to 15,000 users per server, while an Enterprise Edition pool can support up to 100,000 users per pool, supporting 20,000 users per server. This level of scalability heavily outweighs IBM's Sametime solution, which typically can support up to 12,000 users per server.

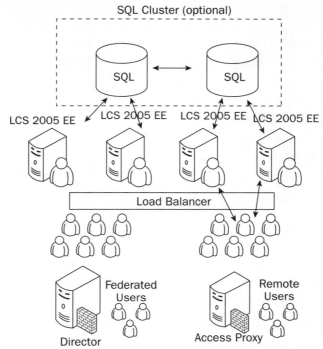

Figure 2-1

The following table provides a matrix of supported users per Microsoft LCS server edition:

Total Number of Users	Required Number of LCS SE or EE Servers	Required LCS Load Balancer	LCS Standard Edition or LCS EE Pool	Maximum Number of Users per Server
0–15,000	1	N	LCS SE Server	15,000
20,000	1	N	LCS EE Server	20,000
30,000	2	Y	LCS EE Server	20,000
50,000	3	Y	LCS EE Server	20,000
100,000	5	Y	LCS EE Server	20,000

IBM Sametime did not pay particular attention to the area of scalability, which has led to customer attrition based on the number of servers that are required to support a Sametime environment. The enterprises that I have worked with dealt with this situation by deploying geographical-based Sametime servers so that the Wide Area Network/Local Area Network connection is closer to the actual user, as Sametime does not provide an "enterprise pool-like" solution whereby users can connect to a centrally managed, load-balanced pool of Sametime servers.

Understanding the User Interface

Deploying an easy to use and attractive communications client to your users is critical. Not only do users desire a client application that works, but Instant Messaging users have matured and expect a plethora of features within their IM clients. Both IBM and Microsoft provide an intuitive client, but there are some major differences between the two in terms of usability and features available directly within the client. With Microsoft Office Communicator, integration with the Office system has been built in. Conveniences such as presence notification, updating your status as "In a Meeting," occur automatically if your Outlook calendar has you scheduled in a meeting. You can also e-mail a contact directly from Communicator in a one-touch manner. These conveniences create a better user experience as well as an addictive user base, which has led to the recent choice of IM over e-mail for electronic communication. Communicator also provides one-touch launching of video and voice communications, enabling you to use the Communicator client as a digital phone to receive, forward, or provide advanced voice communications. Other convenient features include the Address Book service, which provides users with the capability to search for contacts that are not in their buddy list to view presence status and contact users immediately.

These solutions are non-existent in IBM's Sametime client. Simple conveniences such as the Communicator's presence awareness, are color coded like a stoplight to assist with the visibility of a contact's presence when they are away, busy, in a meeting, etc. The IBM Sametime client presentation of a user's status is in accordance with its other features, i.e., they are proprietary in nature. A user must become acquainted with its symbols to recognize the status of a contact.

Figure 2-2 compares the Microsoft Office Communicator and IBM Sametime clients.

Understanding Telephony and VoIP Integration

Of the two solutions, the Microsoft UC platform is the only solution that provides Private Branch Exchange (PBX) and Voice over Internet Protocol (VoIP) functionality. IBM has not made any telephony investments to create additional integrated components to its Sametime solution.

With the Microsoft UC solution, enterprise users can utilize their Office Communicator clients as a phone to contact colleagues, as well as a call manager to route inbound calls or to apply rules to calls. Figure 2-3 shows a sample of the Communicator telephony features available out of the box.

Understanding the Development Platform

While most enterprises are interested in providing a real-time, collaborative platform for their users, they are also interested in providing a solution to build applications that leverage real-time technologies to integrate their line of business applications. Two enterprise customers that I have worked with were analyzing both IBM Sametime and Microsoft Live Communications Server in an effort to provide real-time applications for their financial trading departments, while several others were exploring better solutions for call center functionality. Each of these customers decided on the Microsoft UC solution due to the open-source capabilities that Microsoft provides with the available server application programming interfaces (APIs).

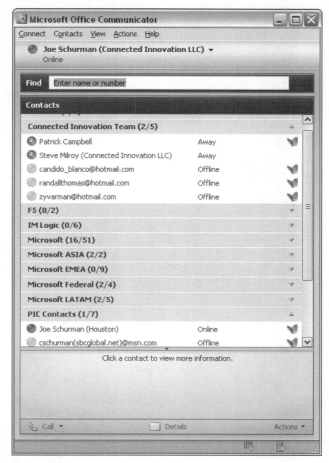

Figure 2-2

With this same approach to leverage the APIs, several Microsoft vendors and customers have developed industry-specific solutions for compliance, niche messaging applications, presence controls, and integration into existing line of business applications for HR, Finance, Operations, and so on. An example of these open-source capabilities includes the development call center applications and tracking applications, which leverage these APIs. These applications can now tap into the rich presence and integrated telephony features of LCS to enhance the features of customer-focused sessions.

Microsoft focused not only on delivering quality products, but also on providing a foundation upon which customers can build. With a massive development support focus, including training events, educational websites, and online seminars, Microsoft has provided more benefit to the development community than any other vendor in the marketplace.

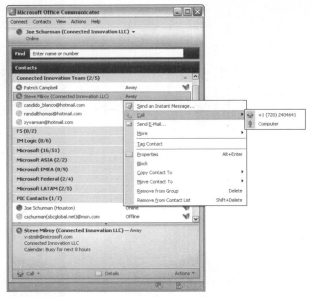

Figure 2-3

Summary

This chapter contained a high-level look at how to approach introducing Live Communications Server to the enterprise by providing examples of the selling and deployment process, including a competitive analysis. As a consultant in the field and a Microsoft MVP, I have worked with several Fortune 500 and Global 1000 customers. The customers I have assisted in providing migration strategies and UC consulting services have assisted me in providing this information to other organizations that are faced with making sound decisions about which platform they should invest in for their companies. In my professional opinion, Microsoft has proven to be the only quality solution with investment opportunity in the marketplace today. A number of other organizations such as Google, Yahoo, AOL, and Skype have made recent moves to develop enterprise-ready communications applications, but the investment is nowhere close to where Microsoft is headed: real-time connectivity, available anytime and anywhere.

3

Microsoft Office
Integration

One of the major differences between Live Communications Server 2005 SP1 and its competitors is its integration with the Microsoft Office suite of products. Microsoft developed the Unified Communications (UC) platform correctly by building a foundation of integrated desktop applications such as Microsoft Office Outlook, Word, Excel, PowerPoint, Live Meeting, and SharePoint. Microsoft realized that millions of users started their day out in Microsoft Office. I personally spend most of my time in Microsoft Outlook or, in the case of writing this book, Microsoft Word. Having the capability to quickly find and communicate with my peers, partners, and customers with one click is simply awesome. I increase my productivity ten-fold knowing that I do not have to look up someone in my contacts list in a separate application to communicate with them or switch between multiple applications, and lose my train of thought. Microsoft Live Communications Server 2005 SP1 and the entire Microsoft Unified Communications suite of products (Live Meeting 2005 and Communicator 2005) are part of the Microsoft Office system. This integrated approach enables the Office applications to be used with the UC applications right out of the box. The purpose of this chapter is to showcase the integrated LCS features within the Office system. In this chapter you will see how presence is represented in Microsoft Outlook, Word, Excel, PowerPoint, and SharePoint.

Microsoft Office Outlook 2003

One of the richest features of Live Communications Server 2005 SP1 and Communicator 2005 is the integration with Microsoft Outlook 2003. The out-of-the-box integration between these products includes calendar-based presence with free/busy information, one click access to e-mail, and contact integration.

With calendar integration, the Communicator 2005 client not only shows when you are offline, online, away, busy, and so on, but also displays "in a Meeting" status, as shown in Figure 3-1.

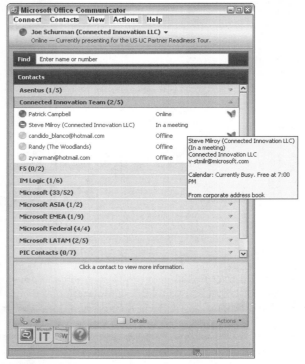

Figure 3-1

The Out of Office option, as shown in Figure 3-2, indicates to contacts who are trying to reach you that you are currently unavailable.

When someone can determine that you are in a meeting or otherwise unavailable, they don't have to waste anyone's time trying to contact you. Knowing when and when not to contact someone still takes a little educating, but we're getting there with Instant Messaging etiquette.

Within Microsoft Outlook, you can communicate with your contacts directly by clicking a contact's name and using communication features available to you within Communicator, such as sending an instant message, calling them on one of their published phone numbers, as well as setting up a Live Meeting conference and conference call. Figure 3-3 displays the menu available to you when you click on a contact's name within Outlook 2003, with Microsoft Office 2003 Service Pack 2.

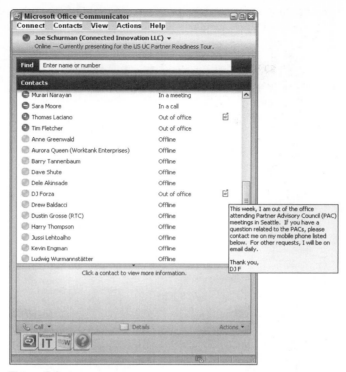

Figure 3-2

Also within Microsoft Office Outlook 2003, you can determine whether a person is online by viewing the presence icon adjacent to the contact's name in the e-mail program (this is enabled using Microsoft Office 2003 Service Pack 2). If you right-click the person's name, you get options to call them, can see their calendar schedule, and can even send them an instant message. Having presence in your Outlook mail makes your mail that much more efficient, because sometimes it is extremely difficult to wait for responses to important questions while trading messages back and forth. The capability to see an e-mail message and immediately ask questions about it without having to wait for a response represents a big step toward making your office run more efficiently; and if you are as impatient as I am, it saves you the time of clicking the Send/Receive button repeatedly, waiting for a response. Given that most individuals spend a larger portion of their time in Outlook than in any other application, Outlook 2003 integration is feature rich and extremely powerful. The time-saving factor in setting up a meeting or having direct communication functionality within the application is something you have to experience to truly appreciate.

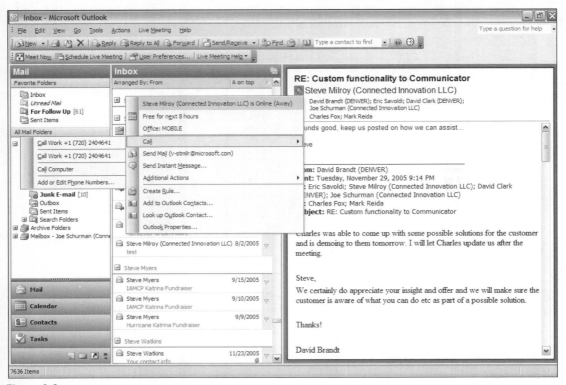

Figure 3-3

Microsoft Office Word 2003

After hours of reading and responding to e-mail, actual work has to be done. In my case, I write a lot of documentation, courseware, and contracts. When creating contracts, I usually need the assistance of my business partner and co-founder of my company to ensure that each contract is within our guidelines. Before Communicator and LCS, I had to find my partner's phone number or send him an e-mail to contact him regarding the document. Now, using Communicator and LCS, I can contact my partner directly within Microsoft Office Word 2003. With direct LCS integration, I can type the name of my partner within the document and have his name light up with the Communicator presence icon and menu or I can leverage the new Office *shared workspace,* available in Office 2003. With the shared workspace, I can contact anyone who is associated with this document if it is published within a SharePoint website. The great thing about using this feature is that I don't lose my train of thought or my place in the document while trying to contact a colleague. I can directly communicate with them whenever I am stuck on an issue or need assistance with it.

Figure 3-4 depicts the LCS and Communicator integration within Microsoft Word 2003 with Office 2003 Service Pack 2.

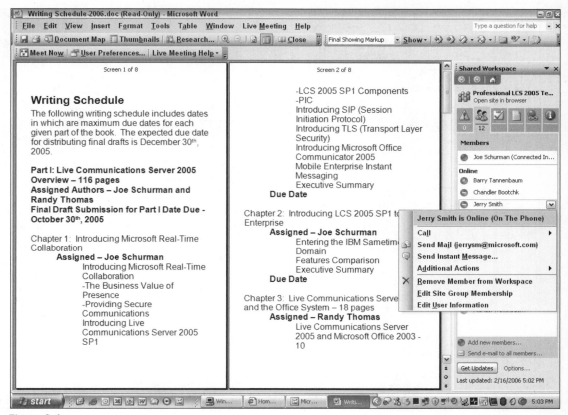

Figure 3-4

Microsoft Word 2003 becomes a lot more powerful when you are able to use all of the additional features of Communicator shown in Figure 3-4. Notice the options you have for contacting the owner of the document via phone, Instant Messaging, text messaging on a mobile device, or e-mail. If your work would progress more quickly within a meeting, you have the capability right within Word 2003 to start a Live Meeting session. The capability to share the document in a meeting enables you to make edits while you are discussing them with the other meeting attendees, bypassing the need to circulate the document later and wait for it to come back before making your changes and verifying them.

Microsoft Office Excel 2003

Whether you are creating a budget analysis, running statistical analysis, or simply reviewing spreadsheets, the integrated features provided within Microsoft Office Excel 2003 will save you an incredible amount of time by enabling direct access to your contacts. This integration offers many of the same features offered in Word, such as the capability to schedule meetings, Instant Messaging, and e-mail. Additionally, each row in the spreadsheet holds a name within it and offers options for contacting the individual. Figure 3-5, which depicts how Communicator is integrated within Microsoft Excel with Office 2003 SP 2, demonstrates Excel's capability to function as a complete office collaboration tool.

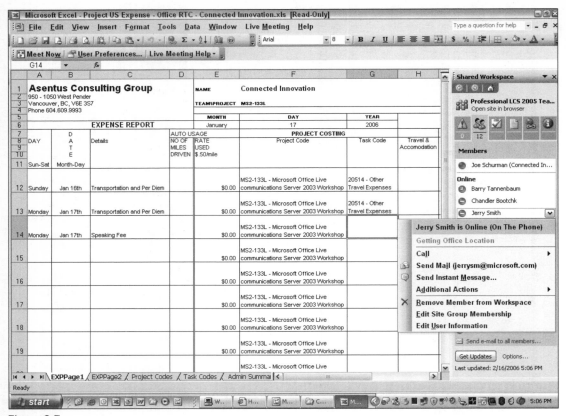

Figure 3-5

Real-world examples of productivity gains in organizations that have deployed LCS abound. For instance, I have worked with enterprise energy trading firms that have deployed LCS, and their commodity traders noticed immediate value because they spend most of their time working within Excel to review pricing and other tasks. Having the capability to contact a colleague, customer, or buyer directly within Excel saved at least five minutes for every occasion that required finding the appropriate contact related to a particular deal.

Microsoft Office PowerPoint 2003

Everyone knows how long it takes to build a nice presentation and make it accurate, and Microsoft has helped streamline that process by adding presence and the capability to schedule Live Meeting sessions directly from Microsoft Office PowerPoint 2003. You are now able to actually share your presentation with your team members and make modifications to it while they watch. Image the time that this feature can save you by avoiding the need to e-mail the presentation back and forth to make sure it is correct or make minor changes.

Other powerful benefits of UC integration within PowerPoint include training and marketing. With UC integration, you can schedule a Live Meeting session to train thousands of attendees without leaving your home office. Many Microsoft customers have realized this benefit already, and the popularity of this solution has reached even consumer media — for example, in the form of ads on the popular television show "The Apprentice" on NBC. With the UC integration within PowerPoint, you can now express ideas, provide training, and perform other tasks in real time.

Figure 3-6 depicts how communicator is integrated within Microsoft PowerPoint 2003 with Office 2003 Service Pack 2.

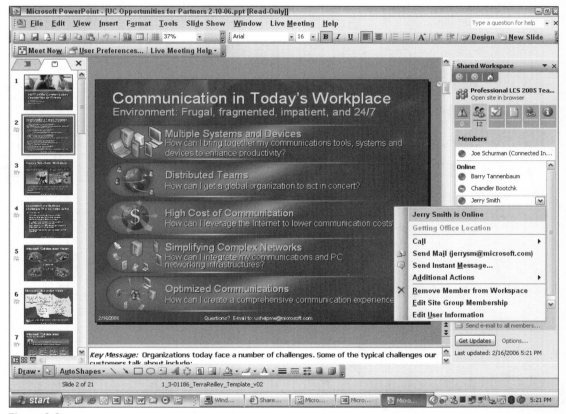

Figure 3-6

Microsoft Office SharePoint Portal Server 2003

In my opinion, SharePoint Portal Server 2003 and Microsoft Windows SharePoint Services are incomplete products without UC integration with LCS and Communicator. SharePoint provides data-driven sites and collaboration, but with LCS integration, SharePoint also acts as a real-time communication and collaboration powerhouse. Within Microsoft Office SharePoint Portal Server 2003, portal users have direct access to user presence and Instant Messaging functionality tied to a user's name, as with Microsoft Outlook. SharePoint provides access to information in an organized, easily retrievable way, and information is generally tied to subject matter experts or individual content contributors. Communicator supplies presence to your contacts to enable easy access to an individual involved in a given scenario so you can ask questions pertaining to the material. You an also add an individual expert to your Communicator contacts list. Additionally, SharePoint Portal Server 2003 and Windows SharePoint Services make use of the Office shared workspace feature for documents you open from a SharePoint site. The Microsoft Office 2003 Shared Workspace tab is opened automatically if enabled, showing team members, tasks, and other features relating to the site in which the document is located. Communicator presence is also supplied within the shared workspace to provide an information worker with access to an entire team or only an individual user within the site.

Figure 3-7 depicts how Communicator presence functionality is embedded within SharePoint Portal Server 2003 with Office 2003 Service Pack 2, as well as the shared workspace feature within Word, Excel, and PowerPoint when viewing SharePoint documents.

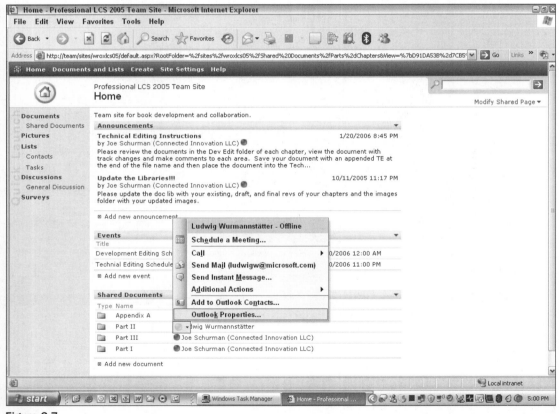

Figure 3-7

Microsoft Office Live Meeting 2005

Microsoft Office Live Meeting 2005 is part of the Office system and Unified Communications (UC) suite of products. There has been a ton of public media around Live Meeting with television commercials and the product's exposure on the NBC show "The Apprentice." Who better to market your product than Donald Trump, eh? The media showcased the product's capability to reduce travel and increase productivity through the use of online meeting technology that provides PowerPoint presentations to the masses across firewalls in order to offer training, support, marketing awareness, and many more presentation options. With Live Meeting's tight integration with Communicator, LCS, and now Microsoft Office 2003, including add-in toolbars, setting up a meeting takes seconds. Compare that to the time required to set up a conference bridge and upload presentations. Additional time savings result from enabling this from your home or wherever an Internet connection is available. With Live Meeting, you can upload your presentations, provide audio conference calls, record meetings, provide training and live demonstrations, and enrich your presentations with the real-time features such as live question-and-answer sessions.

The Microsoft Office Live Meeting 2005 console is depicted in Figure 3-8.

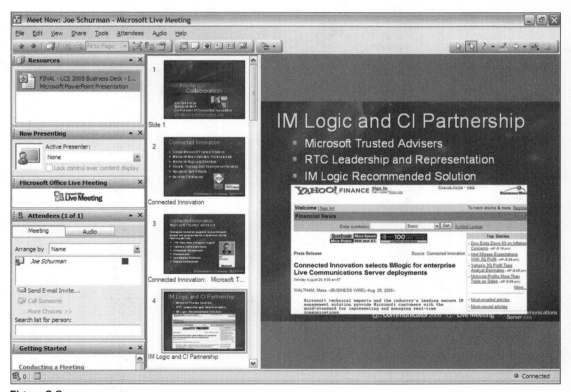

Figure 3-8

Another powerful feature of Live Meeting is remote desktop. I can't count the number of times I have worked with colleagues and customers in supporting their LCS deployments by having the local engineer log in to Live Meeting and allow me to review and correct LCS settings within a test, pilot, or production environment to get an LCS service up and running. The remote control feature within Live Meeting provides this functionality across firewalls and only takes seconds to set up using the Meet Now feature.

The integration with LCS and Communicator enables you to initiate a Live Meeting session within Communicator with one click. This feature is useful when you are having a video, voice, or Instant Messaging conversation and need to share a presentation or remote desktop. Within Communicator, all you have to do is click the Live Meeting option in the Communicator menu and you are ready to go with a Live Meeting session and conference call bridge.

Figure 3-9 illustrates how to start a Live Meeting session from the Communicator 2005 client.

Figure 3-9

"Better Together" Scenario

This section illustrates how real-time collaboration is realized within Microsoft Word, PowerPoint, SharePoint Portal Server 2003, and integration with Microsoft Exchange Server 2003. The purpose of this imaginary scenario is to give you an understanding of how to use UC products as a part of your daily routine to build an understanding of true collaboration.

This scenario demonstrates how a marketing manager named Davis will work with his product management team to market a new solution to his customers. To start, Davis needs to build marketing collateral so he decides to build a presentation that he will use in a meeting session where he will show his customers the new features of his company's product. Davis opens Microsoft Office PowerPoint 2003 and builds slides that include a marketing message and product specifications. Unfortunately, Davis does not know all of the important technical specifications that he needs to complete his presentation. He opens Microsoft Office Communicator 2005 to find his product marketing manager, Paige. Because Paige is in Davis' contact list and her status is set to online, Davis sends an instant message to Paige requesting the information he needs to build his presentation. Paige responds that her colleague, Bailey, developed a specification document, which is available for review on the company's intranet portal. Paige sends Davis the link to the SharePoint Portal website where the document is stored. Davis visits the site and finds the document within the site's document library. This entire process takes only three minutes.

Davis opens the document from within the portal, where he is able to view it. Unfortunately, the document is extremely long and he only needs a bit of information. Luckily, Davis is using Microsoft Office Word 2003, which has the Office 2003 shared workspace. Within the Members tab of the shared workspace to the right of the document is a list of site members, which includes Bailey. This is great, because Bailey is not in Davis' contact list, so he doesn't have to spend time finding her contact details to communicate with her. Davis notices that Bailey is online so he sends her an instant message from within the shared workspace. Bailey responds immediately and Davis messages that he needs her assistance navigating the document to find the information he needs. Bailey opens the document sharing feature and shows Davis where to find the information. Davis thanks Bailey, closes the session, and then copies the information out of the Word document and pastes it into the PowerPoint presentation he is developing. He closes the Word document and then finishes his presentation.

Now, using the PowerPoint presentation he created, Davis is ready to schedule an online meeting to present to his customers the new product that his company is releasing. He opens Microsoft Outlook 2003 and uses the Live Meeting 2005 toolbar to set up a Live Meeting session. Automatically, the meeting details are created, and all Davis has to do now is add his customers' e-mail addresses to the attendee list. Davis sends out the Live Meeting request to his customers, which is one hour from the current time. Davis puts his game face on, gears up for the presentation, and then logs into Live Meeting to attend the meeting. He decides to use Communicator as his phone for the call and dials into the Live Meeting session. Once in the meeting, Davis' customers show up one after another to the meeting. He begins the meeting by introducing himself and the agenda. During this time, one of his customers sends him an instant message using his AOL IM application. Even though the customer is not a Communicator user, Davis can communicate with him because he is federated through Public Instant Messaging Connectivity (PIC). The message informs Davis that he needs to be prepared to answer detailed technical questions regarding the product. Alarmed, Davis realizes that he needs to bring in Paige or Bailey to assist. He quickly adds Paige and Bailey to his Communicator session and asks them both if they can join the conference. Luckily, Paige and Bailey are both available. From within Communicator, Davis clicks on the Live Meeting invite feature and the meeting details are sent to Paige and Bailey automatically. This short exchange saved both time and grief. With everyone now in the meeting together, Paige, Bailey, and Davis present to the customer and Bailey responds to technical questions using the Live Meeting Question Manager feature. When the meeting is over, each customer agrees to trial the product. Davis ends the Communicator session, closing out the meeting. Within two hours, Davis created a presentation with the collaborative assistance of his development team and presented it to his top customers without having to leave his home.

Summary

The integrated features of LCS, Communicator, and Live Meeting within the Microsoft Office system described in this chapter have given you an overview of what is available in terms of features and functionality. In addition, you have seen how these combined products increase productivity, reduce travel, and save time immensely. Please note that for the integrated features described in this chapter to work correctly, you must install Microsoft Office 2003 with Service Pack 2.

You also looked at a typical sample scenario, which highlighted the "Better Together" principle of Unified Communications within the Microsoft Office system. In the next chapter, you will learn how to plan for your LCS deployment to enable this functionality within your own environment.

4

Preparing Your Environment for Live Communications Server 2005 with Service Pack 1

When deploying Live Communications Server 2005 SP1 within an enterprise environment, several network settings need to be modified to enable the properties that LCS requires for installation and connectivity. This chapter describes how Live Communications Server leverages network resources within Microsoft Active Directory; Group Policy Object (GPO) settings; Domain Name Service (DNS); and a digital certificate infrastructure in preparation of a deployment to ensure stable connectivity. You will also be introduced to the appropriate hardware specifications that are required to run Live Communications Server 2005 SP1 and Microsoft Office Communicator 2005.

Live Communications Server 2005 and Microsoft Active Directory

Live Communications Server utilizes Active Directory for more than just authentication. LCS 2005 with SP1 extends the Active Directory schema with 15 classes and 54 attributes, 13 of which are members of the partial attribute set replicated by the Global Catalog. In addition, LCS 2005 with SP1 adds six management groups to the Active Directory. During the preparations, a new container, RTC Service, is added to the System\Microsoft container within Active Directory. The LCS 2005 administration tools provide additional features that enable the system administrator or user administrator to manage the LCS servers within their forest and domains, leverage the Active Directory Users & Computers console to see the Live Communications tab, and manage LCS users in Active Directory. Active Directory may also be leveraged to utilize enterprise certificates and to replicate DNS information.

Active Directory Schema

As it applies to Live Communications Server 2005 with Service Pack 1, the Active Directory schema is extended to hold the 15 classes and 54 attributes associated with LCS. This section describes the changes made to the Active Directory schema. Later in the chapter, the methods related to how those changes are instantiated and verified will be reviewed.

Generally, a service pack does not require a schema extension. However, in an effort to improve the product and add new features to LCS, a schema extension is included with Service Pack 1. The original LCS 2005 schema, as well as the schema additions for Service Pack 1, have been rolled up into a single schema update that is part of the LCS 2005 with SP1 installation CD. The schema preparation does not increase the Active Directory database, or ndts.dit file, significantly. However, when all users in a medium-size organization are enabled for Live Communications, expect to see an increase of approximately 12 to 15 percent.

The Active Directory schema is extended with new classes and attributes associated with LCS 2005 with SP1. A total of 15 classes are created in the Active Directory schema:

❑ **msRTCSIP-Archive:** This class is used to define and hold settings related to the LCS Archiving Service servers in the forest associated with your Live Communications Server with Service Pack 1 deployment.

❑ **msRTCSIP-ArchivingServer:** This class is used to define and hold settings specific to each LCS Archiving server.

❑ **msRTCSIP-Domain:** This class is used to define and hold settings for the domains that are configured as part of the forestwide LCS deployment.

❑ **msRTCSIP-EdgeProxy:** This class is used to represent Access Proxy servers, which are part of the LCS deployment but are generally not domain members in Active Directory because the LCS Access proxy resides in the demilitarized zone (DMZ) or perimeter network and many organizations block Active Directory connectivity to the DMZ.

❑ **msRTCSIP-EnterpriseServerSettings:** This class is used to define settings for LCS servers within the LCS deployment, including whether a server hosts Enterprise Services, or homes users.

❑ **msRTCSIP-Federation:** This class is used to define and hold settings related to federation. This includes relationships between organizations federating connections as well as federation to the Public IM Connectivity (PIC) providers.

❑ **msRTCSIP-GlobalContainer:** This class is used to define and hold settings related to the LCS deployment in a forest. Several of the classes listed in this section are subordinate to this class.

❑ **msRTCSIP-Pool:** This class is used to represent an LCS 2005 Standard server, which is also considered a single-server pool.

❑ **msRTCSIP-Pools:** This class is used to define and hold settings related to LCS 2005 Enterprise Edition pool deployments.

❑ **msRTCSIP-PoolService:** This class is used to define attributes and settings related to the pool to which a user is homed, specifying the service connection point of the pool.

❑ **msRTCSIP-Registrar:** This class is used to define attributes and settings used by the registrar service, which is leveraged for presence, including client subscription to presence (adding a contact).

❑ **msRTCSIP-Search:** This class is used to define attributes and settings used for search operations against the Active Directory, including the number of results that may be returned by a directory search.

❑ **msRTCSIP-Server:** This class is used to define and hold the settings for each LCS server in the forest.

❑ **msRTCSIP-Service:** This class is used to define information related to the LCS service in the forest. It is responsible for the global settings and the msRTCSIP-Domain containers, located in the "Implementing Prep Forest" section of this chapter.

❑ **msRTCSIP-TrustedServer:** This class is used to define and hold attributes related to trusted servers, as well as the msRTCSIP-TrustedServerData attribute, which has been defined for later use.

There are 54 schema attributes associated with these 15 classes. These attributes enable enterprise settings to be stored in, and read from and/or written to, Active Directory. This allows information to be shared across an enterprise environment in a common system, rather than requiring a separate server be configured just to store the Live Communications Server settings.

The following new schema attributes are being added:

❑ msRTCSIP-PrimaryUserAddress

❑ msRTCSIP-UserEnabled

❑ msRTCSIP-PrimaryHomeServer

❑ msRTCSIP-TargetHomeServer

❑ msRTCSIP-OriginatorSid

❑ msRTCSIP-UserExtension

❑ msRTCSIP-FederationEnabled

❑ msRTCSIP-InternetAccessEnabled

❑ msRTCSIP-EnterpriseServices

❑ msRTCSIP-PoolAddress

❑ msRTCSIP-ServerData

❑ msRTCSIP-MaxNumSubscriptions PerUser

❑ msRTCSIP-MinRegistrationTimeout

❑ msRTCSIP-DefRegistrationTimeout

❑ msRTCSIP-MaxRegistrationTimeout

❑ msRTCSIP-MinPresenceSubscription Timeout

❑ msRTCSIP-MinPresenceSubscription Timeout

❑ msRTCSIP-DefPresenceSubscription Timeout

❑ msRTCSIP-MaxPresenceSubscription Timeout

❑ msRTCSIP-MinRoamingData SubscriptionTimeout

❑ msRTCSIP-DefRoamingData SubscriptionTimeout

❑ msRTCSIP-MaxRoamingData SubscriptionTimeout

❑ msRTCSIP-NumDevicesPerUser

❑ msRTCSIP-EnableBestEffortNotify

❑ msRTCSIP-UserDomainList

❑ msRTCSIP-GlobalSettingsData

❑ msRTCSIP-DefaultRouteToEdgeProxy

❑ msRTCSIP-DefaultRouteToEdge ProxyPort

- ❏ msRTCSIP-EnableFederation
- ❏ msRTCSIP-SearchMaxResults
- ❏ msRTCSIP-SearchMaxRequests
- ❏ msRTCSIP-MaxNumOutstandingSearchPerServer
- ❏ msRTCSIP-DomainName
- ❏ msRTCSIP-DomainData
- ❏ msRTCSIP-TrustedServerFQDN
- ❏ msRTCSIP-TrustedServerData
- ❏ msRTCSIP-BackEndServer
- ❏ msRTCSIP-PoolType
- ❏ msRTCSIP-PoolDisplayName
- ❏ msRTCSIP-FrontEndServers
- ❏ msRTCSIP-PoolData
- ❏ msRTCSIP-EdgeProxyFQDN
- ❏ msRTCSIP-EdgeProxyData
- ❏ msRTCSIP-SchemaVersion
- ❏ msRTCSIP-ArchivingEnabled
- ❏ msRTCSIP-ArchiveDefault
- ❏ msRTCSIP-ArchiveFederationDefault
- ❏ msRTCSIP-ArchivingServerData
- ❏ msRTCSIP-TrustedServerVersion
- ❏ msRTCSIP-ArchiveDefaultFlags
- ❏ msRTCSIP-ArchiveFederationDefaultFlags
- ❏ msRTCSIP-OptionFlags
- ❏ msRTCSIP-Line
- ❏ msRTCSIP-LineServer
- ❏ msRTCSIP-PoolVersion

Active Directory Groups

Live Communications Server 2005 with SP1 adds six domain global groups and two domain local groups within Active Directory, two of which are utilized for day-to-day operations: RTCDomainUserAdmins and RTCDomainServerAdmins and are global security groups. The remaining four domain global groups are leveraged by LCS services. These groups — RTCABSDomainServices, RTCArchivingDomainServices, RTCHSDomainServices, and RTCProxyDomainServices — are also global security groups. The two domain local security groups are RTC Local Administrators and RTC Local User Administrators. In addition to these six domain groups and two domain local security groups, seven security groups are local to the server and are used to nest the domain security groups. Depending on the services that you install, you may not see all of the groups on your server or in Active Directory.

The six domain global security groups are added during the *domain prep* process and are created in the Users container within Active Directory. Because they do not have a static well-known GUID assigned, like the Domain Admins and Schema Admins groups, they are searched for by name and should be left in the Users container and should not be renamed. This section describes the functions of each of these groups:

- ❏ **RTCABSDomainServices:** This group provides access for the Address Book Service account(s). The Address Book Service is a new feature that provides an offline address book that Microsoft Office Communicator clients can utilize to search for other users enabled for LCS. The RTCABSDomainServices group is assigned permissions to the LCS user database and to Active Directory, allowing the offline address book to build. Only the service account(s) assigned to the Address Book Service need to be added to this group.

❑ **RTCArchivingDomainServices:** This group is used to provide access for the LCS Archiving Service account(s). It is assigned database access permissions to the LCSIMArchive and LcsLog SQL databases when the Archiving Service is installed. The default account used for archiving in LCS is the LCArchivingService, which is a member of this group. It is entirely possible to add the LCService account to the RTCArchivingDomainServices group and leverage it for this group as well as the RTCDomainServerAdmins group.

❑ **RTCDomainServerAdmins:** This group is one of two groups that administrators leverage for day-to-day management of the LCS environment. It provides access to implement and modify forestwide settings such as the SIP Domains, Access proxies, federation, and archiving. These users can install and administer Enterprise pools and Standard Edition servers. RTCDomainServerAdmins also have permissions to implement and maintain additional services and features, including implementation of Public IM Connectivity. In addition to these responsibilities, the RTCDomainServerAdmins group also has full permissions for managing users. This group is one of only two groups that have default access to the rtc and rtcconfig databases. If the server admins will be SIP-enabling user accounts, they will need to utilize the RTCDomainUserAdmins group.

❑ **RTCDomainUserAdmins:** Much like the RTCDomainServerAdmins group, the RTCDomainUserAdmins admin group is another group commonly used for day-to-day administration of the LCS environment. In this case, the RTCDomainUserAdmins permissions will likely be assigned to the account management team or the help desk, as well as to the members of RTCDomainServerAdmins, who will be tasked with SIP-enabling and managing user accounts. A member of the RTCDomainUserAdmins group has the rights and privileges to enable a user for access to a Live Communications Server or Enterprise Pool, to enable a user to federate with an outside partner, or to enable a user to remotely access the environment. The RTCDomainUserAdmins group also has the rights to enable a user account for archiving, if the archiving service is implemented. Likewise, what the RTCDomainUserAdmins group can enable it can also disable or remove.

❑ **RTCHSDomainServices:** This group enables service accounts, such as the LCService account, to access information in Active Directory and in the LCS database. Specifically, the RTCHSDomainServices group is granted database access permissions to the rtc and rtcconfig databases. The LCService account is the default account name utilized for Live Communications services, and it is created when you activate an Enterprise Edition pool or a Standard Edition server. This account is made a member of the RTCHSDomainServices group. In addition, this group is granted rights to read from and write to the Microsoft Message Queue (MSMQ), which is used to archive IM conversations to the Archiving server. Likewise, the RTCProxyDomainServices are granted similar permissions.

❑ **RTCProxyDomainServices:** This group is used to give accounts utilized for an LCS 2005 with SP1 Proxy server or Access Proxy server the access to submit messages to the MSMQ so that they can be written to a LCS 2005 with SP1 Archiving server within the forest.

Local Server Groups

While not a part of the Active Directory groups that are created during the domain prep, five groups are created locally on the LCS 2005 servers during product installation. Two additional local security groups are created when the Archiving Service is installed.

These groups are used for administration of the local server, be it a home server, Access Proxy, back-end server, Archiving server, or director. The relevance to Active Directory is that the domain groups, created during the domain prep step, will be nested into these local groups on the server(s). These groups are RTC ABS Server Local Group, RTC Local Administrators, RTC Local User Administrators, RTC Server Applications, and RTC Server Local Group.

The domain global group must be nested into the system's Local Group. The following table shows the Local Group and the domain global group that is a member.

Server Local Group	Domain Group
RTC ABS Service Local Group	DOMAIN\RTCABSDomain Services
RTC Archiving Agents	DOMAIN\RTCSHDomainServices DOMAIN\RTCProxyDomainServices
RTC Archiving Services	DOMAIN\RTCArchivingDomainServices
RTC Local Administrators	DOMAIN\RTCDomainServerAdmins
RTC Local User Administrators	DOMAIN\RTCDomainUserAdmins
RTC Server Applications	No default domain group is nested.
RTC Server Local Group	DOMAIN\RTCHSDomainServices

User Authentication

Live Communications Server with SP1 utilizes two authentication protocols to authenticate domain users enabled for Live Communications: Kerberos and NT LAN Manager (NTLM). With Kerberos, the client connects to the Key Distribution Center (KDC) — in this case, a domain controller in their domain — to obtain their Kerberos ticket, which allows them to authenticate to the LCS server. With NTLM, the authentication traffic can be wrapped in a Session Initiation Protocol (SIP) packet and the user can be authenticated even if they do not have access to a domain controller.

Generally, the NTLM protocol is used when external users, or remote users, do not have access to a domain controller. These are generally users who access the LCS environment through either an Access Proxy server connected to the Internet, a customer's office via a direct link, or even a development lab that does not interface with the production Active Directory. This NTLM traffic is encrypted and sent, via the SIP protocol, to the LCS home server, which authenticates the user with the domain controller.

Do not install an Access Proxy on a domain controller. Placing a domain controller on the Internet is dangerous, compromises security, and is definitely not advised. Doing so would negate any benefit that the Kerberos authentication protocol would provide.

As long as we're on the topic of security and authentication, there is one caveat that folks working in environments with two-factor authentication, smart-card authentication, and random token authentication will want to note: The LCS Service account(s), generally LCService, and the service account for the SQL 2000 back-end server should not be enabled for smart cards. A smart card type of authentication system will change the password frequently, and does not update service accounts on systems. As such, the LCService account and the SQL Service account will quickly become locked out, generally causing the associated services to not start up, or to stop functioning.

Preparing Active Directory for LCS 2005 SP1

Preparing the Active Directory is a relatively simple process made possible through the new LCS 2005 deployment tools. The Active Directory domain controllers and global catalog servers require either Windows Server 2003 or Windows 2000 Server with Service Pack 4.

It is important to note that large enterprise environments and environments with multiple Active Directory sites, large Active Directory infrastructures, or Active Directory domain controllers located across slow links will have to plan for replication traffic, as the changes need to propagate across the Active Directory sites.

If the target schema has been extended for LCS 2005 previously, LCS 2005 with SP1 adds additional enhancements that require a schema extension in order to enable and support those features. Thus, a schema extension will have to be performed.

Understanding Administration Tools

Prior to performing any of the preparations to the forest or the domain(s), it is recommended that the LCS 2005 administration tools be installed on a domain controller or administrative workstation or administrative server, whichever is used by your support organization.

When installed, the LCS 2005 administration tools give designated administrators access to the Live Communications tab within the Active Directory Users and Computers application, once the domain prep has been completed for that domain. The changes to Active Directory, which create the tab and define the possible settings, are added as part of the schema prep process. While you do not have to install the LCS 2005 administration tools in advance, you should do so on domain controllers and administrative workstations. This will make administration easier and reduce confusion once the Live Communication tab is available, advice based upon experience in the Microsoft support newsgroup microsoft.public.livecomm.general. Note that you can't install the server application with the administration tools pre-installed on the target LCS server(s). In addition, the LCS 2005 server application should not be installed on a domain controller, as it is not a recommended configuration.

In order to install the administration tools, insert the LCS 2005 with SP1 CD. If Autolaunch is disabled, browse to `<CD>:\setup\i386` and launch `Setup.exe`. Click the Administration Tools menu option. This will launch the LCS 2005 Administration Tools installer. As you go through the installer, you will notice that the administration tools default to `C:\Program Files\Common Files\Microsoft LC 2005\`. It is not possible to change the installation path of these files. In addition to installing in that location, the tools also install an administration template for Active Directory Group Policy. That template, `rtcclient.adm`, as well as a partner template that ships with Microsoft Office Communicator, `communicator.adm`, are covered later in this chapter.

While several methods may be utilized to prepare Active Directory for the installation of the first LCS 2005 SP1 server, the GUI-based deployment tool is the easiest. However, it is possible to utilize a command-line tool, LcsCmd.exe, or functions within the LCS 2005 administration tools to perform the prep forest and prep domain commands.

In order to get to the Prep menu items, insert the LCS 2005 with SP1 CD. If Autolaunch is disabled, browse to <CD>:\setup\i386 and launch Setup.exe. If your LCS 2005 with SP1 CD is the Standard Edition CD, then click the Standard Edition Server menu item. If your LCS 2005 with SP1 CD is the Enterprise Edition CD, then click the Enterprise Pool menu item. This will bring up a screen like the one shown in Figure 4-1.

Figure 4-1

The process starts with a cursory review of the preparation state, followed by the Prep Schema command.

Implementing Prep Schema

The Active Directory schema is updated via a routine that imports a Lightweight Directory Interchange Format, or LDIF, file into the directory. Some organizations have established change control procedures that may require the review of the updates being made to the Active Directory environment. The LDIF file, schema_lcs2005.ldf, is located in the <CD:>\Setup\i386 folder and may be viewed with any text viewer, such as notepad.exe. The LCS 2005 SP1 schema is the same for Live Communications Server 2005 with SP1 Standard Edition and Enterprise Edition.

To extend the Active Directory schema to support Live Communication Server with Service Pack 1, the account being used to extend the schema must be a member of the Schema Admins group and a member of the built-in local Administrators group for the domain in which the Schema Master FSMO role is located. In many large enterprise environments, this is likely the forest root domain. In SMB and mid-size enterprise environments, there is likely only a single Active Directory domain. In either scenario, the Schema Master FSMO role holder and a Global Catalog server should be accessible.

> It is much easier to add the account performing the Prep Schema, Prep Forest, and Prep Domain tasks for the forest root domain to the Schema Admins, Enterprise Admins, and Domain Admins groups as well as the built-in local Administrators group for the forest root domain in which these preps will be performed.

Once these permissions have been granted, you are ready to prepare the schema. As mentioned earlier, once the LCS 2005 with SP1 CD is launched, click the Standard Edition Server menu item or the Enterprise Pool menu item. This brings up the part of the tool that performs the preparations. Here you click Prep Schema. Once it has completed, a notification window will appear, notifying you of success or failure. This notification window also has a button that enables you look at the log, which is particularly useful if the process failed. Optionally, you can utilize the command-line tool:
`<CD>:\Setup\i386\LcsCmd.exe /forest /action:SchemaPrep`

> If the Schema Master FSMO role holder is not available, you may receive one of two generic messages during the Prep Schema step. The error message is `Failure [0x8007203A] The server is not operational` in the LCS 2005 deployment log, or `Action failed with error code 0x8007203A. The server is not operational`. Likewise, if the Remote Registry service is installed or disabled, you will receive the error message `Failure [0x80070035] The network path was not found` in the deployment log, and a pop-up `Action failed with error code 0x80070035. The network path was not found`. These are two of the most common errors noted in the support newsgroups regarding the Active Directory schema preparations.

Once the schema update has completed, the changes need to replicate to other Active Directory domain controllers in the forest. The time needed for the changes to replicate is largely dependent upon the Active Directory site hierarchy and link speed between sites.

While the deployment tool will show you the status of the Prep Schema function, the status may also be checked with the command-line utility `LcsCmd.exe`. The syntax of this tool is `<CD>:\Setup\i386\LcsCmd.exe /forest /action:CheckSchemaPrepState /l:c:\LCSSchemaCheck.html`. Once this tool has finished running, open the resultant log file, `C:\LSCSchemaCheck.html`, and review the Schema Prep state. It should note `LCS 2005 with SP1` if the schema update has completed successfully.

At this point you have successfully extended the schema for LCS 2005 with SP1 and you should be ready to perform the Prep Forest step.

Implementing Prep Forest

The Prep Forest command, also referred to as ForestPrep, readies the Active Directory forest to support Live Communications Server with Service Pack 1. Like the Prep Schema command, the Prep Forest command only needs to be run once in the Active Directory forest.

To prepare the Active Directory forest to support Live Communications Server with Service Pack 1, the account being used to prepare the forest must be a member of the Enterprise Admins group and should also be a member of the built-in local Administrators group for the forest root domain. As mentioned in the preceding section, there may be scenarios in which only a single domain exists within an enterprise environment.

During the Prep Forest, a new container named RTC Service, of the type msRTCSIP-Service, is added to the `System\Microsoft` container within Active Directory. If the Microsoft container does not already exist, it is created as part of the Prep Forest function. The RTC Service container will repose the LCS configuration information for the forest, SIP domains hosted in the forest, LCS pools, and LCS servers. To see this change, click View⇨Advanced Features within Active Directory Users and Computers. These changes can be seen in Figure 4-2.

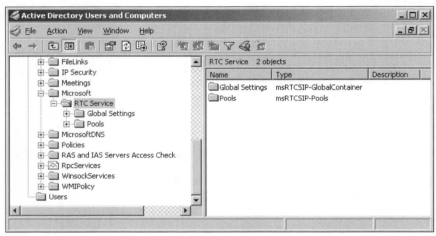

Figure 4-2

Below the RTC Service container are two additional containers: a Global Settings container of the type msRTCSIP-GlobalContainer; and Pools, of the type MSRTCSIP-Pools. Subordinate to the Global Settings container is a GUID of type msRTCSIP-Domain. While this might not make sense at first glance, this GUID actually references the forest root domain, and is the first SIP domain. You can see the domain that this represents by launching the LCS 2005 administration tools (Start⇨All Programs⇨Administration Tools⇨Live Communications Server 2005) and right-clicking on the forest. In addition, once your LCS Servers and Enterprise pools have been configured, the `msRTCSIP-TrustedServer` objects will be stored there as well.

Other items, which may not be readily noticeable, are added to the Configuration container for the Active Directory. An example of this is the addition of a GUID, `{AB255F23-2DBD-4bb6-891D-38754AC280EF}`, to the User-Display properties located under the Configuration container. In this example, the Configuration container is part of a single forest/domain structure named `domain.forest.local`. This specifier would be visible under the `adminContextMenu` properties of the Display Specifiers container. This container is located in `CN=user-Display,CN=409,CN=DisplaySpecifiers,CN=Configuration,DC=domain,` `DC=forest,DC=local`. This property is generally viewed only through the ADSIEdit tool.

Additional items added to the Active Directory Configuration container include the following:

❑ An `RTCPropertySet` object of type `controlAccessRight` under Extended-Rights that applies to the `User` and `Contact` classes

❑ An `RTCUserSearchPropertySet` object of type `controlAccessRight` under Extended-Rights that applies to `User`, `Contact`, `OU`, and `DomainDNS` classes

❑ An `msRTCSIP-PrimaryUserAddress` under the `extraColumns` attribute of each language organizational unit display specifier (`CN=organizationalUnit-Display,CN=409,CN=` `DisplaySpecifiers`) and copies the values of the `extraColumns` attribute of the default display (`CN=organizationalUnit-Display, CN=409,CN=DisplaySpecifiers`)

❑ The `msRTCSIP-PrimaryUserAddress`, `msRTCSIP-PrimaryHomeServer`, and `msRTCSIP-` `UserEnabled` filtering attributes under the `attributeDisplayNames` attribute of each language display specifier for `Users`, `Contacts`, and `InetOrgPerson` objects (for example, in English: `CN=user-Display,CN=409,CN=DisplaySpecifiers`)

To run the Prep Forest command you need Enterprise Admins permissions. Insert the LCS 2005 with SP1 CD into your CD-ROM drive. The deployment tool should launch. When it does, click the Standard Edition Server menu item or the Enterprise Pool menu item. This will bring up the part of the tool that performs the preparations. The tool should launch and check the deployment state. Once it completes there should be a checkbox next to Prep Schema.

Here you will click Prep Forest in order to prepare the Active Directory Forest for LCS 2005 with SP1. Once it has completed, a notification window will appear, notifying you of the success or failure of the installation. On this notification window is a button that enables you look at the log. This is particularly useful if the process failed. Optionally, you can utilize the command-line tool:
`<CD>:\Setup\I386>LcsCmd /forest /action:ForestPrep`.

Once this has completed, you are ready to prepare your child domains with the Prep Domain and Domain Add to Forest Root functions.

Implementing Prep Domain

The primary purpose of the Prep Domain step is to create the domain global security groups that were reviewed in the Active Directory Groups section earlier in this chapter. In addition to creating these groups, the Prep Domain also creates access control lists (ACLs) for these groups so that they can be used to administer users.

The permissions needed for the account being used to perform the Prep Domain function are Domain Admins for the domain the Prep Domain is being performed. The Prep Domain should be performed for every domain that will host LCS 2005 with SP1 servers as well as the forest root domain. When the Prep Domain function is run in the forest root domain, it extends ACLs to LCS server and user properties that are only in the forest root domain.

An example of this is the `RTCUserSearchPropertySet`, which is located in the Extended Rights container. The Extended Rights container is a subordinate of the Configuration container for the forest. The `RTCUserSearchPropertySet` contains information about the user, including the user's name and SIP URI. This object is used by administrators and end-users alike. The well-known security principle "Authenticated Users" has a default read ACL assigned to it. This is what allows users to search for other LCS-enabled users in the forest. The search methodology differs slightly where the Address Book Service has been deployed. In addition to allowing users to search for other SIP-enabled users, this key also allows the server to search for users and their SIP URI, enabling users to authenticate.

> While this is not relevant to the Prep Domain, it is important to mention that in some hosted LCS scenarios, or scenarios in which access to some domains in an enterprise forest are restricted, some papers may advise adding a Deny to the Authenticated Users ACL. Do not add a Deny to the ACL, as a Deny is explicit and could both prevent users from logging in and prevent administrators from making changes.

Because the domain global groups used to administer LCS implementations in the domain are not from a well-known GUID, do not rename the group or move it out of the Users container. If, for whatever reason, one of the global groups is deleted accidentally, insert the LCS 2005 with SP1 CD, and rerun the Prep Domain command. If a group is missing, then the Prep Domain command will not have the checkmark. Instead, it will be blue and can be selected. Optionally, you can use the command-line tool: `<CD>:\Setup\I386>LcsCmd /domain /action:DomainPrep`. This command will rerun the Prep Domain, creating the missing groups; and it will re-apply the domain ACLs and ACEs to that group. Local permissions may need to be changed.

Implementing Domain Add to Forest Root

Whenever a forest contains multiple domains, the Domain Add to Forest Root procedure needs to be performed. This function sets permissions for the child domain to enable access to objects in the forest root domain. This process grants permissions in the forest root to child domain administrators, child domain servers and Enterprise pools, and message queues to be able to access Live Communications Server information stored in the root.

To perform the Domain Add to Forest Root, you must have Domain Admins access in the child domain and Enterprise Admins access in the forest root domain. The Domain Add to Forest Root function is available through the deployment tool. Optionally, the command-line tool, `LcsCmd.exe`, can be used to perform the Domain Add to Forest Root. Note that in the following example, `forest.local` signifies the forest domain and `domain.forest.local` signifies the child domain:

```
<CD>:\Setup\I386>LcsCmd/domain:forest.local/action:DomainAdd/refdomain:domain
.forest.local
```

Working with Resource Forest and Multi-Forest Scenarios

Some organizations maintain several forests used primarily for resources, with one of the forests being utilized for user accounts. Generally these are found in larger organizations. These forests are remnants of upgraded NT4 domains and the domains have not been collapsed. Some organizations make the conscious choice to keep their applications and their user accounts separate. Either way, it works well for the organization and Microsoft has recognized this.

Tools such as Microsoft Identity Integration Server (MIIS) and the MIIS Active Directory Identity Integration Feature Pack (IIFP) may be utilized to synchronize a user account in one forest with a user account or contact object in another forest.

Microsoft has put together a great document regarding this centralized, or resource forest, model. Within the LCS 2005 with SP1 Resource Kit is a directory, `C:\Program Files\Microsoft LC 2005\ResKit\LcsSync`, that contains documentation and example XML files for implementing the resource forest model utilizing MIIS. The resource kit contains a document that provides guidance for implementing this model. This document, `Deploying_in_a_Multiple_Forest_Environment.doc`, is also located in the `LcsSynch` directory along with the example XML files mentioned.

Live Communications Server 2005 SP1 and DNS

LCS uses DNS to enable automatic connectivity to LCS Standard Edition or Enterprise Edition servers without manually configuring the client to communicate with a specific Internet Protocol (IP) address or fully qualified domain name (FQDN) of a server. LCS also uses DNS to enable federation and Public Instant Messaging Connectivity (PIC) to provide communication between LCS Access Proxy servers, as mentioned in Chapter 1. To enable automatic configuration of the Microsoft Office Communicator 2005 client, you need to create the appropriate DNS records to identify the servers and protocols used to connect the client to the specified LCS server. This section identifies the required DNS records used by LCS to ensure a successful deployment.

DNS Host A Records

When installing LCS, the initial steps to deploy the software include preparing your Active Directory for LCS. In doing so, you will update the Active Directory schema, create new LCS properties and accounts within the Active Directory domain and forest, and create an LCS pool (if using LCS Enterprise Edition). When you create the LCS pool or install a LCS Standard Edition server, you need to have a residing DNS host "A" record for the pool available in DNS prior to this step or you will receive a warning in your LCS installation log file. This does not prevent you from creating an LCS pool or server, but you will still need to create the record before Communicator 2005 automatic configuration will work. The client, when enabled with automatic configuration, will perform a DNS query, searching for the name of the server or pool in DNS. If the host A record is not present, the client will not be able to sign in to the service. The query is performed using the lookup of the data listed after the "@" sign portion of the user's sign-in name. For example, if the user's sign-in name is john.doe@company.com, the client will look for a corresponding DNS host A record for company.com. Figure 4-3 displays the flow of the client querying DNS for the host A record of the LCS server or pool.

To enable automatic configuration and to create a DNS host A record for your LCS Server or pool, you must create the a record like the following:

```
Company Name = ConnectedInnovation.com
DNS A Host Record for a pool = LCS.ConnectedInnovation.com
DNS A Host Record for a Server = Server1.ConnectedInnovation.com
```

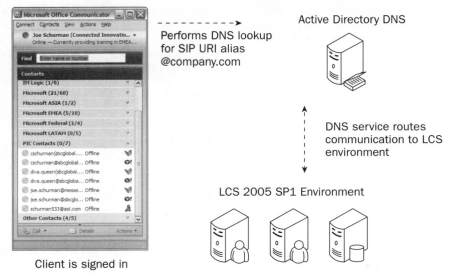

Figure 4-3

When you create a DNS host A record, the key properties you fill out are the name and IP address of the record. When creating a DNS host A record for an LCS Server, you create the record and give it the name of the server. The fully qualified domain name (FQDN) of the server should match the FQDN field of the record, as shown in Figure 4-4.

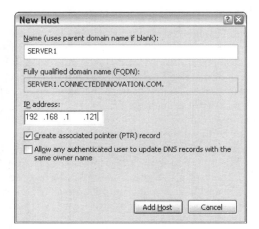

Figure 4-4

When creating a DNS host A record for an LCS pool, you create the record and give it the name of the pool. The fully qualified domain name (FQDN) of the pool should match the FQDN field of the record, as shown in Figure 4-5.

Figure 4-5

To create a DNS host A record for your server or pool, complete the following steps:

1. Log in to a server that has access to the DNS server that resides within your LCS infrastructure.

2. From the Windows Start menu, select All Programs⇨Administrative Tools, and click DNS (see Figure 4-6).

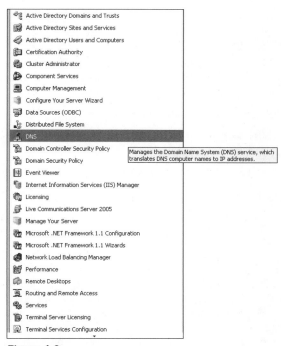

Figure 4-6

3. Expand the tree menu on the left to display the Domain on which you are deploying LCS.

4. From the Actions menu, select New Host (A), as shown in Figure 4-7.

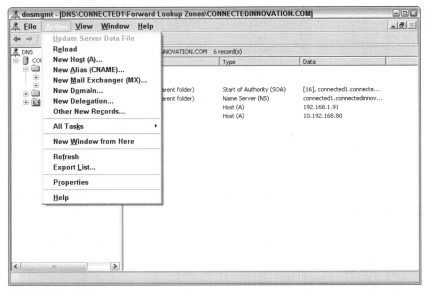

Figure 4-7

5. The New Host window will open (refer to Figure 4-5).

6. In the Name field, enter the name of the LCS server or the LCS pool name. Just enter the name of the server or pool, not the FQDN of the pool or server. The grayed out FQDN field will automatically create the FQDN for you.

7. In the IP address field, enter the address as follows:

    ❑ If the DNS host A record is for a server, enter the IP address of the server.

    ❑ If the DNS host A record is for a pool, enter the IP address of either the load balancer or a LCS pool server, depending on whether you have deployed only one pool server or a load-balanced pool.

8. Click the Add Host button.

DNS SRV Records

To complete the automatic configuration process, DNS SRV records must be applied within DNS. The purpose of a DNS SRV record is to assign a specific protocol for the connection. As an example, most of us know of Transmission Control Protocol (TCP). TCP is a specific protocol that is used to send data packets. Transport Layer Security (TLS) is another protocol used to send data packets over a secured connection. SRV records provide actual network service records to enable you to find network resources within a specific domain based on the connection or protocol type. LCS uses DNS SRV records for automatic configuration so that when the client performs its DNS query and finds the associated DNS host A record, the client will be connected to a DNS SRV record to identify the protocol that the client will use to communicate between users. If you enable TLS within your LCS infrastructure and you are using automatic configuration, you will need to create a DNS SRV record to enable the client to sign into the LCS service using the TLS protocol. If you enable only TCP connectivity to your LCS environment, you will need to create a DNS SRV record for the TCP connection.

The following table outlines the required DNS SRV records based upon the transport and client application used:

LCS Use	Protocol Type	Example of DNS SRV Record	Client Application
Internal	TCP	_SIPINTERNAL._TCP.COMPANY.COM	Communicator
Internal	TCP	_SIP._TCP.COMPANY.COM	Windows Messenger 5.1
Internal	TLS	_SIPINTERNALTLS._TCP.COMPANY.COM	Communicator
Internal	TLS	_SIP._TLS.COMPANY.COM	Windows Messenger 5.1
External	TLS	_SIP._TLS.COMPANY.COM	Both
Federation	TLS	_SIPFEDERATIONTLS._TCP.COMPANY.COM	Communicator

The following steps demonstrate an example of creating a DNS SRV record for an internal TLS connection for Microsoft Office Communicator:

1. Log in to a server that has access to the DNS server that resides within your LCS infrastructure.

2. From the Windows Start menu, select All Programs⇨Administrative Tools, and click DNS (refer to Figure 4-6).

3. Expand the tree menu on the left to display the domain to which you are deploying LCS.

4. From the Actions menu, select Other New Records (refer to Figure 4-7).

5. The Resource Record Type window will open, as shown in Figure 4-8.

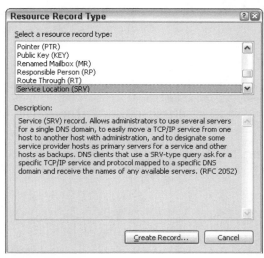

Figure 4-8

6. Scroll down to select Service Location (SRV).

7. Click the Create Record button.

8. The New Resource Record window will open, as shown in Figure 4-9.

Figure 4-9

9. In the Service field, type **_SIPINTERNALTLS**.

10. Leave the Protocol field as _TCP and enter the protocol port as **5061**.

11. In the Host offering this service field, enter the name of the host.

12. Click OK.

Deploying LCS in Multiple Domains

While most LCS deployments for single domains are accomplished in labs and proof of concept environments, in the real world most organizations have multiple domain name spaces due to separation of entities, purpose of the domain (test, development, production, and so on), or for security reasons.

Using an LCS director, you can support multiple SIP URIs and multiple domains for automatic configuration using the Certificate Subject Alternative Name. The Subject Alternative Name is a field property of the certificate that can be set when ordering your certificate and completing the certificate provisioning process.

Figure 4-10 shows a sample certificate with the Subject Alternative Name.

Figure 4-10

You may already be familiar with the Common Name or Friendly Name of a certificate. If not, it's the primary name of the certificate. The client using a defined SIP URI such as user@company2.com using autoconfig is looking for a DNS matching record of company1.com. The same goes for user@company3.com and user@company4.com. However, suppose that the primary use of this LCS deployment is for user@company.com and this type of convoluted deployment is going to leverage one LCS environment for these multiple domains, SIP namespaces, and SIP URIs. In this case, you set the certificate for your LCS director's TLS listening address port of 5061. Apply the certificate with a Server Authentication EKU and a common/friendly name of lcs.company.com (which matches the DNS host record for this entry). Then, in the Subject Alternative Name field, re-enter the original name or lcs.company.com and enter your company2.com, company3.com, and company4.com entries. Then you are set and can enable multiple SIP URIs and namespaces for one entry, one port.

LCS DNS Best Practices

The following items highlight DNS best practices when deploying LCS:

- ❑ Deploy LCS within a central or resource forest if available. Having a solid and controlled, centrally managed infrastructure will speed up the deployment process.

- ❑ Choose a simple SIP URI. The SIP (Session Initiation Protocol) URI (Uniform Resource Identifier) is the ID that your users will use to log in to Communicator or Windows Messenger 5.1. Using the organization's e-mail address is the most common choice for the SIP URI and results in easier deployment of DNS host A records.

- ❑ Always verify your records before you install and deploy LCS. Make sure that you have the appropriate DNS host A records and SRV records applied.

Understanding Live Communications Server 2005 GPO Settings

Client management and meeting client management goals as set forth by the executive and managing sponsor(s) supporting the LCS investment are perhaps some of the more complex tasks that an administrator will have to perform. Through the Group Policy feature of Active Directory, and through the administration template, `rtcclient.adm`, included in LCS 2005 with SP1, this process greatly reduces the need to go desktop to desktop to meet some of the requirements. Additionally, Microsoft Office Communicator comes with its own template, `communicator.adm`. In this section, the configuration settings of the default `rtcclient.adm` file are covered at a high level.

This template can be applied to either the local system policy, through `GPEdit.msc`, or through an Active Directory Group Policy object. Because this chapter focuses on Active Directory, this section concentrates on utilizing the Active Directory Group Policy Object Editor to leverage the administrative changes allowed through the administration template and your organization's investment in Active Directory and Live Communications Server 2005 with Service Pack 1. If your organization has implemented the Group Policy Management Console, the steps to creating a GPO are similar. At the end of the section, a brief example of this is included.

In instances where resource forests are used, the Group Policy object needs to be configured in the same domain in which the workstation and user account are located. If the workstation is not a member of a domain, Group Policy will not be applied for either the user configuration settings or the computer configuration settings.

Using the rtcclient.adm Administrative Template

The `rtcclient.adm` template that will be reviewed in this section is included as part of LCS 2005 with Service Pack 1. This is the default template used for administering Windows Messenger 5.*x* clients within the Active Directory environment.

The `rtcclient.adm` administrative template is installed in the `%windir%\inf` directory when either LCS 2005 Enterprise or Standard Edition is installed on a server, and when the LCS 2005 administration tools are installed on a workstation or server. Generally this directory is `C:\windows\inf` or `C:\winnt\inf`.

This section begins with a table listing the settings associated with this template. After a description of the settings, the section provides a brief description of what the template feature allows the administrator to perform. The Computer Configuration Settings modify policy registry keys and registry values in the following path:

    HKEY_Local_Machine\ Software\Policies\Microsoft\Messenger\Client

Likewise, the User Configuration Settings modify policy registry keys and registry values in the following path:

    HKEY_Current_User\ Software\Policies\Microsoft\Messenger\Client

The `rtcclient.adm` template settings, listed in the following table, apply to the English language Windows Messenger 5.0 and 5.1 client versions:

Computer Configuration Settings
Windows Messenger Feature Policies
Prevent users from running Windows Messenger
Prevent initial, automatic start of Windows Messenger
Prevent connection to .NET Messaging Service
Prevent connection to SIP Communications Service
Prevent connection to Exchange Messaging Service Properties
Prevent video calls
Prevent computer-to-computer audio calls
Prevent computer-to-phone audio calls
Allow computer-to-phone calls
Prevent file transfer
Prevent collaboration features
Prevent NetMeeting
Specify instrumentation
Prevent automatic update from .NET Messaging Service
Prevent Ink in instant messages
SIP Communications Service Policies
Require logon credentials
Allow additional server DNS names
Specify encryption for computer-to-computer audio and video calls
Require SIP high-security mode
Allow storage of user passwords
Specify transport and server
RTC Client API Policies
Limit bandwidth for audio and video calls
Specify dynamic port ranges
Enable Certificate Revocation List Checking

Table continued on following page

User Configuration Settings
Windows Messenger Feature Policies

Prevent users from running Windows Messenger

Prevent initial, automatic start of Windows Messenger

Prevent connection to .NET Messaging Service

Prevent connection to SIP Communications Service

Prevent connection to Exchange Messaging Service Properties

Prevent video calls

Prevent computer-to-computer audio calls

Prevent computer-to-phone audio calls

Allow computer-to-phone calls

Prevent file transfer

Prevent collaboration features

Prevent NetMeeting

Specify instrumentation

Prevent automatic update from .NET Messaging Service

Prevent Ink in instant messages

SIP Communications Service Policies

Require logon credentials

Allow additional server DNS names

Specify encryption for collaboration features

Specify encryption for computer-to-computer audio and video calls

Require SIP high-security mode

Allow storage of user passwords

Specify transport and server

One thing that you might notice is that the Computer Configuration Settings and the User Configuration Settings for the `rtcclient.adm` administrative template are nearly identical to each other. The Computer Configuration Settings have an additional feature for RTC Client API Policies. Although these settings can be applied in the Computer Configuration as well as the User Configuration, unless otherwise specified, the policy set in the Computer Configuration takes precedence over the User Configuration. Because they are so similar, both will be reviewed as a single policy item. Again, if a Computer Configuration policy is applied, then it takes precedence over the User Configuration.

The next section contains information about each of the policy settings. As a default, the template implements all settings as Not Configured.

Understanding the Windows Messenger Feature Policies

The Windows Messenger Feature Policies are available for configuration in the Administrative Templates section of the policy, both in the User Configuration and Computer Configuration hierarchy of the policy object. The settings in this policy enable system administrators to control how Windows Messenger acts within their environment. Remember that settings configured under Computer Configuration take precedence over those in the User Configuration:

❑ **Prevent users from running Windows Messenger:** With this policy enabled, users will not be able to launch or run Windows Messenger. When disabled, or not configured, users will be able to launch or run Windows Messenger.

❑ **Prevent initial, automatic start of Windows Messenger:** This policy, when enabled, prevents Windows Messenger from launching when the user logs into the workstation. When disabled, or not configured, this setting is not used, and the user preferences for Run Windows Messenger when Windows starts, within Windows Messenger, take precedence.

❑ **Prevent connection to .NET Messaging Service:** This policy, when enabled, removes the capability of a workstation (Computer Configuration), user, or group of users (User Configuration) to configure Windows Messenger to connect directly to the .NET Messaging Service. This also removes the Accounts tab option for .Net Passport Account. When left to the default of Not Configured, or set to Disabled, users and workstations to which this policy applies will be able to utilize the .NET Messenger service.

This applies to Windows Messenger, but does not control access via .Net Messenger or third-party applications, such as Trillian. This does not prevent users or workstations from using Public IM Connectivity if it has been configured for your organization.

❑ **Prevent connection to SIP Communications Service:** This policy, when enabled, removes the capability of a workstation (Computer Configuration), user, or group of users (User Configuration) to configure Windows Messenger to connect to a SIP server. This also removes the Accounts tab option for SIP Communications Service Account. Because Live Communications Server is a SIP server, one of the few scenarios in which this policy feature would be used is when your organization has programmed an application to provide presence and Instant Messaging access separate from the Windows Messenger application. When left to the default of Not Configured, or set to Disabled, users and workstations to which this policy applies will be able to utilize the SIP Communications Service.

❑ **Prevent connection to Exchange Messaging Service Properties:** This policy, when enabled, removes the capability of a workstation (Computer Configuration), user, or group of users (User Configuration) to configure Windows Messenger to connect to an Exchange Messaging Service server. This also removes the Accounts tab option for Exchange Account. When left to the default of Not Configured, or set to Disabled, users and workstations to which this policy applies will be able to configure Windows Messenger to utilize an Exchange Messaging Service server. This feature is based on the Rendezvous Protocol, or RVP, which was introduced with Exchange 2000.

❑ **Prevent video calls:** This policy, when enabled, prevents Windows Messenger from starting or receiving computer-to-computer video calls. When left to the default of Not Configured, or set to Disabled, Windows Messenger can receive and initiate computer-to-computer video calls.

❑ **Prevent computer-to-computer audio calls:** This policy, when enabled, prevents Windows Messenger from starting or receiving computer-to-computer audio calls. When left to the default of Not Configured, or set to Disabled, Windows Messenger can receive and initiate computer-to-computer audio calls.

❑ **Prevent computer-to-phone audio calls:** This policy, when enabled, prevents Windows Messenger from receiving or initiating computer-to-phone audio calls. This setting overrides the "Allow computer-to-phone audio calls" policy configuration.

The comments in the rtcclient.adm template specifically note that this feature is outdated and that using it should be avoided.

❑ **Allow computer-to-phone calls:** This policy setting, when enabled, allows Windows Messenger to initiate and receive computer-to-phone calls. When left to the default of Not Configured, or set to Disabled, Windows Messenger cannot initiate or receive computer-to-phone audio calls.

❑ **Prevent file transfer:** This policy setting, when enabled, prevents Windows Messenger from being used to transfer files. If this policy setting is left Not Configured, or is set to Disabled, Windows Messenger can be used to send and receive files.

❑ **Prevent collaboration features:** This policy setting, when enabled, prevents Windows Messenger from being used to whiteboard and share applications, including the desktop of another machine. If this policy setting is left Not Configured, or it is set to Disabled, Windows Messenger can be used to whiteboard and share applications.

❑ **Prevent NetMeeting:** This policy setting, when enabled or left Not Configured, prevents Windows Messenger from being used to start the NetMeeting application. As noted in the rtcclient.adm template file, this is the default behavior. If this policy setting is disabled, then Windows Messenger is allowed to start the NetMeeting application.

❑ **Specify instrumentation:** This policy setting, when enabled, prevents Windows Messenger users from disabling instrumentation, or the capability to record the user's actions. If this setting is Disabled, then the user can't enable instrumentation and instrumentation is left disabled. If this policy is Not Configured, then the user can choose to either enable or disable the instrumentation setting.

❑ **Prevent automatic update from .NET Messaging Service:** This policy setting, when enabled, prevents Windows Messenger from downloading and updating to a new version of Windows Messenger, which is provided by the .NET Messaging Service. This will not replace Windows Messenger with .NET Messenger. If left Disabled or Not Configured, Windows Messenger will automatically download and update to a new version presented by the .NET Messaging Service.

❑ **Prevent Ink in instant messages:** This setting, when enabled, prevents users from sending or receiving IM messages that contain "Ink." Ink is the term for the handwritten text received from someone who is using Windows Messenger. This is generally found by users who have a Tablet PC. A Tablet PC is not required for someone to receive instant messages containing Ink. If this policy setting is left Not Configured, or it is set to Disabled, Windows Messenger can be used to receive and send messages containing Ink.

Understanding the SIP Communications Service Policies

The SIP Communications Service Policies, much like the Windows Messenger Feature Policies are available for configuration in the Administrative Templates section of the policy, both in the User Configuration and Computer Configuration hierarchy of the policy object. These policies enable system administrators to control items related to the SIP configuration of Windows Messenger. Remember that settings configured under Computer Configuration take precedence over those in User Configuration:

❑ **Require logon credentials:** This setting, when enabled, will require the Windows Messenger user to provide a username and password, instead of Windows Messenger utilizing the existing Kerberos ticket, or authenticating the user via NTLM. If this policy setting is left Not Configured, or it is set to Disabled, Windows Messenger will authenticate based upon the credentials for the user currently logged in. These settings can be particularly useful when a shared account, such as a help-desk account, is being used. While sharing an account is generally a bad idea, it still happens on some shared PCs.

❑ **Allow additional server DNS names:** This policy setting is used when Windows Messenger is set to "automatic" and utilizes the `_sip._tls.company.com` SRV record to connect to a Live Communications Server with a DNS name that is not standard.

For example, if your user's SIP URIs end in `@Company.com`, then the SRV record must resolve `_sip._tls.company.com` to either `LCSservername.company.com` or `server.sip.company.com`.

If the LCS server is in a resource domain, the server would be `LCSservername.resource.company.com`. Enabling this registry key allows the Windows Messenger client to acknowledge that the LCS Server or LCS Enterprise Pool may be in a different domain. Disabling this setting, or leaving it as Not Configured, does prevent the Windows Messenger client from connecting to servers where the FQDN is not standard. It also prevents a possible man-in-the-middle attack.

❑ **Specify encryption for computer-to-computer audio and video calls:** This policy setting, when enabled, has three additional options: Support Encryption (default), Require Encryption, and Don't Support Encrypt. If the policy setting is enabled and Support Encryption (default) is selected, the Windows Messenger client will support both encrypted and nonencrypted audio and video data streams. If Require Encryption is selected, only encrypted audio and video data streams are allowed. Other, nonencrypted streams are disallowed and automatically declined by Windows Messenger.

If this policy setting is Disabled or set to Not Configured, Windows Messenger sends and receives audio and video data whether or not it is encrypted. This is the default functionality of Windows Messenger.

❑ **Require SIP high-security mode:** This policy setting, when enabled, requires Windows Messenger clients to send and receive SIP messages via Transport Layer Security, or TLS, and authenticate using Kerberos or NTLM authentication protocols. Neither the TCP nor the UDP protocol guarantee secure Instant Messaging traffic for SIP-based clients. This setting also requires that messages pass from a client to a server and back to a client. Client-to-client SIP communication is not allowed when this setting is enabled, and SIP IM traffic is not allowed to pass through a Universal Plug-and-Play NAT translation device. When this setting is disabled or left set to Not Configured, Windows Messenger can be configured to communicate via TLS, TCP, or UDP. Please note that Live Communications Server does not support SIP over UDP.

❑ **Allow storage of user passwords:** This policy setting, when enabled, allows Windows Messenger to store passwords at the request of the user. If this policy setting is set to Disabled, Windows Messenger is not allowed to store a password. If the policy is set to Not Configured and the user account logs on to an Active Directory domain, Windows Messenger will not store the user's password. If the user does not log on to a domain but is configured to log on to the workstation, Windows Messenger is allowed to store the password.

❑ **Specify transport and server:** This policy setting, when enabled, allows the administrator to specify the transport that the Windows Messenger client will use—either TCP, TLS, or UDP. LCS 2005 allows only the TCP or TLS protocols to be used for instant messages and presence registration.

This policy setting, when enabled, also allows the administrator to specify the DNS name or IP address of the server. While it does say DNS name or IP address of the server, when using LCS the Windows Messenger application should always be configured to point to the DNS name of the Enterprise pool if LCS is connecting to LCS 2005 with SP1 Enterprise Edition. If the Windows Messenger application is connecting to LCS 2005 with SP1 Standard Edition, the DNS name should be that of the Standard Edition server, be it a Proxy or Access Proxy.

This policy is particularly useful when configuring Group Policy settings via Active Directory sites in a large enterprise deployment where multiple LCS 2005 Standard Edition servers and Enterprise pools may be available.

When this policy is set to Disabled or Not Configured, there are two options. The first is to use the default Automatic Configuration, which relies upon the DNS SRV records to provide connection information. The second is to allow users, or their desktop administrator, to manually configure Windows Messenger.

Understanding the RTC Client API Policies

The RTC Client API Policies are available for configuration only in the Computer Configuration portion of the Administrative Templates section of the GPO. The three policies in this section enable the system administrator to control advanced features related to ports and bandwidth, such as audio and video communication, certificate revocation checking, and ports used by the audio, video, and SIP features.

❑ **Limit bandwidth for audio and video calls:** This policy setting, when enabled, allows the administrator to limit the maximum amount of bandwidth that will be used by Windows Messenger for audio and video calls. The maximum bandwidth will not extend the amount of bandwidth that Windows Messenger uses beyond what is necessary.

When set to Disabled or Not Configured, Windows Messenger will utilize the maximum amount of bandwidth that is necessary to pass traffic for peer-to-peer audio and video calls.

❑ **Specify dynamic port ranges:** This policy setting, when enabled, enables the administrator to set the Minimum SIP dynamic port and Maximum SIP dynamic port as well as the Minimum RTP dynamic port and the Maximum RTP dynamic port. Maximum limits the maximum amount of bandwidth that will be utilized by Windows Messenger for audio and video calls. The maximum bandwidth will not extend the amount of bandwidth that Windows Messenger utilizes beyond what is necessary.

When set to Disabled or Not Configured, Windows Messenger will utilize the maximum amount of bandwidth that is necessary to pass traffic for peer-to-peer audio and video calls. Based upon past experience, this is generally less than 100K, but may peak to 300K on occasion.

❑ **Enable Certificate Revocation List Checking:** This policy setting, when enabled, enables the administrator to make the client check for the CRL. Administrators can enable three settings: Enabled (default), Disabled, and Strictly Enforced. When the CRL checking is Enabled, the client attempts to obtain the certificate revocation list and check the CRL against the server certificate. If the policy is Enabled, but CRL checking is disabled, it has the same effect as setting the policy to Disabled or Not Configured. The client does not check for CRL revocation. Lastly, if the policy is Enabled and set to Strictly Enforced, then the client must obtain the CRL and must verify that the server certificate is valid before establishing a TLS connection.

Implementing a Group Policy Template for Testing

This section covers the steps to create a Group Policy object and utilize the `rtcclient.adm` template. This brief implementation will apply to a test policy created in a test OU, using the default tools available through Active Directory Users and Computers. However, the Group Policy Management Console is acknowledged and can be leveraged as well.

When implementing the `rtcclient.adm` template for the domain, you should create an additional policy for managing Windows Messenger clients at the domain level, rather than make changes to the default domain policy, even if it is in a test environment. If at all possible, avoid modifying the default domain policy. The following steps assume that the account creating the policy has the appropriate rights to do so within the Active Directory test environment.

Implementation of any Group Policy should include testing, management communication, help desk communication, and communication with the end-user community. This section covers creating a test policy within your own test environment only.

In this test, we are going to implement a policy to prevent a test user from having access to the .NET Messenger and Exchange Messaging features of Windows Messenger:

1. On a system with the LCS 2005 administration tools installed, check the `%windir%\inf` directory to ensure that `rtcclient.adm` is located in it.

> **This system could be a domain controller with the tools, an administrative workstation, or even an LCS 2005 Standard Edition server or LCS 2005 Enterprise Edition front-end server.**

2. Open Active Directory Users and Computers either by selecting Start⇨Run and typing **<dsa.msc>** or by selecting Start⇨Programs⇨Administrative Tools⇨Active Directory Users and Computers.

3. Create an organizational unit named `RTCClientTest` by right-clicking your domain in Active Directory Users and Computers and selecting New⇨Organizational Unit.

4. In that OU, create a test user account and a group named RTCClient Policy Test Group, using the default of a global security group.

5. Once the group is created, add the test user to the RTCClient Policy Test Group.

6. If the test user account has an e-mail address, right-click on the user and select Enable Users for Live Communications. Otherwise, open the Properties page for the user, select the Live Communications tab, select the checkbox Enable Live Communications for This User, and provide a SIP URI and a server or pool name for the user.

7. Log into the test workstation with the test user account and configure Windows Messenger so that the test user can log on to the LCS server. This validates that the client can connect to the LCS server:

    a. In order to configure Windows Messenger, you would select Tools⇨Options on the Windows Messenger sign-in page, and select the Account tab.

b. Enter the SIP URI for the sign-in. If you have the SRV records already created, then no further configuration is needed. If you do not have the SRV records already created, enter the server's fully qualified domain name (FQDN) and the method with which you desire to connect, either TCP or TLS. TCP should be fine for these tests. Please note that Live Communications Server does not support a UDP connection for SIP messaging.

8. From within Windows Messenger, select Tools⇨Options. On the Options window that appears, select the Accounts tab. Validate that both .NET Passport Account and Exchange Account are visible.

9. In the Active Directory Users and Computers Group Policy editor, right-click the RTCClientTest OU and select Properties.

10. Select the Group Policy tab and click the New button.

11. Name the new Group Policy object RTC Client Test Policy and press Enter.

12. Select the RTC Client Test Policy and select Properties. When the RTC Client Test Policy Properties dialog box comes up, select the Security tab.

> **Performing this now is a best practice for preventing a policy from being configured and accidentally applied to a client or set of clients, such as Authenticated Users.**

13. Select the Authenticated Users group and uncheck Apply Group Policy. Do not add a Deny, as a Deny is explicit.

> **While a domain Admin, or other privileged account, should not be enabled for Live Communications for the same security reasons it should not be e-mail-enabled, it is possible that a policy may need to be applied, and an explicit Deny would prevent this.**

14. Click the Add button, search for the RTCClient Policy Test Group, and click OK. This should add the group to the list of group or usernames within the policy's Properties box.

15. Ensure that read permissions are set to Allow. Select the Allow checkbox for Apply Group Policy.

16. Validate that no other groups or users have Apply Group Policy and then click Apply and OK.

17. Select the RTCClient Test Policy and click the Edit button. This will launch the Group Policy Object Editor.

18. Right-click on the Administrative Templates folder under either Computer Configuration or User Configuration and select Add/Remove Templates.

19. On the Add/Remove Templates dialog box you will see several current policy templates. Select all of those templates and then select Remove (this is being performed because we are only interested in the `rtcclient.adm` policy template).

20. Select the Add button. This will bring up the Policy Templates dialog box. Select the `rtcclient.adm` template and click the Open button. Select the Close button on the Add/Remove Templates dialog.

21. Click the + box on the Administrative Templates folder, which is subordinate of User Configuration, and select the Windows Messenger Feature Policies folder.

22. Double-click Prevent Connection to .NET Messaging Service. Optionally, this can be right-clicked and then Properties selected. This will bring up the Properties dialog box. Select Enabled and click Apply and OK.

23. Double-click Prevent Connection to Exchange Messaging Service. Optionally, this can be right-clicked and then Properties selected. This will bring up the Properties dialog box. Select Enabled and click Apply and OK

24. Close the Group Policy Object Editor. Note that there are no Save or Save As options, as the changes are automatically saved.

25. Close the RTCClient Test Properties dialog box by clicking OK.

26. Log the test user off of the test workstation and then back on to the test workstation.

27. Launch Windows Messenger and select Tools⇨Options. Click the Accounts tab. Both the .NET Messenger Account and the Exchange Account options should be gone.

Communicator.adm Administrative Template

This section describes the configuration options available through the `communicator.adm` template, which ships on the Microsoft Office Communicator CD. One thing you may notice is how many additional features the `communicator.adm` template contains compared to the `rtcclient.adm` template. Administrators will also notice that the `communicator.adm` template contains many of the same setting options as the `rtcclient.adm` template.

The `communicator.adm` template for Microsoft Office Communicator is located in the `Support` directory on the Microsoft Office Communicator CD. Generally, this directory is `D:\Support` or `<CD>:\Support`.

The Computer Configuration Settings modify policy registry keys and registry values in the following path:

    HKEY_Local_Machine\ Software\Policies\Microsoft\Communicator

Likewise, the User Configuration Settings modify policy registry keys and registry values in the following path:

    HKEY_Current_User\ Software\Policies\Microsoft\Communicator

The following two tables list the settings available in Computer Configuration as well as the settings available in the User Configuration. The `communicator.adm` template settings, as listed in these tables, apply to the English language version of Microsoft Office Communicator 2005. The first table lists the settings available in the Computer Configuration portion of the Administrative template.

Computer Configuration Settings
Microsoft Office Communicator Policy Settings
Microsoft Office Communicator Feature Policies
Prevent users from running Microsoft Office Communicator
Prevent video calls
Prevent computer-to-computer audio calls
Enable conferencing
Enable computer-to-phone calls
Prevent file transfer
Prevent users from saving instant messages
Prevent collaboration features
Specify instrumentation
Prevent Ink in instant messages
Permit hyperlinks in instant messages
Disable Calendar presence
Enable phone control
Disable presence note
Disable call presence
Allow remote assistance
Help menu
Tab URL
Disable Live Meeting integration
Block IMs from federated contacts
Set maximum allowed number of contacts
Launch Microsoft Office Communicator Tour
Require logon credentials
Allow additional server DNS names
Specify encryption for computer-to-computer audio and video calls
Configure SIP security mode
Enable UPNP
Allow storage of user passwords

Computer Configuration Settings
Microsoft Office Communicator Policy Settings
Microsoft Office Communicator Feature Policies
Specify transport and server
Limit bandwidth for audio and video calls
Specify dynamic port ranges
Disable certificate revocation list checking
Allow Microsoft Office Communicator to transfer unencrypted files
Disable emoticons in instant messages
Warning text
Address book URL fallback logic
Address book server inside URL
Address book server outside URL

The next table lists the settings available in the User Configuration portion of the Administrative template. As with the `rtcclient.adm` template, the User Configuration settings in the `communicator.adm` template can be overridden by the Computer Configuration settings.

User Configuration Settings
Microsoft Office Communicator Policy Settings
Microsoft Office Communicator Feature Policies
Prevent users from running Microsoft Office Communicator
Prevent video calls
Prevent computer-to-computer audio calls
Enable conferencing
Enable computer-to-phone calls
Prevent file transfer
Prevent users from saving instant messages
Prevent collaboration features
Specify instrumentation
Prevent Ink in instant messages

Table continued on following page

User Configuration Settings
Microsoft Office Communicator Policy Settings
Microsoft Office Communicator Feature Policies
Permit hyperlinks in instant messages
Disable Calendar presence
Enable phone control
Disable presence note
Disable call presence
Allow remote assistance
Help menu
Tab URL
Disable Live Meeting integration
Block IMs from federated contacts
Set maximum allowed number of contacts
Launch Microsoft Office Communicator Tour
Require logon credentials
Allow additional server DNS names
Specify encryption for computer-to-computer audio and video calls
Configure SIP security mode
Enable UPNP
Allow storage of user passwords
Specify transport and server
Allow Microsoft Office Communicator to transfer unencrypted files
Disable emoticons in instant messages
Warning text
Address book URL fallback logic
Address book server inside URL
Address book server outside URL

To view the new features of the `communicator.adm` template, you can open the template locally on a workstation using `gpedit.msc` or by creating a test GPO in Active Directory. Because we are concentrating on the environment, the focus will be on utilizing a test GPO:

1. Insert the Microsoft Office Communicator CD into the CD drive of the system that was used in the previous exercise.

2. Copy the `communicator.adm` template file to your `%windir%\inf` directory; generally, this directory is `C:\windows.inf`.

> This is not a completely necessary step as the template file is copied into a policy contained within the Active Directory `SYSVOL`.

3. In the Active Directory Users and Computers Group Policy editor, right-click on RTCClientTest OU and select Properties.

4. Select the Group Policy tab and click the New button.

5. Name the new Group Policy object "Communicator Client Test Policy" and press Enter.

6. Select the Communicator Client Test Policy and select Properties. When the Communicator Client Test Policy Properties dialog box appears, select the Security tab.

> As noted when the `rtcclient.adm` template was implemented in the preceding section, this is being performed now because it is a best practice to prevent a policy from being configured and accidentally applied to a client or set of clients, such as Authenticated Users.

7. Select the Authenticated Users group and uncheck Apply Group Policy. Do not add a Deny, which is explicit.

> While a domain Admin, or other privileged account, should not be enabled for Live Communications for the same security reasons it should not be e-mail enabled, it is possible that a policy may need to be applied, and an explicit Deny would prevent this.

8. Select the Add button and search for the RTCClient Policy Test Group, clicking OK. This should add the group to the list of group or usernames within the policy's Properties box.

> This group is being reused from the `rtcclient.adm` template testing performed earlier in this section.

9. Ensure that read permissions are set to Allow. Select the Allow checkbox for Apply Group Policy.

10. Validate that no other groups or users have Apply Group Policy and then click Apply and OK.

11. Select the Communicator Client Test Policy and click the Edit button. This will launch the Group Policy Object Editor.

12. Right-click on the Administrative Templates folder under either Computer Configuration or User Configuration and select Add/Remove Templates.

13. On the Add/Remove Templates dialog box you will see several current policy templates. Select all of those templates and then select Remove (this is being performed because we are only interested in the communicator.adm policy template).

14. Select the Add button. This will bring up the Policy Templates dialog box. Select the communicator.adm template and click the Open button. Select the Close button on the Add/Remove Templates dialog.

15. Click the + boxes on the Administrative Templates folder, which is a subordinate of User Configuration and Computer Configuration.

16. Click the + boxes next to Microsoft Office Communicator Policy Settings.

17. Click Microsoft Office Communicator Feature Policies. From here, the individual policies and their functions can be reviewed.

Understanding LCS and Certificates

LCS requires digital certificates if you deploy Transport Layer Security (TLS) for client connectivity or if you have multiple LCS servers within your environment using Mutual Transport Layer Security (MTLS). As described in Chapter 1, LCS uses TLS to encrypt Instant Messaging communications between users and networks. LCS requires MTLS to provide server-to-server communication between LCS servers. TLS, like its predecessor, Secure Sockets Layer (SSL), requires a certificate at the server level tied to a certificate root chain. This issuing chain provides authoritative trust for servers within an LCS infrastructure.

Figure 4-11 shows the flow of communication across a TLS-encrypted pipe, with each endpoint's required certificate.

The TLS certificate requirements within a LCS deployment include the following:

❑ All client machines that will connect to the LCS service must have a trusted Root Certificate Authority (CA) certificate installed on their desktop. Most personal computers ship with default Root CA certificates such as VeriSign, EnTrust, and others. The client machine does not need a user-specific certificate; it's only necessary that the client trusts the Root CA from which the LCS server certificates were generated.

❑ Each LCS Server to which the client machines will connect using TLS must have a Server Authentication EKU (Enhanced Key Usage) certificate. These certificates are requested for each physical machine. Note that when requesting a certificate for a LCS pool or LCS server, the common name (CN) of the certificate must match the name of the server or pool (for front-end servers). If not, the connection between client and server or pool will not work.

❑ If you are enabling federation or Public Instant Messaging Connectivity (PIC) within your LCS environment to provide communication capabilities with public IM networks such as MSN, AOL, Yahoo, or other LCS environments, you need a certificate for your LCS Access Proxy servers. The purpose of this is to enable authentication between networks.

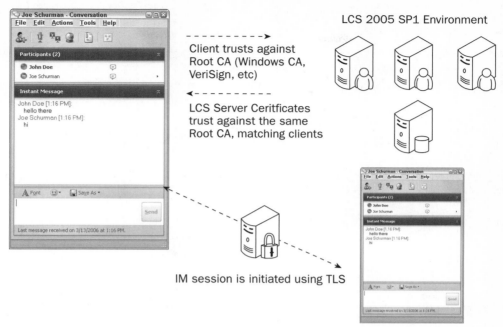

Figure 4-11

Certificate Types

You can select from several certificate EKU (Enhanced Key Usage) types when creating a digital certificate. Prior to LCS 2005, the requirement for an LCS Server Certificate was a Server and Client Authentication EKU certificate. With LCS 2005 SP1, only a Server Authentication EKU certificate is required because the chain is not actually authenticating a user certificate; it is authenticating that the client trusts the Certificate Authority.

The Server Authentication EKU certificate is used to authenticate the LCS Standard Edition or Enterprise Edition servers within the Root CA chain. Figure 4-12 shows an example of an LCS Enterprise Edition Pool Server certificate.

LCS Certificate Properties

When requesting certificates for your LCS servers or LCS pools, several properties are extremely important. If these properties are not set correctly, your LCS environment will not work and much time will be lost in the process of going back again and requesting the right certificate. This is a huge concern for organizations that purchase public certificates and do not order the correct certificate the first time.

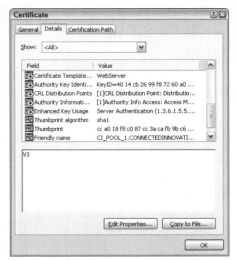

Figure 4-12

The following properties are of critical importance when requesting a certificate for an LCS server or pool:

- ❑ Common name or subject name
- ❑ Enhanced Key Usage
- ❑ Validity period
- ❑ Subject alternative name

Common Name or Subject Name

The common name or subject name of a certificate is an optional property to set when requesting a certificate. However, it is required when requesting a certificate for an LCS server or pool. The subject name/common name correctly identifies the name of the LCS server or pool as the name of the certificate. Correctly identifying a certificate common name or subject name is absolutely critical when requesting a certificate for your LCS server or pool because when an LCS client signs in, the service checks to make sure that the server or pool into which the client is logging matches the name of the certificate. If the name does not match, the client will not connect. If you understand this process, you will be able to master the most confusing element in deploying Live Communications Server 2005 SP1.

Enhanced Key Usage

The Enhanced Key Usage (EKU) field is the property of a certificate that identifies what the certificate is being used for. There are several EKU types, but when working with LCS, the requirement for the EKU of an LCS server or pool is Server Authentication. If LCS were authenticating a client certificate based on a user's name, the EKU would be Server and Client Authentication, but as explained earlier in this chapter, LCS does not require a specific user certificate, but only that the machine into which a user is signing with LCS trusts the certificate Root CA or chain. Recall that pre-LCS 2005 SP1 servers required both the Client and Server Authentication EKU type, but with LCS 2005 SP1, only a Server Authentication EKU type is required.

Validity Period

In some cases, when a client cannot connect, it is due to the validity period of the certificate. The validity period of a certificate identifies when a certificate is active and when it will expire. Some organizations enable Certificate Revocation Services so that certificates within their network infrastructure automatically expire based on a specific rule or time frame. When requesting your LCS certificates, it is important to set the validity period correctly and to keep track of the expiration date so that the certificate can be renewed. If you have Microsoft Operations Manager 2005, you will be alerted that the certificate has expired; otherwise, you will only start to see problems in your environment when clients cannot connect or servers cannot authenticate with one another.

As an example, the following table outlines the properties of a certificate that will be used for an LCS 2005 SP1 Enterprise Edition Pool Server or LCS 2005 SP1 Standard Edition server:

Server or Pool	CN / Friendly Name	EKU	Valid From/To
Server	LCSServer1.Company.com	Server Authentication	01/01/2006 – 01/01/2007
Pool	LCSPool1.Company.com	Server Authentication	01/01/2006 – 01/01/2007

Certificate Deployment

There are several ways to request certificates for servers and client machines. The following sections describe the most commonly used processes for requesting certificates within a Microsoft Windows Server infrastructure.

Certsrv Website

Some organizations that deploy an internal Windows Certificate Authority will enable a feature within Microsoft Internet Information Services (IIS) for certificate enrollment. This is a new feature enabled within Microsoft Windows 2003. This feature provides a web-based application that enables a user to request a certificate and fill out the certificate properties online.

To use the IIS Certsrv website to request a certificate for your LCS pool or server, perform the following steps:

1. Open Internet Explorer.
2. Browse to the URL of your Certificate Services website, such as `https://server/certsrv`.
3. The Microsoft Certificate Services site will open (see Figure 4-13).
4. Under the Select a Task section of the main page, click the Request a Certificate link.
5. On the Request a Certificate page, click the Advanced Certificate Request link.
6. On the Advanced Certificate Request page, click the "Create and submit a request to this CA" link, as shown in Figure 4-14.

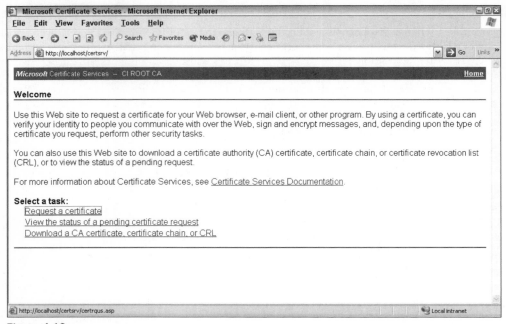

Figure 4-13

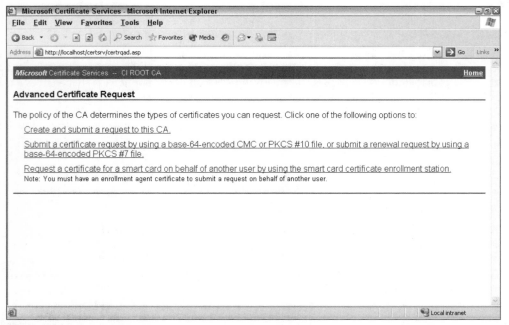

Figure 4-14

7. On the Advanced Certificate Request form, fill out the required fields for your certificate as follows:

❏ **Certificate Template:** Choose the appropriate template, such as the Web Server template.

   If you want the key automatically stored within the local machine's personal certificate store, select the "Store certificate in the local computer certificate store" checkbox.

❏ **Friendly Name:** Enter the FQDN of your LCS server or pool in this field, as shown in Figure 4-15, e.g., LCSPool1.Domain.Company.com, LCSPool1.Company.com, LCSServer1.Company.com, etc.

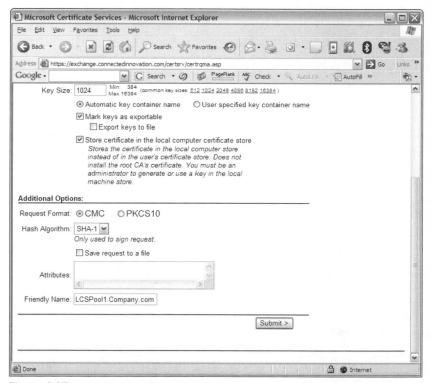

Figure 4-15

8. Click the Submit button.

9. The Potential Scripting Violation warning message may appear. Click the Yes button.

10. The Certificate Issued page, shown in Figure 4-16, will open. Click the Install This Certificate link to install the certificate.

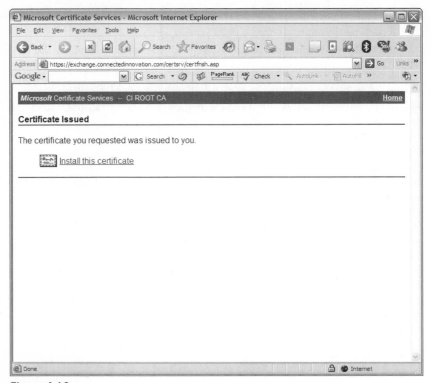

Figure 4-16

11. Another Potential Scripting Violation warning message may appear. Click the Yes button.

12. The Certificate Installed page will open, as shown in Figure 4-17, if the install was successful. Close Internet Explorer.

Certificate Automatic Enrollment

One of the new features of Windows Server 2003 is the Certificate Auto-Enrollment feature. If a new server is added to a domain, the server will automatically receive a certificate with the FQDN of the server as the common name. This is great if you are not running a multi-pool server LCS environment because you would still need a certificate for the actual pool, and its corresponding pool FQDN entered as the common name of the certificate.

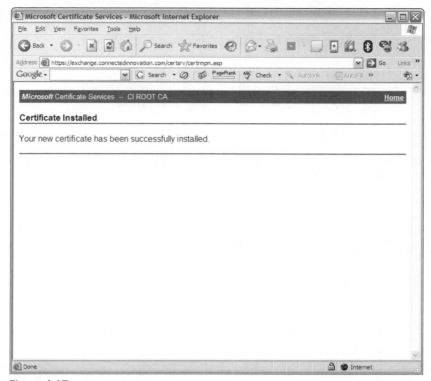

Figure 4-17

Certificate Templates

When requesting certificates for your LCS servers or pools, you select from a Certificate template. A certificate template is a pre-built set of certificate properties that reduces the time involved in requesting the certificate you need. When requesting an LCS certificate for your servers and pools, the Web Server Certificate template is often used because its configuration matches the one required for a certificate used within an LCS environment enabled with TLS. The only properties that would then need to be filled out include the subject name or common name, the validity period, and other custom fields. If you are not satisfied with the Web Server Certificate template, you can create a customized template of your own.

Certificate MMC Console

Within each Windows desktop or server operating system, you have the capability to request a certificate, import certificates, export certificates, and add additional functionality. Using the MMC console, a client machine can request or import the Root CA certificate that is required for its mutual trust. From an LCS server, you can also use the MMC console to request, import, or export the certificate required to run on the server.

Follow these steps to use the Windows Certificate MMC console to request a certificate for a LCS server:

1. From the Start menu, select Run, enter **MMC,** and press Enter (see Figure 4-18).

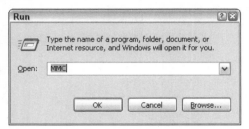

Figure 4-18

2. The MMC console will open. From the File menu, select Add/Remove Snap-in (see Figure 4-19). The Add/Remove Snap-in console will open.

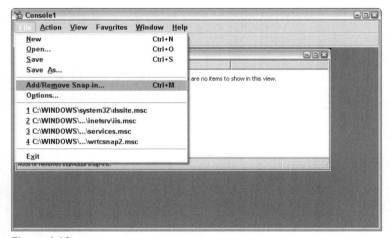

Figure 4-19

3. Click the Add button (see Figure 4-20). The Add Standalone Snap-in console will open.

4. Select the Certificates Snap-in and click the Add button (see Figure 4-21). The Certificates Snap-in window will appear.

Figure 4-20

Figure 4-21

5. Select Computer Account and click the Next button, as shown in Figure 4-22.

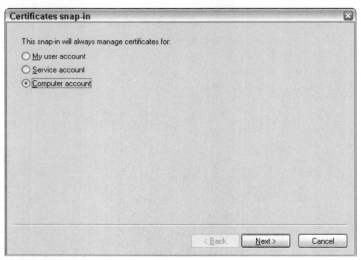

Figure 4-22

6. In the Select Computer window, shown in Figure 4-23, choose the machine from which you are requesting the certificate. The default is the local computer, which is the machine to which you are currently adding the snap-in. When finished, click the Finish button.

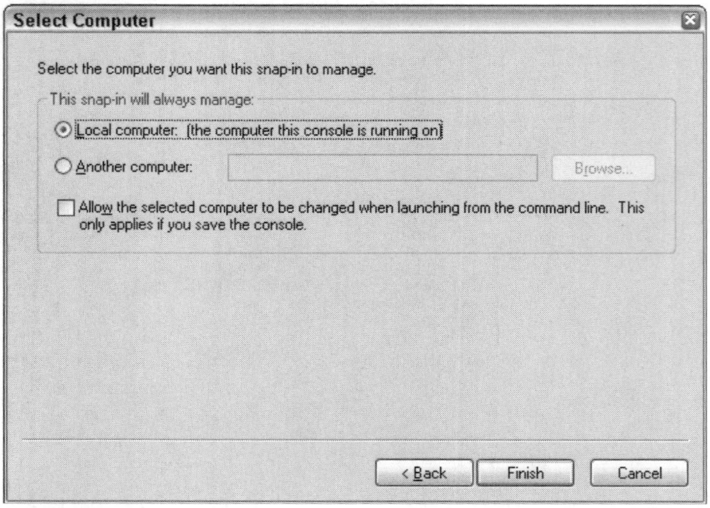

Figure 4-23

7. The Select Computer window will close and the Add Standalone Snap-in console will still be open. Click the Close button.

8. In the Add/Remove Snap-in console, click the OK button.

9. Now the Certificates snap-in has been added to your MMC console. You can save this MMC configuration for future use by selecting Save from the File menu.

10. Within the console, expand the tree from Certificates to Personal, and then click the Certificates folder (see Figure 4-24).

Figure 4-24

11. From the Action menu, select All Tasks, and then select Request New Certificate, as shown in Figure 4-25.

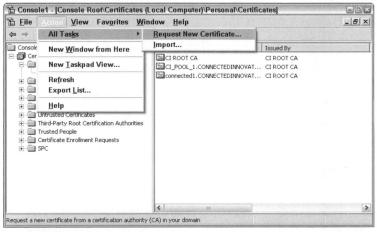

Figure 4-25

12. The Certificate Request Wizard will open, as shown in Figure 4-26. Click Next.

Figure 4-26

13. Select the Domain Controller Authentication certificate type and click Next (see Figure 4-27).

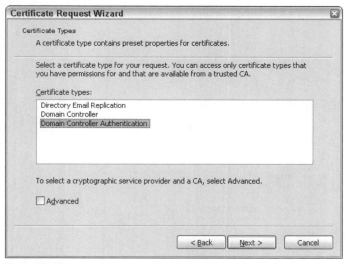

Figure 4-27

14. Enter the name of your corresponding DNS host A record, pool, or LCS server in the Friendly Name field (see Figure 4-28). The Description field is optional. Click Next.

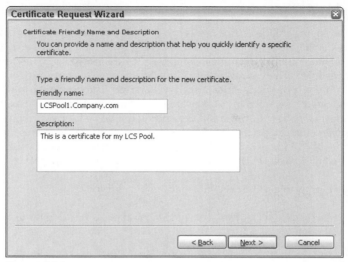

Figure 4-28

15. Verify that the settings for your certificate are correct and then click the Finish button (see Figure 4-29).

Figure 4-29

The certificate you requested, if automatically approved, will appear in your Certificates folder.

Public Certificates

Purchasing and deploying public certificates is just as easy, but may not be as cheap, as deploying an internal Windows Certificate Authority. The main benefit of using a public certificate from companies such as VeriSign is that you know that most computer devices possess a trusted root certificate from the provider already installed. There is absolutely nothing you have to configure for your users regarding certificates if you deploy a public certificate such as VeriSign. The downside to using a public certificate is cost. Certificates can cost as much as $1,000, although sometimes they can cost as little as a few hundred dollars per certificate based on use and depending on the vendor you choose. Other than the cost, the difference between using a public certificate versus an internal Windows certificate is the deployment process. You will still identify the same properties as you would with your internal certificates, but you will have to install them on each server instead of using some of the options listed previously.

Follow these steps to import a public certificate on an LCS server:

1. From the Start menu, select Run, enter **MMC,** and press Enter (refer to Figure 4-18). The MMC console will open.

2. From the File menu, select Add/Remove Snap-in (refer to Figure 4-19). The Add/Remove Snap-in console will open.

3. Click the Add button (refer to Figure 4-20). The Add Standalone Snap-in console will open.

4. Select the Certificates Snap-in and click the Add button (refer to Figure 4-21). The Certificates Snap-in menu will open.

5. Select Computer Account and click Next (refer to Figure 4-22).

6. In the Select Computer window, choose the machine from which you are requesting the certificate. The default is the local computer, which is the machine to which you are currently adding the snap-in. When finished, click the Finish button (refer to Figure 4-23).

7. The Select Computer window will close and the Add Standalone Snap-in console will still be open. Click the Close button.

8. In the Add/Remove Snap-in console, click the OK button.

9. Now the Certificates Snap-in has been added to your MMC console. You can save this MMC configuration for future use by selecting Save from the File menu.

10. Within the console, expand the tree from Certificates to Personal, and then click on the Certificates folder (refer to Figure 4-24).

11. From the Action menu, select All Tasks⇨Import (see Figure 4-30). The Certificate Import Wizard will open.

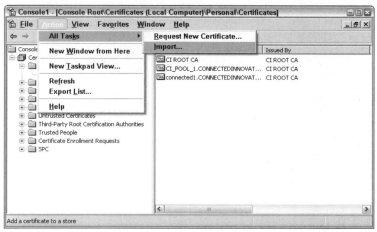

Figure 4-30

12. Click Next (see Figure 4-31).

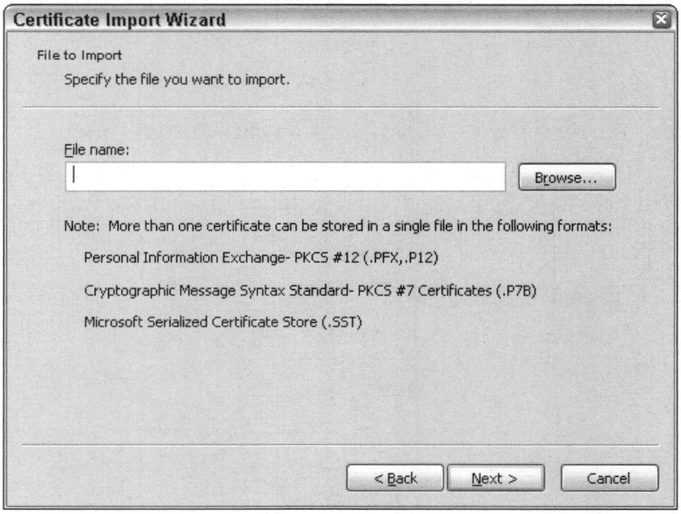

Figure 4-31

13. Browse to the public certificate file. Click the Open button after the file is selected (see Figure 4-32).

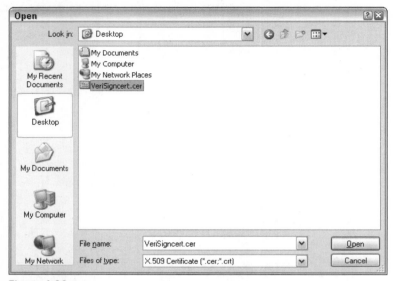

Figure 4-32

14. Back in the Certificate Import Wizard window, click the Next button.

15. Select the "Place all certificates in the following store" option, and ensure that the field displays the Personal store. If not, click the Browse button and select the Personal folder (see Figure 4-33). Click Next.

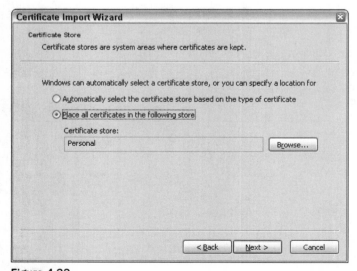

Figure 4-33

16.   Verify the settings and click the Finish button (see Figure 4-34).

Figure 4-34

Understanding Live Communications Server and SQL Server

One of the primary components of an LCS 2005 enterprise pool is the SQL back-end. SQL is utilized to store information regarding users and their contacts, and cache information from Active Directory. It may also be used for the LCS Archiving Service. This section covers installation, permissions, and the user replicator process.

Generally, an LCS 2005 Enterprise Edition deployment, along with the associated SQL back-end, should be used in environments with over 10,000 users or in environments where redundancy and/or high availability is required and a hardware load balancer will be installed along with multiple LCS 2005 Enterprise Edition home servers. In environments with fewer than 10,000 users; environments with a single front-end server; and environments in which there will not be redundant LCS servers with a hardware load balancer, LCS 2005 Standard Edition with SP1 should be utilized.

A frequent question asked in the user community is "Can I install LCS 2005 Enterprise Edition on a single server?" While not recommended, the answer is yes — it is possible. LCS 2005 Enterprise Edition does not require two front-end servers to be implemented. Again, due to the load placed on the SQL server and the LCS server in an enterprise environment, it is recommended that you install the front-end server function on a separate server than the enterprise pool back-end.

Installing LCS with SQL Server

LCS 2005 and LCS 2005 with SP1 both utilize Microsoft SQL Server 2000. In addition, both require installation of either SQL 2000 SP3, which is called out specifically in the Microsoft LCS whitepapers, or SQL 2000 SP4. This author has successfully tested and utilized SQL 2003 SP4 with LCS 2005. As of the writing of this book, LCS 2005 with SP1 was not supported on the SQL 2005 Server platform, and it has not been certified by the SQL or RTC product groups. However, it is entirely possible to use SQL 2005 as the SQL back-end for LCS 2005 with SP1 Enterprise Edition pools.

LCS 2005 does not require that you install the Archiving Service on a pool back-end. It is entirely fine to install the Archiving Service on a separate SQL Server or SQL cluster. If the SQL Server being used is shared between applications, it is important that ports 5060 and 5061 remain available and not be used by any other applications.

Having noted that, the installation process of SQL Server 2000 is pretty straightforward, and can be installed by taking the defaults. LCS 2005 will function with either the default SQL instance or with a named SQL instance. The service account that is being used for the SQL server should be a member of Domain Users and should be granted local Administrators rights on the SQL Server box or SQL Server cluster. It is recommended that this service account not be used as the LCS service account.

There are a few caveats to note during the installation. If your back-end SQL box has been identified and it is an existing SQL 2000 server with SP3a or SP4 running on Windows 2000, the updated version of Windows Scripting Host (WSH) should be downloaded and installed. The other caveat is related to the two authentication methods that are available during the installation of SQL, as shown in Figure 4-35. While LCS 2005 can function happily in Mixed Mode, it is recommended that you use Windows Authentication Mode during the installation of SQL 2000 for the Enterprise pool back-end server(s) and/or Archiving server(s).

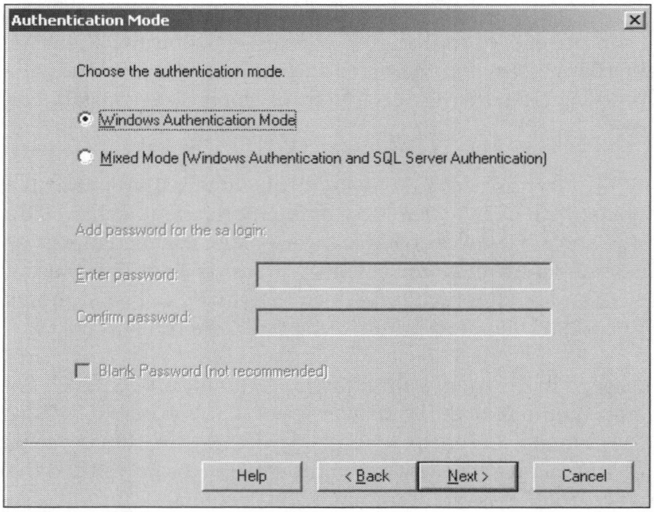

Figure 4-35

Once Microsoft SQL Server 2000 has been installed, SQL 2000 Service Pack 3a and the appropriate hotfixes, such as MS03-31, should be installed. It is recommended that SQL 2000 Service Pack 4 be installed and patched with the appropriate security patches. In addition, SQL Server 2000 with SP4 should be used for LCS Enterprise pools, LCS Archiving, and LCS Enterprise Directors, as it provides enhancements for security and SQL. While not a caveat for the SQL installation, if the SQL server has the C: drive encrypted or compressed, then the Temp variable will need to be changed to a drive that is not encrypted or compressed.

Speaking of secure environments, note that the service account required for SQL Server 2000 and the Enterprise pool account do not need any special rights other than to be a member of Domain Users in the domain, and a member of the local Administrators group on the LCS server.

Understanding Permissions

One of the reasons for Mixed or Windows Authentication on the SQL server is the use of domain groups to assign permissions to functions within the LCS Enterprise pool back-end. Within each SQL server the domain-level groups, which are created during the domain prep procedure, are granted permissions within the SQL server.

Several of the Active Directory groups created during domain prep are granted access to the rtc and rtcconfig databases. These groups, as shown in the user properties for each database, are domain\rtcabsdomainservices, domain\rtcdomainserveradmins, and domain\rtchsdomainservices. The rtcabsdomainservices group is granted public and ReadOnlyRole access within the rtc database. The rtcdomainserveradmins group is granted public access and AdminRole access within the rtc database, and public and ReadWriteRole within the rtcconfig database. The rtchsdomainservices group is granted public and ServerRole rights to the rtc database, and public and ReadOnlyRole rights to the rtcconfig database. The rtcdomainuseradmins group is granted public and ReadOnlyRole access to the rtcconfig database. In both the rtc database and the rtcclient database, the local SQL user, dbo, is granted db_owner rights to the database and is the database owner. The other administrative user local to the SQL database is the sa account.

If archiving is implemented, the domain\rtcarchivingdomainservices global group will be granted public database role access as well as ServerRole database role access.

Understanding the LCS Databases and Database Functions

Within the LCS 2005 with SP1 Enterprise Edition environment, two databases are configured on the SQL pool back-end: rtc and rtcconfig. If you have archiving deployed, then the LcsLog database will be on the back-end SQL server that supports the Archiving Service. Figure 4-36 depicts the rtc and rtcconfig databases within the Microsoft SQL Server Enterprise Manager.

The rtc database, and the rtcconfig and LcsLog databases, are efficient in their storage of information. An example of this is the user accounts. In the rtc database, the SIP-enabled users are called *resources*. Within the Resource table, the LCS user is given an ID, which is associated with that user's SIP URI. Instead of duplicating the SIP URI for the user when the information is required, the ID is referred to within the database. This is an example of one of the many efficiencies that have been implemented within the product.

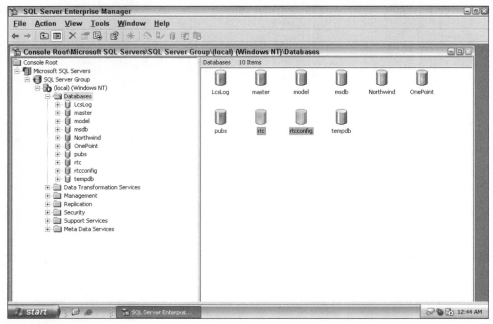

Figure 4-36

Another great example of efficiencies with the database is related to the User Replicator (UR) process. The UR process synchronizes user and contact objects from Active Directory into the rtc database, minimizing the impact between the user and Active Directory. If it finds a user or contact object in Active Directory and can match it to a user or contact in the database, it will synchronize the information. If it does not find an object in the database, but one exists within Active Directory, it will put a placeholder object in the database instead of synchronizing the contact or user object. The UR process is covered in more detail later in this section.

rtc Database

The rtc database is one of the two core databases utilized by the Enterprise pool. This database stores information primarily related to the users. These are items such as the contacts associated with a particular user, the presence information for the users, the pools and front-end servers that exist in the environment, and when the last heartbeat from the front-end servers occurred. In addition, the allow/block list that a user has created, or that an admin has implemented from Active Directory Users and Computers, is also stored here. Note that both the admin and the end-user can modify the allow/block list stored in the SQL database.

In an environment of 25,000 users, the rtc database should only grow to between 1GB and 1.5GB in size. It is possible to load the rtc database into RAM using the Address Windowing Extensions (AWE) feature of SQL server. For more information regarding enabling SQL for AWE mode, please see http://msdn2.microsoft.com/en-us/library/ms190673.aspx.

rtcconfig Database

The `rtcconfig` database complements the `rtc` database. When reviewing your implementation, it is clear that the `rtcconfig` database does not grow much. As the well-known cliché states: "This is by design." The `rtcconfig` database is used to store pool settings, routing information, system information, proxy information, and information related to the Address Book configuration. It is also possible to load this database into RAM using SQL AWE.

LcsLog Database

The `LcsLog` database is likely to get its fair share of attention. This database stores archived message text and session initiation data for voice, video, and file sharing.

Because only the message text is archived, as well as some session initiation data, expect the `LcsLog` database to grow by 150K–300K per user per day based upon utilization. Voice conversations as well as video, remote access, file transfers, and whiteboard sessions are noted when initiated, but the data for these is not stored in the archiving database.

Exporting the LcsLog Archiving Database

In the initial implementation archiving, you may need to export the `LcsLog` database to ensure that it is archiving correctly. Because this chapter covers environment preparation, following are the instructions for performing some initial exports.

You must have permission to the database `LcsLog`. Even at the beginning of the implementation, this database may contain confidential information, and any exported data should be treated with kid gloves. If it is exported to a text file, this text file should be tightly controlled. If it is exported to an Excel spreadsheet, it is best to password protect it with a strong password and ensure that it is tightly controlled.

These directions assume that the account being used has access to the `LcsLog` database. Accounts that are members of `RTCArchivingDomainServices` have rights to extract data from the `LcsLog` database in this manner.

1. On the back-end SQL box, open SQL Enterprise Manager.

2. Drill down through `Microsoft SQL Servers\SQL Server Group\(local)(Windows NT)\ Databases` and expand the + box next to LCSLog.

3. Right-click and select All Tasks⇨Export Data.

4. The DTS Import/Export Wizard window will appear. Click Next.

5. The Choose a Data Source window will appear with the data source, authentication, and database information. Click Next.

6. A window will appear up with the destination source. Change the source to Microsoft Excel 97-2000 and provide a filename such as `C:\Temp\LcsLog.xls`. If the `C:\temp directory` or other destination directory does not exist, the export will error out.

7. At this point you can copy the tables and views from the database or use a query. For this example we will export all the tables and views. Leave the top radio button selected and click Next.

8. On the Select Source Tables and Views dialog, click the Select All button and click Next.

9. While it is possible to set the export for later, leave Run Immediately selected and click Next.

10. Click the Finish button in order to complete the export.

11. Transfer the Excel file to a system with Microsoft Excel or use the free Microsoft Excel Viewer.

If a lot of data exists in the `LcsLog` **database, i.e., it exceeds 65,535 lines, Excel will truncate the data.**

---

12. View the Computers tab to see what computers were used as part of the archive.

13. View the Users tab to see what SIP URI matches to the user ID.

14. View the Messages tab to confirm that messages are being archived, the user ID number and computer ID number are valid, and the content is being archived.

Understanding User Replicator

Live Communications Server utilizes a process in which the user information for Active Directory is synchronized to the local `rtc` database. To store this data, LCS 2005 Enterprise Edition utilizes a SQL back-end, and LCS 2005 Standard Edition utilizes a MSDE back end.

Whenever a user is enabled for LCS, or the parameters of the user's LCS account change, the User Replicator (UR) process updates the SQL database. This `dirsync` process occurs approximately every minute, contacting Active Directory for updates and propagating the updates into the `rtc` database in SQL or MSDE. Initially all of the objects are searched and marked when a server is installed. According to the Microsoft Live Communications Server 2005 SP1 documentation, the User Replicator process can process 50 users per second during its initial replication cycle. Additionally, when a large number of users is enabled, each user object must be marked, and the information replicated, through the UR process. Once that has occurred, LCS looks only for changes that have occurred since the last UR `dirsync`. The benefit to searching for changes is that it minimizes the impact on Active Directory once the first UR process has executed.

For this reason, the LCS home server must have rights to read information from all domains within a forest in order for the UR process to execute properly. The UR process authenticates via the service account(s) for LCS in each domain. These accounts are part of DOMAIN\RTCHSDomainServices, and this group must have read rights across the forest. This goes back to the Domain Add to Forest Root function and the importance of performing the Active Directory preparations first.

Understanding Software Requirements

In the previous sections we talked about various utilities and management consoles. Obviously, those management consoles are loaded onto a system as part of the installation process. Only Windows 2000, Windows 2003, and Windows XP will support the administration tools. While not a requirement, it is very important to have a disaster recovery strategy in place as well as appropriate backup software and licenses if the product is not the built-in `NTBackup` application and the built-in `dbbackup` application.

Live Communications Server 2005 with Service Pack 1 requires an Active Directory infrastructure with all AD domain controllers running Windows Server 2003 or later or Windows 2000 Server with SP4 or later. LCS 2005, and its predecessor LCS 2003, will not function with an Active Directory Application Mode (ADAM) environment.

The Enterprise Edition of Live Communications Server 2005 with SP1 requires a SQL 2000 back-end pool running SQL Server 2000 with SP3 or SP4. SQL Server 2005 and the SQL Server 2005 Express Editions are presently not supported. The SQL 2000 back-end pool will run on versions of Windows 2000 Server and Windows 2003 Server. As with the Active Directory requirement, Windows 2000 SP4 is the minimum requirement. The pool will run on Windows Server 2003, Standard Edition, Enterprise Edition, or Datacenter Edition. Windows 2003 Service Pack 1 is suggested. The SQL back-end may also be hosted on Windows 2000 Server Standard Edition, or Advanced Edition with SP4 or later. While the SQL back end may also be installed on Windows 2000 Datacenter, this is not recommended. The back-end pool can reside on a clustered SQL server, which has its own set of requirements, such as Windows 2000 Server Advanced Edition, Windows Server 2003 Enterprise Edition, shared storage, public and private network configurations, and so on.

The Standard Edition of Live Communications Server 2005 comes with the Microsoft SQL Desktop Engine (MSDE), which functions in lieu of the SQL server. While MSDE can run happily on several of the other Windows platforms, Windows Server 2003 is required for LCS 2005.

Once the Active Directory is prepped and ready, and the SQL server has been installed and configured in an Enterprise deployment, LCS is ready to be installed on a Window 2003 Server. While the administration tools will function on a Windows 2000 server, LCS requires Windows Server 2003 Standard Edition, Enterprise Edition, or Datacenter Edition in order to function. LCS 2005 Enterprise Edition can run in Windows Server 2003 Standard Edition; it does not require the Enterprise Edition of Windows 2003 Server.

If the Archiving component of LCS 2005 with SP1 is to be implemented, SQL Server 2000 with SP3 or SP4 is required, as is the Microsoft Message Queue (MSMQ) product. The Archiving component is not designed to be installed on a MSDE database, but a full SQL database.

Depending on how your backup solution is licensed, you may need to plan on acquiring appropriate backup licenses and backup tapes for each LCS Server as well as a SQL connector license for the SQL back end.

Recommended Hardware Configurations

Live Communications Server 2005 with SP1 has two versions: Standard Edition, which is a single server deployment, and Enterprise Edition, which encompasses a multi-server deployment coupled with a SQL back end. The LCS 2005 Archiving Service can function with either LCS 2005 Standard or Enterprise Editions because it is a service installed on a SQL server and an MSMQ endpoint.

An LCS 2005 Standard Edition server can support up to 15,000 users. Several servers and a hardware load balancer may be used in order to support up to 125,000 users on an Enterprise Edition deployment, supporting 20,000 users per each Enterprise Edition server. Because the Enterprise Edition home servers do not have the local SQL database, they can support more users per server than an LCS 2005 Standard Edition.

Capacity planning, both as a paper exercise as well as lab testing, is crucial for sizing large deployments. Fortunately, Microsoft provides a tool for capacity planning: the Microsoft Office Live Communications Server 2005 Service Pack 1 Capacity Planning Toolkit. The kit is available through the Microsoft download center, as well as through the Microsoft KB article KB907862, both of which can be found through the following links:

```
www.microsoft.com/downloads/details.aspx?familyid=F249A48A-FC42-4D30-B60B-
CB91BF8F2191&displaylang=en
```

```
http://support.microsoft.com/kb/907862
```

> **I highly recommend reading the *LCS Capacity Planning Guide* and using the LCS System Model spreadsheet in your capacity planning. Both of these files are located in the** `C:\Program Files\Microsoft LC 2005\Capacity Planning Tools\Doc` **folder when the toolkit is installed.**

Processors and RAM

The recommendation for the LCS 2005 Standard servers, supporting up to 15,000 users, is a dual processor 2.8 GHz server with at least 1GB of RAM, preferably 2GB of RAM. Smaller deployments may have fewer needs and may not require dual processors or 1GB of RAM.

An LCS 2005 Standard Edition server, acting as an Access Proxy, can function fine on a single-processor 1.2 GHz system with 1GB of RAM, supporting up to 5,000 external users, and potentially more depending upon use and PIC connectivity. However, larger deployments may require additional hardware, including multiple processors and additional RAM.

LCS 2005 Enterprise Edition front-end servers have processor and RAM requirements similar to those of the LCS 2005 Standard Edition servers. The back-end servers, however, are placed under significant load and require larger amounts of RAM and multiple processors.

When sizing the SQL back end, deployments of up to 25,000 users require at least a single-processor 2.8 GHz system with 2GB of RAM, but would benefit from a dual-processor system. A SQL back end with 50,000 users, dependent upon usage, would benefit from a dual-processor 2.8 GHz system with 4GB of RAM. A SQL back end used for deployments to 100,000 users would benefit from a quad-processor system with 2.8 GHz processors, 8GB of RAM, and a storage area network (SAN). Because of the amount of traffic in large Enterprise Edition deployments, a Gigabit NIC and Gigabit switch/router is recommended for the Enterprise Edition home servers and SQL back-end pool servers in an environment larger than 50,000 users or when there will be more than 20,000 users per Enterprise Edition home server. In order to enhance performance in larger deployments, it is possible to use the Advanced Windowing Extensions (AWE) feature of SQL server for the `rtc` and `rtcconfig` databases if the SQL server has more than 4GB of RAM.

Similar to the pool back end, the Archiving server is also a SQL server. Generally, the Archiving server should handle traffic up to five home servers, be it Enterprise or Standard Edition LCS servers. It is recommended that this server be a dual-processor 2.8 GHz system with 2GB of RAM.

Hard Drives

This is always a tricky planning phase, as some smaller servers allow for two drives per server, which is great for an Access Proxy using the Standard Edition of LCS 2005. However, this might not be the optimal configuration for the LCS 2005 Standard Edition server hosting 10,000 users.

If you are limited to four drives, a rule of thumb is to place the operating system, SQL binaries, and LCS binaries on their own logical drive, generally the C: drive. Two 10K, 18GB, or 36GB drives mirrored in a RAID-1 or RAID-1+0 serve this purpose well. A separate logical drive should be used for the database and transaction logs. Two 15K, 18GB, or 36GB drives mirrored in a RAID-1 or RAID-1+0 should be used for the database and transaction logs. While the transaction logs can reside on the same logical drive as the binaries without significant adverse impact, the transaction logs and databases should not reside on the same logical drive on which the pagefile resides. Thus, the database and transaction logs are arranged on the D: drive or E: drive, depending on how the drive letter for the CD-ROM has been configured.

An LCS 2005 Enterprise Edition deployment is a bit different. In this situation there is not a local database on the front-end servers used in the pool. Much like the LCS 2005 Standard Edition deployment mentioned earlier, the operating system, LCS binaries, and pagefile can all sit on the same logical drive. In this instance, two 10K, 18GB, or 36GB drives configured in a RAID-1 or RAID-1+0 will serve quite nicely.

The SQL back end is where drive configuration takes on greater importance. The SQL back end is likely going to be a large server with internal capacity for six or more local disks and/or a connection to a SAN back end. The first two disks should be 10K, 18GB, or 36GB drives mirrored in a RAID-1 or RAID-1+0 and should be configured as a single logical disk. This disk should be used to contain the OS, the SQL binaries, the LCS binaries, and the pagefile. Surprisingly enough, a 100,000-user environment may not use more than 3GB for the configuration and user databases. While large disks are not needed, the back-end server will benefit from fast drives. Thus, these drives should be 15K, 18GB, or 36GB drives mirrored in a RAID-1 or RAID-1+0 and configured as a single logical disk. The transaction logs, and the speed with which they are written to disk, is important.

The most important factor regarding the SQL Archiving databases is to ensure that the Archiving database system(s) have their OS and binaries installed on one logical drive. The transaction logs and databases should be on separate logical disks. When planning for the disk capacity for the LCSLog database, plan on approximately 100KB per day for a light user, 175KB per day for a medium user, and 250KB per day for a heavy user. Because the Archiving database does not archive attachments, the information stored in it is text information only. In an environment with 100,000 users, where 20% are heavy users, 30% are medium users, and 50% are light users, approximately 17GB of data will be archived per day if every user has his or her Instant Messaging sessions archived. If at all possible, use a SAN for larger deployments.

Note that clustered deployments of SQL Server require shared storage. Generally this is a SAN, but it may also be part of a "cluster in a box" solution, or may be external DASD storage. It is recommended to start with faster disks and then move to secondary storage based on use, rather than start on secondary storage and be forced to step up.

Virtual Machines

Some organizations choose to use a virtualized environment for their home servers, using VMWare ESX Server, Microsoft Virtual Server, or VMWare GSX Server. In some cases these virtual servers access a SAN disk for databases or even the OS and databases, booting from the SAN. This works quite well for some organizations and can be utilized quite effectively, allowing for system growth with the flexibility to move the virtual machines to a new server, or even move the data on the SAN from a SATA drive set to a FATA, or fiber-based, disk. The one important item to note is that use of the VM should be monitored, including the processor, the disk, transaction logs, databases, and so on. If the performance starts to suffer, allocate additional resources to the system.

With the licensing enhancements and use rights made available in Windows Server 2003 R2 Enterprise and Datacenter editions, it might be beneficial to speak with your Microsoft account manager and evaluate the option to use Virtual Server or VMWare for server virtualization. VMWare's recent announcement regarding the free edition of their server may make virtualization even more attractive to organizations that have limited hardware or datacenter space.

Network Infrastructure

For the most part, LCS 2005 with SP1 Standard Edition server deployments, including Access Proxy servers, and LCS 2005 with SP1 Enterprise Edition pools with less than 50,000 users, will function just fine on a 100Mbit switched network.

LCS 2005 Enterprise Edition deployments larger than 50,000 users may require a Gigabit backbone with Gigabit cards in the back-end servers as well as the home servers. If the Gigabit infrastructure is not in place, it is entirely possible to add additional home servers. Additionally, large-scale deployments integrating the PBX and PSTN gateways may require a Gigabit infrastructure.

The capacity-planning tools mentioned earlier in this chapter are beneficial in planning your LCS 2005 deployment, and contain information specific to estimated network utilization. The capacity-planning tools do not contain estimates for SIP-to-PSTN gateways and PBX integration.

Summary

This chapter presented a significant amount of information related to the functions of Active Directory, DNS, certificates, SQL, hardware, software, and the preparations required in order to move forward with implementing your Live Communications Server infrastructure. This chapter discussed how Live Communications Server leverages network resources such as Active Directory, Group Policy Object (GPO) settings, Domain Name Service (DNS), and digital certificate infrastructures. This information lays the foundation for the installation of Live Communications Server 2005 with Service Pack 1.

The chapter started with a review of the Active Directory environment, the schema extensions, and the 15 classes and 54 attributes that are created as part of the schema prep. The LCS 2005 with SP1 deployment tool and its prep functions were covered. The deployment tool simplifies the Active Directory preparation process significantly, providing a graphical representation of what needs to be performed and what remains on the checklist.

The chapter continued with coverage of the domain global security groups and their relevance to the Active Directory environment, including how some of these groups are leveraged by the SQL Server. User authentication methods using Kerberos and NTLM were also covered, as well as why the Kerberos protocol cannot be used when connecting to an Access Proxy.

Most important, the DNS records required for automatic configuration were reviewed in detail, including a reference table. Automatic configuration can reduce the administrative burden significantly, as users do not need to be bothered with entering the details of the LCS server or server pool, or the connection type, and the help desk does not have to walk users through configuring this. In addition to easing administrative burden through DNS SRV record configuration, use of the `rtcclient.adm` and `communicator.adm` administrative templates was reviewed.

Securing SIP communication can be performed via certificates. As noted earlier in this chapter, it is possible to use an internal certificate server, or to leverage an outside vendor holding a public trusted root designation, such as VeriSign.

The next chapter covers the installation of LCS 2005 SP1 from the perspective of an experienced LCS consultant.

5

Installing Live Communications Server 2005

In a lab environment, I was able to install and configure Microsoft Office Live Communications Server 2005 SP1 in less than 15 minutes. However, as you will see, installing and configuring LCS in the real world is not as easy as it seems. This chapter focuses on the installation of both LCS Standard Edition and Enterprise Edition. Of course, the purpose of this book is not to repeat existing documentation related to installing LCS, which can be found via the Microsoft LCS website at `microsoft.com/lcs`, but to serve as a guide. This chapter includes information based on our experience deploying the product within production environments.

Live Communications Server: Standard or Enterprise Edition

This first decision you will make when deploying LCS is whether you need the Live Communications Server Standard Edition or Enterprise Edition. Unlike other Microsoft products, the Standard Edition of Live Communications Server actually includes all the features found in the Enterprise Edition. The difference between the versions is that the Standard Edition is a single-server solution, whereas the Enterprise Edition will work with other components — such as hardware load balancers and a clustered Microsoft SQL server environment — to provide a high-availability Live Communications Server environment.

When determining which edition is right for you, consider the following selection criteria:

❑ **Availability of the final design:** Do you require your solution to be up 24-7, or do you only need average availability that a single Live Communications Server can provide?

❑ **Patching your Windows 2003 Server operation system:** Most corporations have scheduled downtime for performing operating system upgrades. Recently, Microsoft has been doing a great job in reducing the need to apply critical patches to the operating system; however, Windows Server still requires some patches. With Live Communications Server Enterprise Edition, a hardware load balancer, and Microsoft SQL clustering, you can actually schedule your system update, so that your client will not suffer any LCS downtime.

❑ **Budgeting for your design:** Live Communications Server is a single-server solution. By design, a single low-end dual-processor server can easily handle up to 15,000 users. Experience has shown that availability is so good that the only downtime that occurs is when you are having Windows server issues or upgrading. Enterprise Edition offers almost perfect availability, but it does require a hardware load balancer and a Microsoft SQL cluster to achieve this level of uptime. Normally, the cluster lives on top of a storage area network (SAN). The combined cost of a redundant load balancer, a Microsoft SQL cluster, and a SAN makes the Enterprise Edition a much bigger investment than the Standard Edition.

❑ **Size of the user population:** A single Standard Edition server can handle up to 15,000 users per server. For the Enterprise Edition, each front-end server can handle 20,000 users, and a single Enterprise Edition pool can support 125,000 users. If you have 30,000 users, you can have two Standard Edition servers or a single Enterprise pool with three front-end servers. The Enterprise Edition solution will guarantee the availability of LCS even if one of the front-end servers is down and you are running at full capacity. When you even out the cost of implementation over 30,000 users, the Enterprise Edition is probably a financially feasible solution.

Other Components Needed for the Install

No matter which edition you choose to install, you will install the basic components you need to host a collaborative environment. At its most basic, the install will provide users connected directly to the server with the capability to communicate via instant messages. On top of that, you can enable audio/ video communication, transfer files, and share applications. However, to support different real-life scenarios, you may have to install other components that are available as part of the Live Communications Server package.

Both the Standard Edition and Enterprise Edition include the other components that will work together with Live Communications Server:

❑ **IM Archiving Service:** The IM Archiving Service enables the administrator to centrally collect usage statistics for instant message text communication. In addition, when the company policy requires it, you can collect the text message content to a SQL database for storage.

❑ **Access Proxy:** The Access Proxy marks the boundary between the internal and external Live Communications Server environment. You can use the Access Proxy to provide connectivity for users outside the corporate network, for business partners who are also running Live Communications Server, and for users from public Instant Messaging services such as MSN, AOL, and Yahoo.

❑ **Director:** In some cases, you may want to install a Live Communications Server but not put any users on it. You can use this server to authenticate users coming in via the Access Proxy, and then redirect users to the Live Communications Server that hosts the users' account. In other cases, you can even use it as a bridge to connect your Live Communications Server environment to the telephony world.

❑ **Proxy:** The Proxy server is the simplest form of Live Communications Server. It understands the SIP protocol and is able to route SIP requests based on static routing rules. However, it doesn't understand the concept of boundary as the Access Proxy does, and it doesn't have the database back end as the home server to host any user on it. The purpose of the Proxy server is simply to concentrate traffic and provide a location for you to put in your custom server-side Live Communications Server application.

❑ **SIP/PSTN gateway:** This is actually not part of the Microsoft Live Communications Server. Live Communications Server gives the client the capability to communicate through PC-to-phone (PC2Phone) calls, or even phone-to-PC calls in some situations. To do this, the system requires a connection to the phone system, which you can achieve by adding a SIP/PSTN gateway to the network. This gateway brokers the communication between SIP and RTP communications on the network side, and is connected to the phone system via T1 or other telephony connections, which can even be an analog or digital phone line.

❑ **Microsoft Office Communicator:** This upscale SIP client from Microsoft is free for Live Communications Server clients using SIP communication. However, if you need to connect the system to your telephony system to achieve remote call control on your phone, you will have to pay an additional licensing fee. This client provides all the high-end features, such as encrypted audio/video communication, encrypted file transfer, remote call control (to your phone), and all the other features, such as application/desktop sharing, and PC2Phone.

❑ **Windows Messenger:** This is a free IM client you can download from Microsoft, or it comes as part of Windows XP. In order for it to work seamlessly with Live Communications Server, use version 5.1 or later. It doesn't support high-end feature such as remote call control, but it does have all the general features, and it concurrently supports MSN and Exchange Instant Messaging systems.

Installing Live Communications Server 2005 Standard Edition

The Live Communications Server Standard Edition installation can be divided into two stages: preparation and the actual installation. You will need different permissions for each procedure. All installation procedures start from the Live Communications Server Standard Edition CD.

The first step of the installation is to prepare the environment for the Live Communications Server, a process that includes the following:

❑ **Updating the Active Directory schema:** This enables new objects and attributes to be added to Windows Active Directory.

❑ **Preparing the Active Directory forest for the Live Communications Server installation:** This step creates the necessary objects and organization unit in the root domain of the Active Directory.

❑ **Preparing the Active Directory domain on which you will install the Live Communications Server as a member server:** To install Live Communications Server in an Active Directory domain, you must create certain groups in the domain and grant appropriate security permission to those groups.

❑ **Adding the domain to the forest root:** This step is required because you created some objects in the Active Directory forest root while the forest root was being prepared for the Live Communications Server installation. Because you created the security group in the domain in which Live Communications Server will be installed, you need to make sure these security groups have access to the OU and objects created in the forest root. If this is a single-level Active Directory, you are installing Live Communications Server in the forest root, so you don't have to perform this domain add procedure. LCS will know it is working on the forest root, and will grant the necessary permission automatically.

After the preparation is done, you can proceed to install Live Communications Server in your environment. The configuration of the server will be discussed in Chapter 6. To start the Live Communications Server installation, you run SETUP.EXE from the I386 directory on the Live Communications Server Standard Edition CD. You will see the screen shown in Figure 5-1.

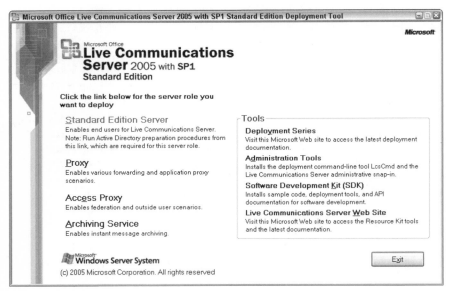

Figure 5-1

Select the server role you want to deploy. To install all the Standard Edition components, simply select Install Files for Standard Edition Server, as shown in Figure 5-2.

This screen will give you all the options to perform the preparation one step at a time. This setup program will actually check the status of the Active Directory and then highlight only the available options for you. In a lab environment, the response is fast; however, if you are in a distributed, large Active Directory environment, you may have to wait a minute or two before the check is completed.

Figure 5-2

This setup screen also lists the security permissions required for each step of the preparation/installation and provides some guidance regarding how to choose the best location from which to run that part of the preparation.

Prep Schema is the procedure that extends the Active Directory schema, so that you can create any new object that is required for Live Communications Server in the Active Directory. In addition, you can add attributes to existing objects, such as User or Contact, to enable Live Communications Server service for these objects. To perform this procedure, the login account needs to have Active Directory Schema Admin rights, and have Local Administrator rights on the Schema Master. To ensure that the procedure is performed correctly, you should do this part of the setup preparations directly on the Active Directory domain controller that hosted the Schema Master role. After the Active Directory schema is updated, depending on the Active Directory topology and network connectivity, it will take some time for the schema to be replicated to all domain controllers. The easiest way to verify that the replication has completed is to run the Live Communications Server setup on the server on which you want to install Live Communications Server code. The setup program will check the Active Directory domain controller to see whether the required schema is available; and if the schema update is available, the Prep Schema option will be grayed out.

Once the Prep Schema is completed, you can proceed to the Prep Forest. It is recommended that you run it on an Active Directory domain controller that is part of the forest root. Typically, the Schema Master is in the Active Directory forest root, so you can also run the Prep Forest on the Active Directory Schema Master. Again, it will take some time for Active Directory replication, and the setup program can verify whether this step is completed correctly.

Now that the Active Directory forest schema and forest root are ready for Live Communications Server, you can move on to the domain to which you plan to add the Live Communications Server as a member. You may have multiple child domains under your Active Directory forest root domain, but you don't have to perform Prep Domain on every domain. It is only needed for the domain on which Live Communications Server will be a member server. A Live Communications Server member server in one of the child domains can service all the Live Communications Server users in other child domains. To run the Prep Domain procedure, you need to have Domain Admin rights on this child domain, and you must log on to one of the domain controllers of this child domain. If you are running it on the Active Directory root domain, you need to have Domain Admin rights on the root.

If you are not adding the Live Communications Server servers to your Active Directory root forest, you have to perform the Domain Add to Forest Root procedure on the child domain. To do so, log on with an account that has Enterprise Admin or Domain Admin rights on the forest root because you need to assign permission for objects that exist on the forest root. However, you need to run it from a domain controller on the Live Communications Server child domain so that the setup program knows where to pick up the groups it needs to grant the permissions.

After each step of the installation/preparation, a hypertext log will be created in the current user directory `%userprofile%\Local Settings\Temp\`. You will also be prompted at the end of each installation/preparation step to confirm that each portion of the installation/preparation is completed correctly. Based on the security settings of Internet Explorer, you may have to allow the content by clicking the information bar on the IE screen. For a large installation, you should read each installation log file and save all these installation log files for future reference.

After all the installation/preparation steps are done, you can start the installation of the Live Communications Server Standard Edition server. Simply select Install Files for Standard Edition Server to start the Setup Wizard, which will walk you through the installation.

The first thing the setup program will do is add the MSDE engine to the server; this is the application version of the Microsoft SQL server, which will be the database engine for the Live Communications Server operation. After that, you will see screens related to the Microsoft licensing agreement, and user and organization name. The first decision you have to make is selecting the installation directory. The default is to put all these directories on the Windows Server system drive. However, for performance purposes, I recommend you change the default.

Before making the decision, you need to understand a little about SQL/MSDE database operations. If you are not familiar with SQL, you should know that the database is composed of two parts: the database part in LC Data, and the transaction (changes to the database) in LC Log. For the database to operate efficiently, you need to make sure that any change/transaction you make to the database can be quickly written to the transaction log file in LC Log directory. Live Communications Server database operation doesn't involve a very large database, but the frequency of instant messages being sent inside the system does require the database to handle high-speed updates of certain counters it contains. To achieve this speed you should separate the database and transaction logs onto two different physical drives, and not put either with the Windows operating system. In general, design the Live Communications Server hardware and file locations as though they were a small Microsoft SQL server.

After you determine where to put the files, simply click through the wizard and finish the installation. When the installation completes, you will be prompted to activate your newly installed LCS server. The activate procedure writes the necessary changes to the server's Active Directory object, and associates a service account with the Live Communications Server service. It also provides configuration on the Live

Communications Server Archiving Service. If you have Archiving Service already enabled, you can add a new server with the Archiving Service enabled from the very beginning. In most cases, it is easier to choose to not start the Archiving Service, and configure that after you confirm that the Live Communications Server is up and running correctly. The last step of the Setup Wizard is a check box that starts the Live Communications Server service after the activation. The activation procedure actually makes changes to the server's Active Directory objects. Because of the Active Directory replication delay, those changes may not be available right after the activation procedure is completed, so the Live Communications Server service will have problems starting. To avoid this problem, clear the Start Service check box and manually start the service after activation is complete.

Keep the following in mind as you work through the activation process:

❑ To perform the activation, the user must log on as member of the RTCDomainServerAdmins and Domain Admins groups. The RTCDomainServerAdmins group is created during the Prep Domain process. If you are using an administrator's user account to perform the activation, make sure you add this user account to the RTCDomainServerAdmins group before performing the procedure.

❑ In most corporate environments, users will not have Domain Admin rights all the time. Nevertheless, adding the necessary extensions to the server's Computer object requires special rights that only Domain Admins will have. If it is next to impossible to get the Active Directory Domain Admins rights in your company, refer to the workaround outlined in the Live Communications Server 2005 SP1 Standard Edition Deployment Guide's Appendix A. Basically, you can group your Live Communications Server in a separate Active Directory organization unit and grant special permissions to the group, so that members of this group can perform the Live Communications Server activation process.

Installing Live Communications Server 2005 Enterprise Edition

One of the major improvements in LCS 2005 is the provision of high availability through the introduction of the new Enterprise Edition of LCS. Through the introduction of network load-balanced front ends, and clustering of the SQL Server back end, Enterprise Edition can provide the high availability required by the most demanding corporate service–level requirements. Although more moving parts are introduced, the installation of LCS Enterprise Edition is still relatively easy.

Installing Enterprise Edition includes the same infrastructure preparation as the Standard Edition. That includes the Active Directory schema update, forest preparation, domain preparation, and domain add preparation if necessary. (Details for these steps are explained in the preceding section, which outlines the Standard Edition installation process.)

One of the most common questions asked by new customers is, "If I have done the Standard Edition preparation work, do I have to repeat the work to add an Enterprise Edition LCS server to the environment?" The answer is no. The Active Directory infrastructure preparation for the LCS Standard Edition and Enterprise Edition are actually the same. Therefore, once the environment has been prepared you can install either the Standard Edition or the Enterprise Edition of LCS. You don't have to redo the preparation.

Nevertheless, if you are upgrading from a previous version—for example, from LCS 2003 to LCS 2005, or from LCS 2005 to LCS 2005 SP1—because of Active Directory schema differences, and object and permission differences, you will have to repeat the entire preparation procedure. If you fail to do so, the setup program will not allow you to install the new version of LCS.

After the preparation is done, you can start setting up your LCS Enterprise Edition pool. The Enterprise Edition pool includes three major components:

❑ The hardware load balancer divides the incoming requests from clients to different front-end servers.

❑ The LCS front-end server listens to client requests and responds to them.

❑ The SQL database back end holds the user information to support LCS operations and store data.

In the Standard Edition, the front-end portion and database back end exist on the same physical server as different logical components of the server. In the case of Enterprise Edition, these components actually exist on different physical Windows 2003 servers. Because of that, you may want to perform different portions of the installation process on different servers.

When you want to create an Enterprise Edition pool, you actually start with a reversed logical sequence. You first create the logical definition of the pool on the SQL database back end. Then you can activate a front-end server and assign it to different Enterprise Edition pools that you have created.

This book concentrates on LCS, so I am not going to describe the SQL cluster installation in detail. In fact, the LCS database back-end operation doesn't check to determine whether the back end is clustered or not. As long as the setup program can access the SQL back end, you can proceed to the LCS pool creation.

To create an Enterprise Edition pool, simply start the Enterprise Edition setup program and select the Enterprise Pool option. The setup program will check the status of Active Directory and provide the available options to you. Because you can create multiple enterprise pools, even on a server that already has LCS installed, you will still see the Create Enterprise Pool Option available.

LCS requires at least SQL 2000 SP3a or later to work. Currently, SQL 2005 is still not officially supported for the LCS operation.

It is recommended that you run this part of the installation on the SQL back end. If you're working in a clustered SQL environment, start the installation on the active node of the SQL cluster.

Once you click the Create/Upgrade Enterprise Edition Pool option, you will be prompted by an installation wizard to create the pool.

This process controls the name of the pool you created. However, it has no bearing on the name of the SIP domains you want to support on this LCS environment. If you didn't install your SQL Server as a new instance, then you will need to put in the SQL Server name; you don't have to put in the \instance portion.

The setup program searches for the DNS record for the pool. If one doesn't exist, the setup log will issue a warning: `Warning [0x03EC78E3] No DNS record is found for the pool FQDN. Please register the pool FQDN with DNS before deploying Live Communications Server in the pool`. Nevertheless, it will still report that the LCS pool was created successfully.

In some cases, your FQDN for the pool may be different from the SQL back-end server DNS domain. If that is the case, you may have name resolution issues when you use only the server name for the SQL Server instance name. You can use the FQDN of the SQL server instead of just the server name.

The next option is to replace any existing database, as shown in Figure 5-3. For new installations, this checkbox will not have any bearing. However, if the scenario involves the recovery of an existing database, make sure the checkbox is cleared. Otherwise, it will remove any existing database from the SQL back end.

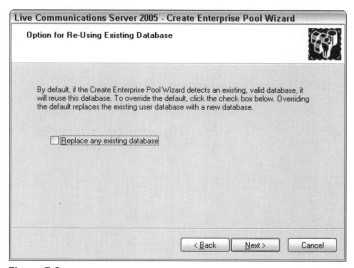

Figure 5-3

The screen shown in Figure 5-4 enables you to control where the setup program puts the SQL database and the transaction log file for the LCS database. To ensure the best performance of the LCS server, you should put the LC Log and LC Data directories on separate drives. The major consideration here is that when the LCS server is in operation, it will need to update the database very rapidly, so you want to ensure that your drive system can keep up with the real-time operation.

This is another reason why you want to run this portion of the installation on the SQL back end. If you run it on the LCS front-end server, the front-end server will not have the correct disk structure. You will not be able to select the drive letter you need for the installation.

Another common problem for this part of the installation occurs if setup is running remotely and doesn't have the SQL connectivity installed. When the setup program is trying to access the SQL back end remotely, it fails to do so.

After the LCS Enterprise Edition pool is created, you can move on to the next step of the installation, which is to install the LCS Enterprise Edition software on the front-end server. Figure 5-5 shows the deployment tool, with all of the previously completed tasks grayed out.

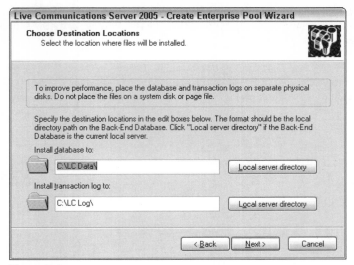

Figure 5-4

Figure 5-5

Simply start the setup program on the front end, and select the Install Files for Enterprise Edition Server option. Follow the user interface and complete the installation. When the installation is completed, the setup application will prompt you to activate the server, as shown in Figure 5-6.

Figure 5-6

To activate a server, you need Domain Admin rights. Make sure you have the correct group membership for the permission. Otherwise, the activation will fail.

If you have the necessary permission, the activation interface will provide a list of LCS Enterprise Edition pools available in this forest. Select one to activate the Enterprise Edition front-end server and attach it to this pool (see Figure 5-7).

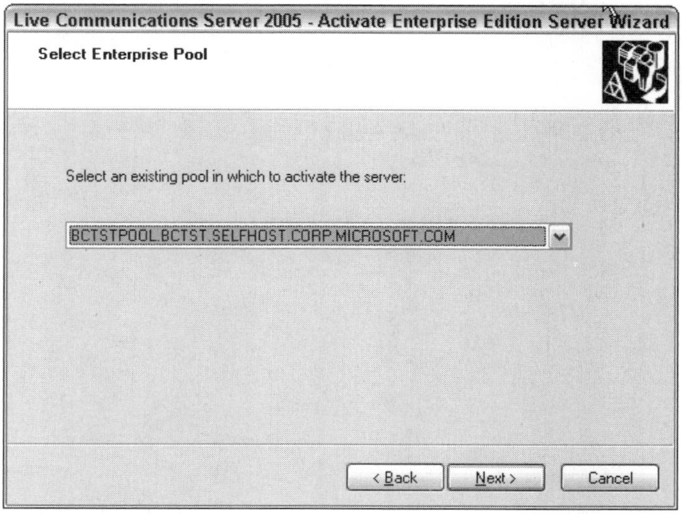

Figure 5-7

This activation is a very interesting point. Before the activation, the front-end servers actually have no association with any Enterprise Edition pool. The association is created by the activation process. Before that, you can actually move the front-end from one Enterprise Edition pool to another simply by deactivating the front end from the first pool and then reactivating it on the second pool. In some situations, you can actually consider using this capability in disaster recovery planning.

The next step is to select a service account for the server (see Figure 5-8). If no service account exists, the system can create one for you. Simply type in a password and create the new service account.

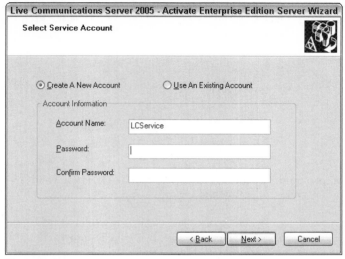

Figure 5-8

Part of the installation process is the option to enable IM archiving (see Figure 5-9).

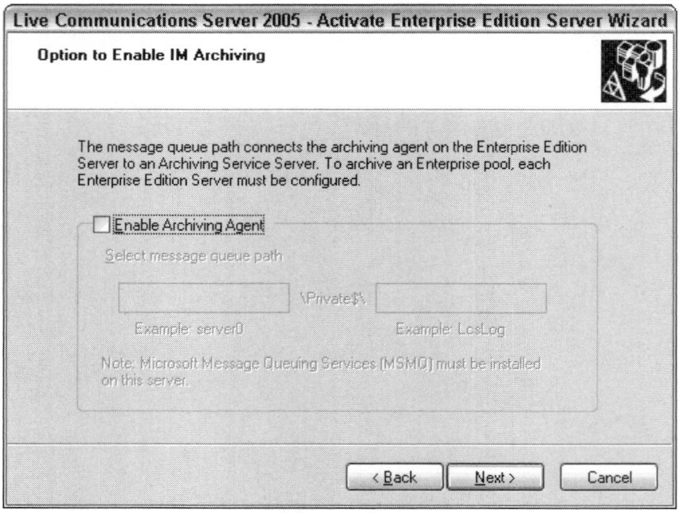

Figure 5-9

Once you enable it, the LCS server will actually check for the MSMQ presence before it can start the service. If you don't have the Archiving server already set up, it would be easier not to enable the Archiving Service during the installation. You can always enable the Archiving server after LCS is installed and in operation.

After the installation is completed, you have the option to start the service, as shown in Figure 5-10. Remember that in order for the application to start, the primary domain controller (PDC) will have to have the server/pool information.

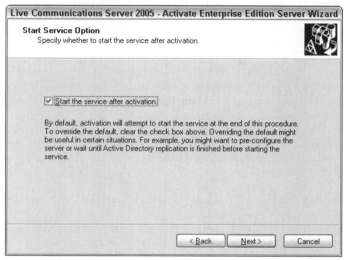

Figure 5-10

In a large Active Directory environment, the replication may take a few minutes to complete. Therefore, the LCS service may not be able to start after activation. My suggestion is to not start the service after the activation. Once the activation is completed, then you can manually start the service.

Installing Live Communications Server 2005 SP1 Additional Components

You have the option to install several additional components to provide enhanced functionality to your LCS environment, as described in Chapter 1. The purpose of this section is to guide you through the installation process of each of the following components:

❑ IM Archiving Service

❑ Access Proxy server

❑ Director server

❑ Proxy server

Installing the Live Communications Server 2005 IM Archiving Service

The purpose of the LCS IM Archiving Service, described in Chapter 1, is to provide the archival and storage of instant messages sent throughout a Live Communications Server environment. This section focuses on the necessary steps to install the service. The IM Archiving Service only archives instant messages. Any peer-to-peer communications such as audio and video, file transfer, or data collaboration are not captured using this service.

Before you install the IM Archiving Service, you need to install the Microsoft Message Queuing (MSMQ) service on the server on which you are installing the IM Archiving Service, as well as on each LCS server for which you will enable the Archiving Service.

The architecture diagram shown in Chapter 1 (refer to Figure 1-6) depicts the IM Archiving Service within an LCS environment. This diagram should make clear the architecture and placement of the service within an LCS environment.

Deploying the Archiving Service for Live Communications Server 2005 involves the following tasks:

1. Deploying the Live Communications Server 2005 Archiving Service in each domain with LCS servers that you want to archive. An Archiving server can archive only IM communications from other servers within the same domain.

2. Enabling and configuring servers to connect to the archiving server. All servers can archive except for the Access Proxy. To archive an Enterprise pool, you must enable archiving on all Enterprise Edition Servers in the pool.

To archive messages, MSMQ is required on the Archiving server and on the Archiving agent. You will start by setting up MSMQ on the Archiving agent.

MSMQ runs on each LCS Server to capture the instant messages that pass through the LCS Server. The messages are then sent to the IM Archiving SQL Server for storage and retrieval. What is awesome about MSMQ is the queuing process itself. This is a great solution if your SQL Server fails. Should this happen, the queue will fire the messages to the server upon startup.

One thing to keep in mind is that the Microsoft LCS IM Archiving Service does not include any reporting on the data that is stored. It is up to you to build customized reporting using SQL Reporting Services or any other method of data retrieval and presentation.

If you require more advanced compliance reporting, Microsoft works with several partners that provide customized reporting and archiving solutions. A list of these partners can be found at microsoft.com/lcs.

Installing a Live Communications Server Access Proxy

The addition of an Access Proxy to the LCS 2005 SP1 environment provides LCS with several capabilities: talking to other LCS installations, public IM connectivity, and the capability for clients to access LCS directly from the Internet, without the need of any VPN connection to the corporate network. The Access Proxy component is also required for federation with other LCS environments, as well as federation with the Public Instant Messaging Connectivity (PIC) service, as mentioned in Chapter 1.

For a secure installation, the Access Proxy should be installed on a workgroup server that has no connection to the Active Directory. All the Access Proxy requires is a connection with the LCS Director server via point 5061, and a connection to the Internet via port 5061 or port 443. Once a client connects to an Access Proxy, the Access Proxy forwards the request to an LCS Server for further authentication and sign-in into the LCS environment.

To start the Access Proxy installation, start from either the LCS Enterprise Edition or the Standard Edition setup program and then select the Access Proxy installation, as depicted in Figure 5-11.

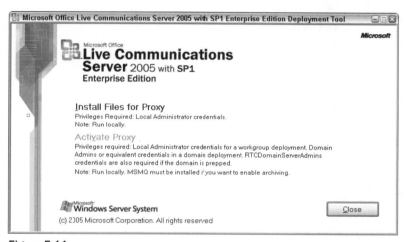

Figure 5-11

The first step is to install the files for the Access Proxy. When the files are installed, the setup program will prompt you to activate the server. It creates a local account on the server as the service account. This installation differs from other LCS activations in that you will not have the option to start the Access Proxy because it is not fully configured.

The most important aspect to understand about an LCS Access Proxy is the service it provides. The Access Proxy provides two edges for communication: There is an external edge that communicates with a public network, and an internal edge that communicates with your internal LCS environment. It is important that you secure these two edges as much as possible — with certificates and SPAM for IM (SPIM) — to protect your internal LCS environment.

The placement of an LCS Access Proxy within an LCS environment is shown in Chapter 1 (refer to Figure 1-1).

Installing a Live Communications Director Server

LCS director servers are simply LCS servers with no user homed on them. In most situations, director servers are Standard Edition servers. You can use an Enterprise Edition pool to act as director server, but that is not a cost-effective way to design LCS.

There are two ways to use an LCS server as a director. The first way is to use LCS as an internal director, and the second way is to use it as an external director.

The internal director eases client configuration. You can point all your clients to the internal director server. The server will redirect your clients to the server on which the clients are actually homed. This way, even if you move your client from one LCS pool to another, you don't have to change the client-side setting.

The external director protects against external access. You can point your Access Proxy to a Standard Edition server that acts as director. The director server can authenticate the requests coming in via the Access Proxy. If the request authenticates successfully with NTLM, the director will forward the traffic to the home server on which the client is actually homed.

To install a LCS director server, simply follow the same procedure you followed when installing the Enterprise Edition or Standard Edition LCS server/pool.

Another important aspect to note about the LCS director server is that it can be used to support multi-domain users. The director can route users, as mentioned above, by their sign-in ID or SIP URI. If a user has a SIP URI of an alternate domain, the director can route the user's connection to the appropriate LCS server or pool.

Installing a Live Communications Server Proxy

Installation of an LCS Proxy server is very similar to installing the Access Proxy. Like Access Proxy, normally the Proxy server is a stand-alone workgroup server. However, you can also make it an Active Directory member server if necessary.

To install a Proxy server, simply start the installation from either the Enterprise Edition or Standard Edition setup program. Select the Proxy server option in the installation wizard.

After the setup program installs the Proxy server, it will go through the activation process just as it did with the Access Proxy. The activation process will create a service account on the local machine. Note that you do have the option to enable archiving on a Proxy server. After you install the Proxy server, you can start the LCS Proxy service.

Installing Live Communications Server 2005 SP1 Client Applications

In the previous section of this chapter, we focused on the installation of additional LCS components to enhance the functionality of an LCS environment. This section focuses on the installation of the client applications used to connect to an LCS environment.

The two client applications described in Chapter 1 include Microsoft Office Communicator 2005 and Windows Messenger 5.1. You may be wondering why there are two clients available for connectivity to an LCS environment. The answer to that is related to versions and availability. Prior to Service Pack 1, Windows Messenger version 5.1 was the only client available to connect to a Live Communications Server server. With Service Pack 1, Microsoft Office Communicator 2005 has taken over as the default and preferred client for LCS. To be as practical as possible, both versions of the client software are covered in this book, which should cover most real-world scenarios.

Installing Microsoft Office Communicator 2005

Installation of MOC 2005 is very simple. As with any other Microsoft Office application, you can simply start the installation from the setup program. Once it is installed, just configure your SIP URI, server name, and connection method, and you will be able to connect to LCS.

In a large corporate environment, you may want to create your own setup script to control the different options available, and have the installation process automatically set up the client-side setting for you. That way, your clients will not have to worry about any client-side configuration. They can simply run the setup program and Office Communicator will already be set up correctly and start automatically for them.

In some client engagements, customers use a push method using software such as Tivoli to package Communicator and deploy it to their users' client machines, while others have provided a pull method whereby users request the Communicator installation package via an intranet site. As you may recall from Chapter 4, it is highly recommended that you use GPO policies to manage the features and experience of Communicator to better control your user environment.

Another important note related to the installation of Communicator is that we recommend Microsoft Office 2003 with Service Pack 2 to fully take advantage of the presence features and icons within the Office system. This Service Pack updates Microsoft Outlook, SharePoint, PowerPoint, Word, and Excel. Unlike Windows Messenger 5.1, Communicator is not a free downloadable client. You must have a license to use and install this software on your desktop. If you do not have Communicator, you can contact your local Microsoft representative or leverage an MSDN subscription-licensed install.

Installing Windows Messenger

Windows Messenger is actually packaged as part of the Windows XP operating system, but this version doesn't work with the LCS server. You will need to download the latest version from Microsoft to ensure that you have the version that will work with LCS 2005 SP1. Hot fixes are available to enable the new version to work seamlessly with LCS 2005 SP1.

As with Communicator, Windows Messenger can be deployed via script, push, or manually; the choice of deployment is up to you. While Communicator provides much more functionality than Windows Messenger 5.1, it is still a functional client for LCS. The confusion surrounding this technology results from the multiple Instant Messaging clients that Microsoft provides. Many customers think that they can use Windows Messenger 4.7 or 5.0, and many are confused with MSN Messenger and the new Windows Live Messenger. Understand that only Windows Messenger 5.1 works with LCS. If the client software is not already installed on your desktop, you can download Windows Messenger 5.1 from the Microsoft download site at `microsoft.com/downloads`.

Summary

This chapter provided guidelines to ensure a successful install of Live Communications Server 2005 SP1 servers and additional components. In the next chapter, we will focus on the configuration of the Live Communications Server environment.

6

Configuring
Live Communications
Server 2005

In Chapter 5, you learned about installing Live Communications Server 2005. As you saw, the installation is very simple. The Standard Edition is a straightforward single-server installation, whereas the Enterprise Edition involves multiple servers and a third-party hardware load-balancing device.

Once the server is installed, you can get to the fun part: configuring the server. Based on different designs and need, you can change your basic Live Communications Server configuration to achieve the targeted result. This chapter covers the configuration of Live Communications Server 2005 SP1.

Live Communications Server 2005 Microsoft Management Console Snap-in

The Live Communications Server team created a Microsoft Management Console Snap-in for Live Communications Server administration. You can perform almost all the server configuration tasks using the LCS Microsoft Management Console Snap-in. The snap-in is installed on the Live Communications Server when you install the server code. If you like to perform administration remotely, you can install the snap-in on a remote server, or even your workstation. Figure 6-1 shows the LCS MMC.

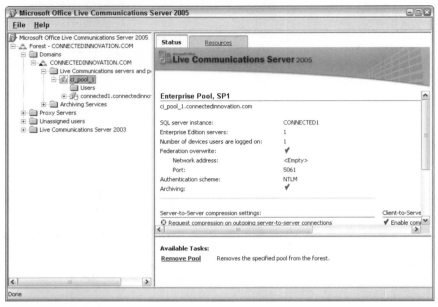

Figure 6-1

The Live Communications Server MMC is divided into four categories: Domains, Proxy Servers, Unassigned Users, and Live Communications Server 2003:

❑ **Domains:** This container is subdivided into different Live Communications Server servers and pools. Each Standard Edition server will show up as a pool with a single front-end server. Each Enterprise Edition pool will have multiple front-end servers assigned to it. Under each pool is a user container showing all the users who are homed on that pool. For an Enterprise pool, the users can connect to the servers via one of the front ends that is assigned by the hardware load balancer, so they are homed based on the Live Communications Server pool, not by the front-end server.

❑ **Proxy Servers:** This container holds all the Proxy servers in the organization. In designs that don't require Proxy servers, this container will be an empty container.

❑ **Unassigned Users:** This container holds all the users who are enabled for Live Communications Server, but aren't assigned to a Live Communications Server pool. Normally, this container should be empty. However, when you are having problems with Live Communications Server — for example, one of your Standard Edition servers just crashed and you have to delete the Live Communications Server Computer object — you will find that all the users who are homed on this LCS server are moved to this container. This enables the Live Communications Server system to tell you that some of your Live Communication Server users are having a problem. You can rehome users in this Unassigned Users container to other existing LCS servers.

❑ **Live Communications Server 2003:** This container holds all the Live Communications Server 2003 version server objects. It is recommended that you don't do any Live Communications Server 2003 server administration work on the Live Communications Server 2005 MMC. The purpose of this container is to enable you to select users from the Live Communications

Server 2003 server. You can do a one-way migration of users from Live Communications Server 2003 to Live Communications Server 2005 simply by selecting the user in this Live Communications Server 2003 container, right-clicking the selected users, and migrating them to Live Communications Server 2005. After the users are on Live Communications Server 2005, you can migrate them back to Live Communications Server 2003.

Configuring Messaging Ports

Now that you know you can configure Live Communications Server using the Live Communications Server MMC, among the first tasks you want to perform is to configure the port(s) that you want your LCS server to listen to for incoming SIP requests.

The port configuration is a LCS server–level configuration. When you want to change the port configuration of a Live Communications Server SE server, or a Live Communications Server EE front end, just drill down to the server level of the Live Communications Server MMS, right-click the server/front end, and select the property of the object (see Figure 6-2).

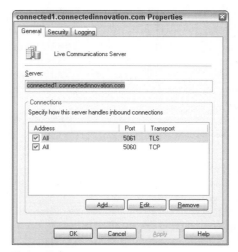

Figure 6-2

During the default installation, the server will be configured to listen on port 5060 for a TCP connection on all available IP connections. Port 5060 is the default SIP port for TCP connections. When we say SIP TCP connection in the Live Communications Server context, we are saying that the content of the communication is not encrypted; anyone with a network sniffing device or application can capture the network traffic and see all the SIP requests in clear text.

In most corporate situations, you will not want to use a SIP connection over TCP without any encryption, so you can edit the default connection or add a secured connection for SIP communication. Simply click the Add button and you will see the Add Connection dialog, shown in Figure 6-3, in which you can add a new connection to the server.

Figure 6-3

You have several options on this window:

❑ **Listen to Address(es):** You can select to listen to all IP addresses available on the server, or you can select to listen to only one of the available IP addresses on the server. In most situations, All Available IP addresses would be an easy option; however, if you have a complex IP network and you want your Live Communications Server not to listen on all IP subnets, you can select only a single IP. Be aware that if the IP address changes, the Live Communications Server configuration will be confused and you will have to reconfigure the server. We would hope that, if you have a complex IP network, you will have fixed IP addresses on each subnet for your Live Communications Server. That way, you don't have to worry about IP changes when you only listen to some of the IP addresses.

❑ **Transport Type:** The two transport types available are TCP and TLS. TCP is an unsecured IP connection. You can use this to connect to other instances of Live Communications Server, or to connect to third-party equipment that allows SIP connections over TCP. The SIP-to-PSTN gateway that allows connection of audio call from Live Communications Server to a telephony network is a good example of such a device. TLS stands for Transport Layer Security. With a TLS connection, the content of the SIP communication is encrypted. Live Communications Server instant text messages actually use the SIMPLE protocol and transfer inside the SIP protocol; with the TLS connection, the text message content is encrypted, and not vulnerable to network sniffing activities, as is the case with most public IM services.

❑ **Listen on this port:** By default, the SIP communication over TCP is on port 5060; however, that doesn't mean that you can't do SIP communication over other ports. As long as both parties know which port to use, you can establish a TCP or TLS connection for SIP over any port number. The Live Communications Server product team kept port 5060 for a TCP connection and set the default for TLS connection to 5061. You can change the inbound TLS port number to match an existing port number, e.g., 443, within this setting.

❑ **Certificate:** This option is grayed out for TCP connections, as a certificate is not needed. However, TLS is a certificate-based encryption, so the server that supports TLS connections will need to have a certificate installed on it. On Live Communications Server 2005, this certificate needs to be a client and server certificate. On Live Communications Server 2005 SP1, it has to be a server certificate. This is the same for any server SSL certificate that is used for any HTTPS-secured web server connection.

Configuring Routes

Routing configuration is a pool-level configuration. Currently, Live Communications Server supports only static routing, and you have the following options for creating a static routing:

❑ **User:** This is the user SIP URI. In most situations, you can use the wildcard, "*".

❑ **Domain:** This represents the target SIP domain of the message.

❑ **Phone URI:** This checkbox is provided to route PC2Phone calls. When you make a PC2Phone call with Window Messenger or Office Communicator, it will put a User=Phone option on the SIP request. This checkbox enables you to specify a routing to the SIP/PSTN gateway.

❑ **Network Address/IP Address:** You can select to put in a network address or IP address for the next hop of the route. If you select Network Address, you can put in an FQDN of the next hop SIP device. You need to ensure that your DNS resolution is working correctly for this FQDN.

❑ **Transport:** You can select TLS or TCP as the transport to connect to the next hop. In fact, when you select TLS, you are actually doing MTLS with the next hop. You need to make sure the next hop does support MTLS. In addition, the name of the certificate must actually match the name you put in the Network address input box. If you select TCP, use the IP address input box, instead of using the FQDN of the next hop.

❑ **Port:** Live Communications Server actually supports the SIP protocol with any port you want. However, it is recommended that you stay with the standard; select 5060 for TCP and 5061 for TLS.

❑ **Replace host in request URI:** This is a confusing option. The idea of this option is to replace the host URI of the server that is used to route the SIP message. One of the simple examples uses an SE server to centralize telephony communication. You may route all your telephony requests to an SE server by setting up a static router on the home server pool. This route can use TLS as the transport, and whether you select "Replace host in request URI" or not will have no bearing, as the request host is the sending host, i.e., the home server. When the request reaches the SE server, it will have to route the request to the SIP/PSTN gateway. If the SIP/PSTN gateway doesn't support TLS, it will have to route the message via port 5060 with TCP. When the SIP/PSTN gateway responds to this message, it will have to respond to the SE server. In order for the SIP/PSTN gateway to respond to the SE, you need to ensure that the message-sending host URI is set to the SE server. That's why you need to make sure you select the "Replace host in request URI" option in this situation.

To manage and edit routes within an LCS pool, use the following steps:

1. Launch the LCS Management Console (refer to Figure 6-1), and then drill down to an LCS pool.

2. Right-click on the pool and select properties.

3. Click the Routing tab (see Figure 6-4).

4. To add a route, click the Add button. Figure 6-5 shows the Add Static Route dialog box.

Figure 6-4

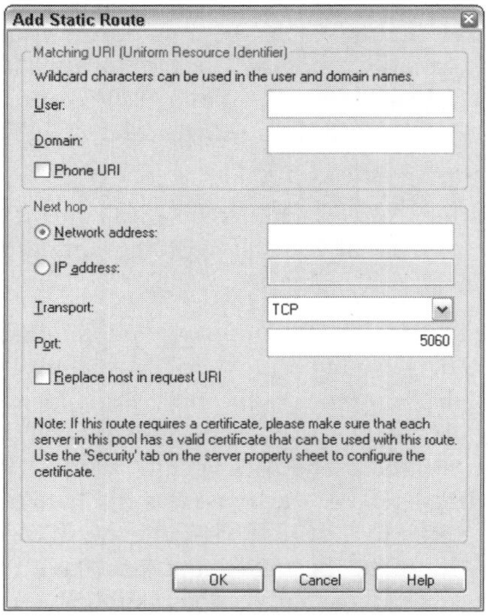

Figure 6-5

Enabling Remote Access

To enable remote access, the configuration starts from the forest level of your Live Communications Server implementation. To edit the forest-level properties, open the LCS Management console and right-click on the Forest name, and then select properties. Click the Access Proxy tab within the forest-level Properties UI, shown in Figure 6-6.

Figure 6-6

You can click the Add button and add the FQDN of the Access Proxy server that will support the clients' remote access. As you can see in the figure, you can have multiple entries to enable more than one Access Proxy for the forest.

No configuration is needed for remote access on the Live Communications Server pool level. However, you need to ensure that the front end has the proper certificate and is listening on port 5061 for the MTLS connection request coming in from the Access Proxy servers.

The next step of the configuration will happen on the Access Proxy server. It is kind of misleading that the Live Communications Server 2005 MMC console is actually added to the Access Proxy server. You can't really perform any Live Communications Server administration because most likely the Access Proxy is not even a member server of the Active Directory. To configure the Access Proxy server, you need to get into the Computer Management console of the local server, as no MMC console is provided for this LCS server role. Use the following steps to access the Computer Management console:

1. Right-click on the My Computer icon on the desktop.
2. Choose the Manage option.
3. Expand Services and Applications.
4. Right-click on the Microsoft Office Live Communications Server 2005 listing and select Properties.
5. On the General tab, shown in Figure 6-7, select the "Allow remote user access to your network" checkbox to enable remote access.

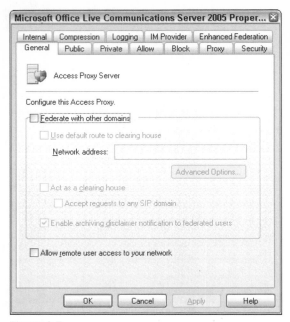

Figure 6-7

6. The next step is to make sure your Access Proxy is listening on the public network for remote access. Select the Public tab (see Figure 6-8).

7. In the Server Name text box, enter the FQDN name that the server is listening as. For example, if you are doing automatic configuration and using the default sip.company.com as host name, you need to add the exact name to this box. It can be different from the actual server name of the Access Proxy.

8. By design, the Access Proxy needs to have more than one address to operate. On the Public tab, select the IP address that is accessible from outside of the corporation.

9. Once you have selected a server name and network address, you need to select a certificate that matches the server name.

10. The last step is to select a port to listen on for the public side of the Access Proxy. You also need to determine whether you want to listen to certain kinds of connections, such as federation connections, or remote access connections, or both (see Figure 6-9).

For remote access, you can select the default port 5061. However, it is recommended that you also listen on port 443 for client connections. In some situations, the clients may be connecting via an Internet Access Proxy server. In those cases, port 5061 is usually blocked. Nevertheless, port 443 will be opened for SSL connection. Live Communications Server will support the client establishing a remote connection via an Internet Access Proxy server to the Live Communications Server Access Proxy server. A lot of Internet hot spots or corporations will allow guests to connect to the Internet via an Internet Access Proxy. In those situations, Live Communications Server clients will be able to establish real-time communication back to their partners in their own company's Live Communications Server system.

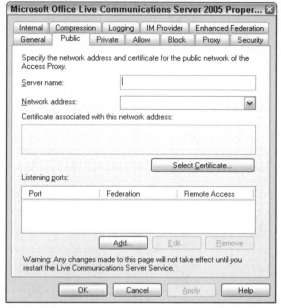

Figure 6-8

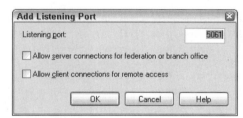

Figure 6-9

Enabling Federation

The procedure to enable federation is very similar to the configuration for remote access. To configure your LCS environment for federation, use the following steps:

1. Open the Microsoft Office Live Communications Server 2005 SP1 Management console from any LCS Standard or Enterprise Edition server and select the Forest node.

2. Right-click on the Forest node and select Properties. Then, select the Federation tab, shown in Figure 6-10.

Figure 6-10

On the Federation tab, you can enable the Live Communications Server federation and public IM con-nectivity. For the Network Address field, enter the FQDN of the next hop for federation traffic. You have the option to go directly to the Access Proxy, which in most situations will be a director server. You can share the same Access Proxy for both remote access and federation connection. In addition, you can actually select a different port number for the federation connection. This is helpful when the next hop is behind a layer 2/3 firewall and you only have certain ports opened. Simply select that port. You have to make sure that the next hop is listening for an MTLS SIP connection at that port number.

After the federation global default route is set up, you don't have to go to each pool and set up federa-tion on the pool level. The only exception to this is when you have a director server. The director server will get the same global default federation route from AD. However, the responsibility of the director is to route all the federation traffic to the Access Proxy. Therefore, if you are using a director server, you should set the default global route to point at the director server. Then, on the pool level for the director server, override the global default route and point it to the FQDN of the Access Proxy. The pool-level Federation tab is just like the forest level — you have the option to select the port to connect to the Access proxy, which is in the DMZ.

The next step of the federation configuration will be on the Access Proxy, and you have several options. First of all, you need to enable federation with other domains. The first option is to use a default route to a clearing house. This option enables you to send all your traffic to a Live Communications Server clear-ing house. The clearing house will handle all the routing of SIP messaging. However, once you select a clearing house, you will get the warning shown in Figure 6-11. You have to disable enhanced federation in Live Communications Server 2005 SP1, and you can't have any entries on the IM Provider tab for the public IM connectivity. If you plan to connect to a public IM cloud, or do any enhanced federation, you can't use the clearing house configuration.

Figure 6-11

You can also select to make your Access Proxy act as a clearing house, and you have the option to accept requests to any SIP domain.

The last option to configure federation is to enable an archiving disclaimer notification to federated users. This option is effective only for the Office Communicator client; the Communicator client knows whether the connection is coming from a federated Live Communications Server partner. If this option is selected on the remote end, the Communicator will pop up a warning to the user that the content for the current IM communication may be archived on the remote end. Nevertheless, if the receiving end is using an older client, such as Windows Messenger, it will not display the warning.

There are two more tabs on the Access Proxy configuration related to federation. The first one is Enhanced Federation, shown in Figure 6-12.

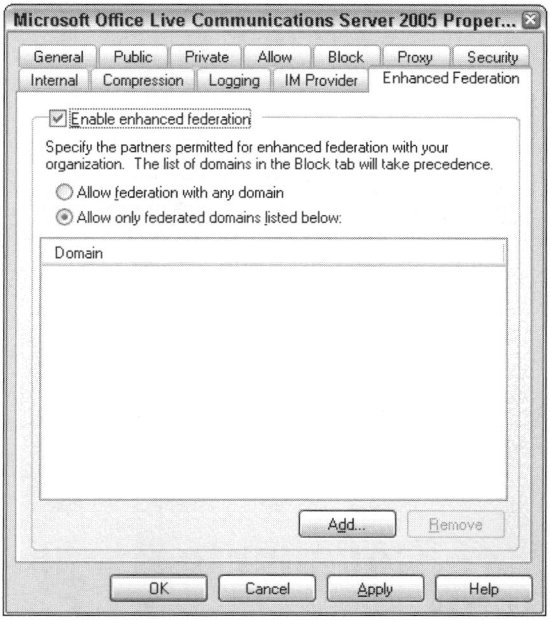

Figure 6-12

Live Communications Server 2005 federation configuration requires administrators to hard-code all the federation connections with the supported SIP domains, and the host that is responsible for the connection. In Live Communications Server 2005 SP1, Microsoft introduces *enhanced federation*. The Access

Proxy will use the target SIP domain of the communication to look for connection information from the DNS. Once the DNS returns the information, the Access Proxy will automatically connect to the target host and establish an MTLS SIP connection. In addition, you have the option to create a list of allowed federation partners. For a more secure configuration, select the list method: Check the "Allow only federated domains listed below" option, and then add the domains you want to federate with. This way, you just have to worry about the domains to which you want to connect, but you don't have to worry about the partner's configuration, as it will be discovered automatically by the Access Proxy.

The last option involved in federation configuration is public IM connectivity. You can select the public IM cloud to which you want to connect from the IM Provider tab, shown in Figure 6-13.

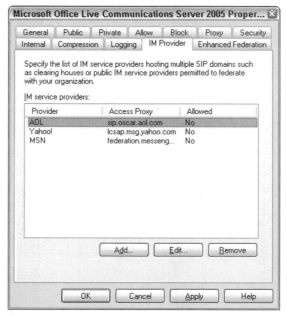

Figure 6-13

Simply select AOL, Yahoo, or MSN, and allow connectivity to these public IM clouds. This feature involves different client licensing fees and registration procedures. You can check the following link for the most up-to-date information on this: microsoft.com/office/livecomm/prodinfo/publicim.mspx.

Integrating Live Communications Server with VoIP

You can integrate Live Communications Server with Voice over Internet Protocol (VoIP) by using Live Communication Server to make PC-to-Phone (PC2Phone) calls, or you can use the MOC client to control your desk phone. Different configurations are required for different features.

The capability of the Live Communications Server client to make a PC-to-phone call has actually been available ever since Live Communications Server 2003; the configuration hasn't changed too much. To make PC2Phone calls, all you need is a SIP-to-PSTN gateway on your IP network. Then, you configure your LCS server routing so it can route the requests to the gateway. Many companies, such as Cisco, Net.com, and Audiocode, use a SIP-to-PSTN gateway. On one side of the gateway is an IP connection to the computer network, and on the other side of the gateway you can have different types of connections — ranging from T1, E1, and analog/digital phone lines to the phone system. The idea is that the SIP protocol will be used from the MOC client to Live Communications Server, and then to the gateway, to establish the call. The audio information will move directly between the MOC client and the gateway. The gateway uses the signaling information to make a call on the phone system, and passes the audio information back and forth from the phone system.

On the client side, you need to make sure you have the right registry setting. Please be careful when editing the registry, as any changes can affect your machine permanently. To access the registry editor on a given machine, select Start⇨Run and enter **REGEDIT**. The Registry Editor will then open. In order for the MOC client to make PC-to-phone calls, you need to add the `EnablePC2phone REG_DWORD` with the value of 1, under `HKLM\Software\Policies\Microsoft\Communicator`. The best way to confirm that your audio/video device is working perfectly is to use the Audio and Video Tuning Wizard. The wizard will walk you through the necessary steps to verify that your audio/video equipment is working with the MOC client.

On the server side, you need to make sure routing is set up for the PC2Phone call. You can set up your server to talk directly to the SIP/PSTN gateway, or you can set it up so it goes through an LCS server. We will discuss the reason for each option, but the configuration is similar in both cases. You need to set up static routing so the Live Communications Server knows how to route any PC2Phone call request. Routing is a pool-level setting; simply access the Properties of the pool, and then select the Routing tab. You can add a static routing by simply using the Add button, after which you will see the dialog shown in Figure 6-14.

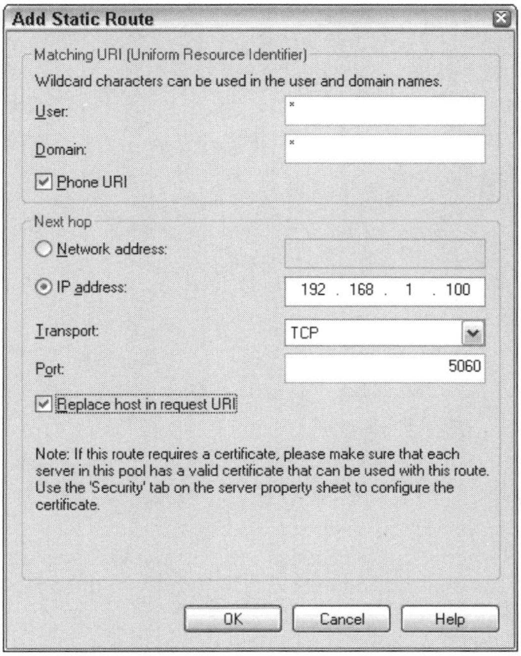

Figure 6-14

You need to put the wildcard "∗" on both the user and domain, and check the Phone URI checkbox. This checkbox will enable the server to detect all SIP requests related to PC-to-phone requests, and route them to the SIP/PSTN gateway. In this setup, we are routing the call directly to the gateway using the IP address, to the port 5060. We also selected "Replace host in request URI"; this way, we can be sure that the gateway knows that the request is from this server.

In this configuration, the target gateway only speaks to SIP over TCP on port 5060; that means your Live Communications Server servers also have to listen to SIP over TCP, most likely on port 5060. To secure your LCS communications, you can put the connection on a LCS server that has no users homed on it — for example, a director server — and only open port 5060 to list to TCP connections on this Live Communications Server director server. Any users who try to connect to the director server using TCP will be connected on TCP, but the director server will then redirect them to connect to port 5060 of the Live Communication Server home server/pool, and that connection will fail. This way, you don't have to worry about any unencrypted IM traffic in your Live Communications Server environment.

If you want to use such a design, you need a different routing on the home server than on the director server. It will look something like what is shown in Figure 6-15.

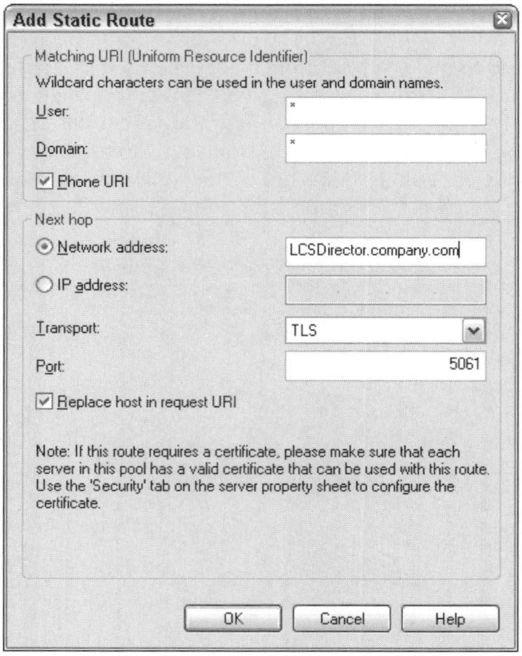

Add Static Route

Matching URI (Uniform Resource Identifier)
Wildcard characters can be used in the user and domain names.

User: ∗

Domain: ∗

☑ Phone URI

Next hop
◉ Network address: LCSDirector.company.com
◯ IP address:

Transport: TLS

Port: 5061

☑ Replace host in request URI

Note: If this route requires a certificate, please make sure that each server in this pool has a valid certificate that can be used with this route. Use the 'Security' tab on the server property sheet to configure the certificate.

[OK] [Cancel] [Help]

Figure 6-15

You can see that the Matching URI is still the same, but the target is now the FQDN of the director server. You select TLS (actually MTLS) as your transport, and use 5061, the default port, for the communication. Make sure the "Replace host in request URI" option is checked on every LCS server on the route, so that the SIP/PSTN will send the response back only to the director, which is the only LCS server listening on port 5060.

An increasing number of gateways are supporting SIP over TLS; if you have one of these gateways, you can simply go directly from the Live Communications Server home server/pool without worrying about encryption issues.

The other phone integration is *Remote Call Control (RCC) integration* (also called Third-Party Call Control, or 3PCC). In fact, strictly speaking, this is not a VoIP integration; there is no voice over IP. All you are doing is establishing a communication between your phone system and your Live Communications Server environment so that you can control your phone, which is connected to the phone system, and you will get information on your phone directly on the MOC client.

To have RCC features, you need to have a gateway that connects your Live Communications Server environment to the phone system. This gateway translates the CSTA request inside SIP to the API that your particular phone system can understand. Different phone systems may behave a little differently. If you have many phone systems in your organization, make sure you find a gateway vendor who can handle all the different types of systems, and that you can effectively manage them.

Each client is assigned a particular gateway according to the phone system to which they belong. The Live Communications Server user administrator can put this information on the Active Directory for the users so they don't have to configure it on the MOC client side (see Figure 6-16).

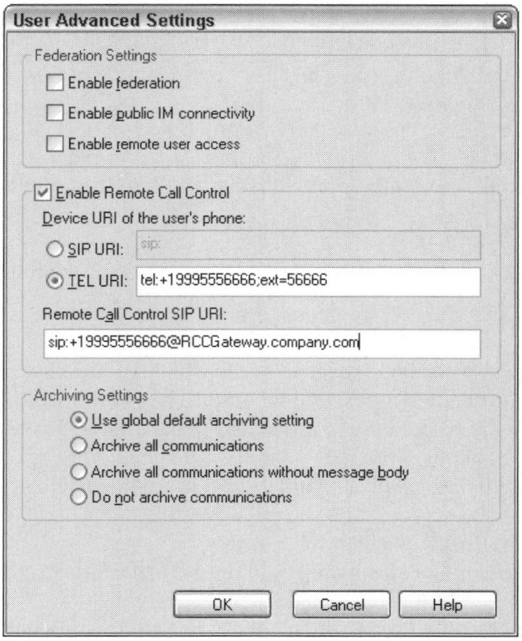

Figure 6-16

Once you set up the client setting, all you need is routing from the Live Communications Server home server/pool to the RCC gateway server. Different from the PC-to-phone setting, the routing is based on the targeted gateway server. Instead of putting in a wildcard for the target host, you need a route, as shown in Figure 6-17.

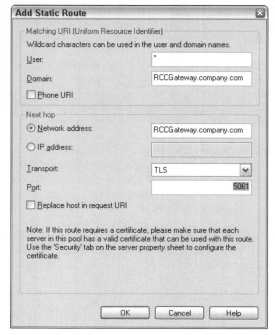

Figure 6-17

There is a Host Authorization tab on the pool's Properties. Use these steps to manage the settings of the Host Authorization tab:

1. Open the LCS Management Console and right-click on an LCS pool.
2. Select Properties and click on the Host Authorization tab, shown in Figure 6-18.

In order for the Live Communications Server to accept the SIP communication coming in to the server, it must be coming in from a trusted source. If you expect SIP communications from any kind of gateway, you need to add this gateway to the list of authorized hosts on the Host Authorization tab.

To add a trusted host, just click the Add button and fill in the form shown in Figure 6-19.

If this is for a routing with IP addresses on the Routing tab, use IP address. If this is a routing with host name and MTLS connection, make sure you put in the FQDN of the target host.

In most cases, you will check only the Throttle As Server and Treat As Authenticated checkboxes, and leave the Outbound Only unchecked, so Live Communications Server will accept inbound SIP messages from the gateway.

Usually, you will have a matching host authorization entry for every route you add that has an endpoint that is not an LCS server.

Figure 6-18

Figure 6-19

Configuring Microsoft Office Communicator

After you have installed Microsoft Office Communicator, you can configure it to allow connectivity to the Live Communications Server environment. If you have automatic client configuration set up properly in your environment, all you need to do is add your sign-in name (see Figure 6-20).

If you don't have automatic configuration established in your Live Communications Server environment, click the Advanced button and manually add the Live Communications Server connection information in the Advanced Connection Settings dialog box, shown in Figure 6-21.

Figure 6-20

Figure 6-21

If your LCS server is configured for TCP connection, you can add the server name or IP address of the server, and select TCP as your connection method. If your LCS server is configured for TLS connection, add the FQDN of the server, and select TLS as the connection.

By default, when you select TCP, your MOC client will try to connect to the server using port 5060. If you select TLS, the default port will be 5061. In some cases, you may have to configure your Live Communications Server to listen on a different port number. If that is the case, you can force the MOC to connect with a particular port using the syntax `FQDN:PortNumber`. For example, adding `Live Communication ServerAccessProxy.company.com:443` forces the MOC to try to establish a connection to port 443 of the Access Proxy server.

Once your MOC can connect to the Live Communications Server, you can manually configure other options on the client. Access the Options dialog box shown in Figure 6-22 by selecting Actions⇨Options.

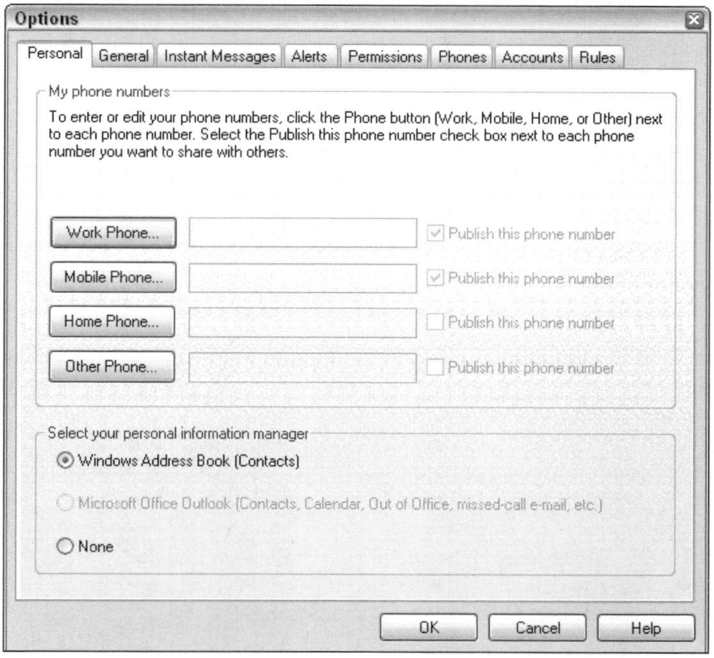

Figure 6-22

The first tab in the configuration options is the Personal tab. Here you can add the phone number you want MOC to use. This is important, as you may want to use MOC to forward incoming phone calls to one of these numbers. You can also select to publish the number to the MOC Address Book, or you can just keep it to yourself.

The General tab, shown in Figure 6-23, controls some of the common settings. For example, you can select to automatically run Communicator when you log on to Windows. Because the main purpose of Live Communications Server is to function as a real-time communicator, it is highly recommended that you select this option.

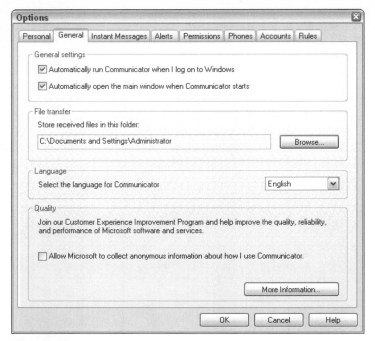

Figure 6-23

You can also automatically open the main windows when Communicator starts. Users will receive a pop-up notification automatically, to give the client more desktop real estate for the user, so it is recommended that you not open the main window every time.

You can also select a location to receive incoming files from MOC file transfer. By default, it will create a My Received Files folder under the My Documents folder to hold these files.

If you have the Multiple Languages Pack for MOC installed on the client, and you have the proper code pack and fonts installed, you can simply select from different languages in the Language option. Once you restart the MOC, it will start with that language interface for you.

The last option in the tab is the Quality option, which enables your MOC clients to send some usage information back to Microsoft, which they can use to improve the product in the future.

In addition to the General settings, you can select fonts and emoticons in your instant messages, and you can configure different alerts. However, it is more important to understand the impact of the Permissions settings (see Figure 6-24).

By default, MOC is set to have All Other Contacts on Notify. That means when someone wants to add you to his/her contact list, you will get a notification. If you deny it, this person will not be able to see your presence. The other two options are Allow and Block. When you select Allow, everyone other than those you specifically added to the block list will be able to add you to their contact list. You will not know who is watching your presence information. If you select Block, unless the other party is specifically added to your list as allowed to see your presence, he or she will not see your presence. For most users, Notify on All Other Contacts will be a good option. Senior staff members who may not want everyone to see their presence can select Block on All Other Contacts, so only those who are specifically allowed on the list will see their presence.

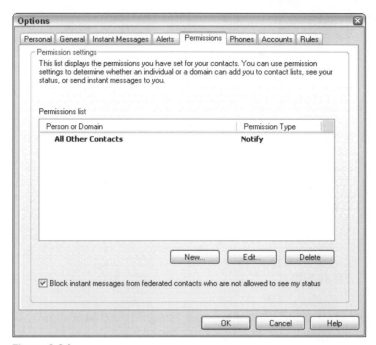

Figure 6-24

Another interesting tab is the Phones tab, shown in Figure 6-25.

There are two phone-related options on this tab. The first specifies the default device for calling phone numbers. If you select Phone as your calling device, when you call a phone number, MOC will actually instruct the phone system to call the number using the desk phone that is integrated using remote call control. If you select Computer as your calling device, when you call a phone number, MOC will use the computer to capture and play audio information. The audio signals will be sent to a SIP gateway and passed on to the telephone world. This is similar to the way most of the VoIP providers behave. The only difference is that with Live Communications Server and MOC, you are doing it inside your corporate network.

The second phone-related option is the configuration for call forwarding. Using the same remote call control capability mentioned previously, you can actually forward your desk phone from the MOC client. You can either turn off call forwarding or forward it to a particular number you have specified on the Personal tab. Even better, you can forward your call based on your location. You can select not to forward while you are using the computer, or forward the call only when you are using the computer. You can even forward the call only when the computer is idle, which means you are most likely away from your desk.

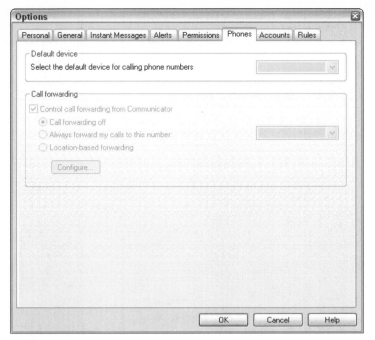

Figure 6-25

Although we have covered the Live Communications Server account configuration, there are other account-related configuration options, as shown in Figure 6-26.

To provide the remote call control feature, the MOC needs to send control commands to the phone system. This is done through the use of a third-party gateway, or directly through the phone system that supports the SIP CSTA. The MOC client will need to know how to access the gateway or phone system. You can configure this information on the client AD entry, or you can have the client set it up manually on the client side.

The conferencing information is for conference service from a service provider such as MCI or British Telecom. When you are in a multiple-party IM session in MOC, you have the option to turn this text communication into a phone conference simply by clicking a button on the MOC. Using the information you put on this Accounts tab, MOC will send the request with your account information, and the information of all the parties in your IM session, to the service provider. The service provider phone system will automatically call all the parties in your IM session and establish a conference call bridge. You don't need to send any conference call information to anyone—just click a button. To configure this option, you need the appropriate information from the service provider, after which you can establish Live Communications Server federation communication with that provider.

The last tab is the Rules tab. You can change the setting according to your needs. You can see that you can actually control a lot of integration with Microsoft Exchange/Outlook inside MOC. You can even pause the Windows Media Player while you are using the PC for audio/video communication.

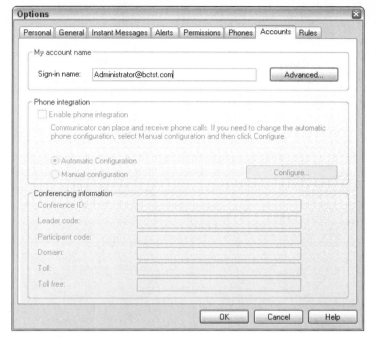

Figure 6-26

Configuring Windows Messenger

The configuration of Windows Messenger is similar to the configuration of Microsoft Office Communicator. The major difference is that Windows Messenger is what is called a *triple-stack client*. That means you can actually log on to three different Instant Messaging systems at the same time using the Windows Messenger.

When you look at the Accounts tab of Windows Messenger, shown in Figure 6-27, you will see the following options available to you:

The .NET Passport Account is for MSN Messenger connectivity. The SIP Communications Service Account is for Live Communications Server Connectivity. The Exchange Account is for Exchange Instant Messaging Connectivity. After you have each service configured, you can actually talk to contacts on any one of the three services.

For security reasons, it is recommended that you only use the multiple-stack option during the migration. Once migration is over, don't allow any multiple-stack operations. This is because when a user is being attacked by an IM virus, if you have multiple stacks enabled, the virus can actually spill from one IM system to another. For example, if a user is infected from the MSN IM system, then the virus can send instant messages to all the Live Communications Server contacts of this user and spread the virus to the Live Communications Server system.

Figure 6-27

To connect to an LCS environment using Windows Messenger, under the SIP Communications Service Account section (refer to Figure 6-27), enter your sign-in name in the field provided and then configure your connection settings to connect to your LCS environment by clicking the Advanced button. When finished, click OK to close the configuration window and then sign in on the main Windows Messenger screen.

Summary

This chapter focused on the configuration of an LCS environment and provided real-world guidance related to each configuration of an LCS server, component, or client application. In the next chapter, you will be introduced to solutions that will help you manage the configuration and health of your LCS environment.

Live Communications Server 2005 Configuration Management

The purpose of this chapter is to provide you with an understanding of how to configure your Live Communications Server environment using the Live Communications Server 2005 SP1 Management Console and Microsoft Operations Manager 2005. Also covered is use of the Live Communications Server 2005 SP1 administration console and how the console assists in managing your entire LCS infrastructure from top to bottom. You will also learn how to use Microsoft Operations Manager 2005 to manage your Live Communications Server environment, including added features for alerting and reporting.

The Live Communications Server 2005 Administration Console

Like many other Microsoft server applications, Live Communications Server has a Microsoft Management Console (MMC) snap-in to administer the LCS environment.

MMC is a productivity utility that enables you to customize the management tools for your environment. The idea is to have all your management tools accessible through a single interface or to display only those that apply to a specific user or group of users. That way, you can add in the snap-ins you need or display only the functionality of the snap-in you require. Figure 7-1 shows where the installation routine creates the link to the Live Communications Server administration console.

Figure 7-1

The LCS 2005 administration console, like any MMC, can be run in author mode. To run the LCS administration console in author mode, simply right-click the Live Communications Server 2005 link in Administrative Tools. The console is installed to run with author mode turned off by default. In addition to launching it from the Administrative Tools program group, you can select Start⟿Run, and then enter **wrtcsnap2.msc.**

As shown in Figure 7-2, the LCS administration console looks much like a Windows Explorer window. Objects that the LCS administrator can access and manage are displayed in the left pane, which is also called the *console tree.* As you select each object in the left pane, the contents of that object are displayed in the right pane, also called the *details pane* or *task pane.* The right pane contains two tabs: Status and Resources. The Resources tab shows helpful information and links to additional documentation. On the lower-right pane of this tab is an Available Tasks section containing tasks such as unprepping for the forest node.

Notice that highlighting the Forest Node object in the left pane displays all the possible options for that object on the right pane.

You navigate through the objects as you would navigate through a Windows Explorer pane; the same shortcuts apply. For example, click a plus sign or a minus sign to expand or collapse it, respectively. Press the Tab key to move between panes or to move from entry to entry in a dialog box. You can open the Properties dialog box by holding down the left Alt key and pressing the Enter key.

The following table provides a little more detail about the objects provided in the LCS administration console.

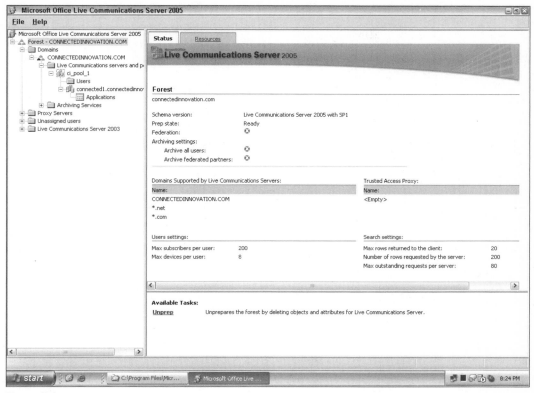

Figure 7-2

Entry in MMC	Description
Microsoft Office Live Communications Server 2005	This Item represents the Microsoft Management Console root entry.
Forest [your forest entry here]	The Forest node is used to manage global settings for LCS, such as the following: • Unprep a forest • Specify search query settings for clients • Specify the maximum number of subscribers and devices for each user • Allow applications to query presence information • Enable federation and remote user access • Specify the TCP/IP port number used for federation • Specify trusted Access Proxies • Archive internal user communication (with or without message body) • Archive federated user communication (with or without message body)

Table continued on following page

Entry in MMC	Description
Domains	This node represents all the Active Directory domains in your organization.
Root Domain [your root domain entry here]	Here you can manage your domain and perform the following tasks: • Prepare a domain • Unprep a domain • Grant cross-domain permissions • Remove a domain
Archiving Services	The Archiving Services node shows all Archiving servers that are joined to a LCS domain. Note that the servers won't be displayed if you are not a member of the RTCDomainServersAdmin group.
Child Domain [your child domain entry here]	Use this node to manage your domain and perform the following tasks: • Prepare a domain • Unprep a domain • Grant cross-domain permissions • Remove a domain The child-domain entry is only available if you have a child domain, as shown in the example organization.
Live Communications Servers and Pools	By expanding this node, you see all the LCS servers and pools in your domain. If you have an empty root domain, this node will have no entries.
Pool [your pool entry here]	This node is for managing your Standard Edition Server or Enterprise pool. The following options will be available: • Specify the maximum number of contacts per user • Override the global route to the Access Proxy • Specify the authentication protocol used by a server or pool • Configure static routes for outbound proxy requests or PSTN gateway calls • Configure client and server compression • Configure authorized hosts • Configure archiving • Manage users hosted on the server or pool

Entry in MMC	Description
Users	The Users node is for managing your Live Communications Server 2005 users in the administration console. Doing so in the snap-in is helpful if you want to have a view of users on a specific server or pool. You can perform the following tasks: • Enable users for LCS • Configure users for LCS • Move users to a different LCS server or pool • Delete users from LCS • Allow users to federate • Block users from federating • Allow users remote access to LCS • Block users from remote access to LCS • View users allow and block list • Edit users allow and block list • Configure archiving settings for users • Manage unassigned users Most of the these tasks can also be done by using the Active Directory Users and Computers snap-in. This can be helpful if you want to see your users based on the organization unit or folder in which they reside. To manage Live Communications Server 2005 users, you must be a member of the RTCDomainUserAdmins group.
Pool Server [your pool server(s) here]	This is for managing your individual Standard Edition or Enterprise Edition Server. The following tasks are available: • Manage connections • Manage certificates • Manage applications running on the server • Start, stop, deactivate, or uninstall Live Communications Server
Applications	Opening this node will show you all installed applications. By default, LCS 2005 SP1 has the IM URL Filter application and Routing application on board. However, you can extend this with your own applications written in a language very similar to C# called Microsoft SIP Processing Language (MSPL) or using managed code written in C++ or C#. Applications can be installed on Standard and Enterprise Edition Servers, Proxies, and Access Proxies. If you design and install a script on one server of an enterprise pool, you should install that script on every server in that pool.

Table continued on following page

Entry in MMC	Description
Proxy Servers	This node shows you all Proxies who joined a domain prepped for LCS.
	The Proxies won't be displayed if you are not a member of the RTCDomainServersAdmin group.
Unassigned Users	This node shows all users enabled for Live Communications Server but not assigned to a server or pool. You can either move these users to functional servers or delete them from the database if they no longer require LCS services. If you delete a user here, that user will not be deleted in Active Directory!
	In order to perform tasks here you must be a member of the RTCSomainUserAdmins group.
Live Communications Server 2003	Last but not least, this node contains all Live Communications Server 2003 servers that exist in your topology. You can view performance counters by using the Performance tab or you can move users from there to Live Communications Server 2005.
	Note that for all other user tasks in LCS 2003, you have to use the Live Communications Server 2003 Administrative snap-in.

The preceding table is only an overview of the options and possibilities Microsoft Office Live Communications Server 2005 offers. Earlier chapters and subsequent chapters dig deeper into the capabilities available, and explain in much more depth how things work and what to do when.

Navigating the Microsoft Office Live Communications Server 2005 administration console is actually quite easy once you get used to it. The hardest part might be finding out where to look for various LCS component settings, especially if you are new to LCS. Give yourself a little extra time to become comfortable with the new MMC.

Microsoft Operations Manager for Live Communications Server 2005

Microsoft Office Live Communications Server 2005 SP1, as with many other Microsoft server products, offers a Management Pack for Microsoft Operations Manager 2005 (MOM).

Microsoft Operations Manager (MOM) is a comprehensive network monitoring solution that radically improves the availability, performance, and security of networks and applications. MOM provides a central monitoring solution. It provides proactive real-time system monitoring for Live Communications Server. It is event-driven, scalable, and offers an immediate and sustainable return of investment (ROI). In addition, it offers advanced security policy enforcement and auditing capabilities, improved system availability and performance tracking, an open and extensible standards-based architecture, and numerous ways to view and report data. MOM is *the* out-of-the-box management solution for proactively monitoring the availability, performance, and security of your Live Communications Server infrastructure. MOM is based on the Microsoft Distributed Network Architecture (DNA): Presenting, Business, Logic, and Data.

The following material assumes you have a basic knowledge of Microsoft Operation Manager 2005 and its functions. Figure 7-3 shows the MOM administration console.

The first thing you have to do is import the Microsoft Office Live Communications Server 2005 SP1 MOM Management Pack. The management pack can be found on Microsoft's Live Communications Server website (at www.microsoft.com/lcs). To install and configure the pack, simply follow the provided wizard. You will be presented with the dialog box shown in Figure 7-4.

Choose the LCS2005MP_MOM2005.AKM file and click Next. After a few seconds the Finish dialog will appear. You may want to save the import log file for future reference and click Finish. After you have installed the management pack on one of your management servers, you have to install the Agent on the Live Communications Server(s) and put your server(s) into the matching computer groups. Figure 7-5 shows this for our example LCS environment.

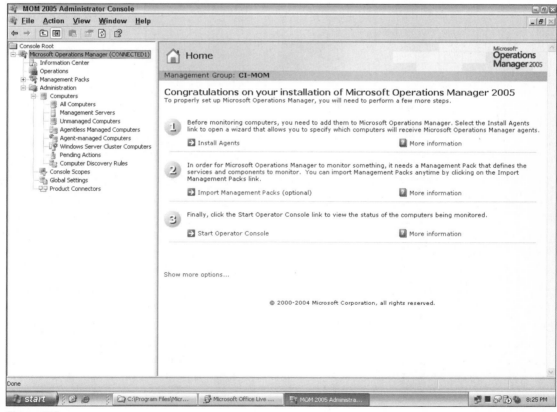

Figure 7-3

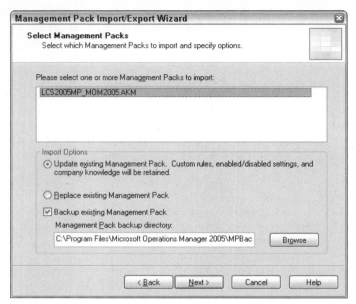

Figure 7-4

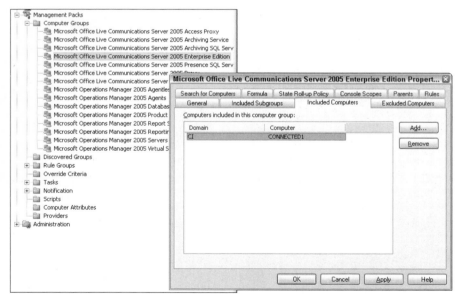

Figure 7-5

For additional configuration of rules and alerts or a more detailed description of Microsoft Management Server, refer to the available MOM product documentation available on the Microsoft Operations Manager website: www.microsoft.com/mom.

For a good starting point, leave the counters as provided by Microsoft. The Microsoft Product Group defined approximately 200 event rules and 30 performance rules. Furthermore, three public views can be used to provide everyone with a server status:

- ❑ **Logged-On End Points:** This view is represented by one counter, which shows the number of users currently logged on to the service.

- ❑ **Machine Health:** This view is represented by two counters, which provide processor data and paging data. The processor data indicates how much load the processor is handling, which can help MOM operators determine whether more users can be added to the server. The paging data indicates whether the server has sufficient RAM.

- ❑ **Connection Health:** This view is represented by three counters: Flow-Controlled Connections, Queue Depth, and Average Holding Time for Incoming Messages. Flow-Controlled Connections is the number of client connections for which the server is restricting messages, which (if it ever exceeds zero) can indicate the need to reduce the number of users assigned to that server. Queue Depth indicates whether the server is queuing requests, which can cause delays in the service and can be an area of concern if the value is greater than zero for an extended period (in general, more than 30 seconds). Average Holding Time for Incoming Messages shows the average number of seconds that each incoming message spends in the server until it is handled, which can indicate delays in the clients and the need to reduce the number of users assigned to that server.

The MOM Management Pack for Live Communications Server does not provide server statistics such as the number of text messages, audio messages, video messages, or short- and long-distance communications at a given time. To provide this information, you have to either add additional counters to MOM or run, for example, the Windows Performance Monitor on a server or use the Live Communications Server archive logs to collect and analyze performance and operation data from services.

To disable or enable counters, open the Microsoft Operations Manager administration console, click on your management server, and select Management Packs⇨Rule Groups⇨Microsoft Office Live Communications Server 2005⇨Microsoft Office Live Communications Server 2005 Enterprise Edition or Standard Edition. You will see the different rule groups and corresponding child rule groups.

Summary

The purpose of this chapter was to show you how to manage a Live Communications Server 2005 environment. This included descriptions of all the MMC console options and entries, as well as an overview of the Microsoft Operations Manager possibilities.

The next chapter offers guidance for deploying Live Communications Server 2005 SP1 and Communicator 2005 based on the cumulative real-world experiences of this book's authors.

8

Enterprise Implementation Lessons Learned

The few, the proud, the elite. No, this is not the Marines we are talking about, but an organization of consultants consisting of Microsoft employees and non-Microsoft employees who have been in the trenches deploying Microsoft Unified Communications solutions and have scars to prove it. With any technology application, problems will be realized during the deployment of the application in a real-world environment. The purpose of this chapter, and the heart and meaning of this book, is to impart some of the common lessons learned while deploying Live Communications Server 2005 SP1 and Communicator 2005 in actual real-world network environments. This chapter includes some of the screamers and some of the not so bad, and we hope that the lessons described in this chapter will help you out if and when you encounter them.

This chapter describes some commonly faced issues when deploying Live Communications Server 2005 SP1 within an enterprise, including concerns with Active Directory, enterprise Instant Messaging migration, remote access, international deployments, and implementing Live Communications Server 2005 SP1 for military or private sector use. It is hoped that after reading this chapter, you will be able to leverage the experience and knowledge it provides to thwart issues that may arise in your own deployments, or to use this information as a warning for risk mitigation within your projects.

Active Directory Concerns

When working with any enterprise organization in deploying LCS, major concerns arise regarding the modification of Active Directory. This section presents a few example scenarios that may arise during this engagement process.

Extending the Active Directory Schema

Every LCS consultant will tell you that at some point in their experience, the issue of extending a customer's Active Directory schema arose. It is my feeling and that of many of my peers that the hollering and screaming about having to extend the Active Directory schema reflects a history of schema extension deployment nightmares with Microsoft Exchange Server. After years of updating the schema, and the extended paranoia of customer network engineers, it was inevitable that the requirement for extending the schema again for LCS enablement would cause an eruption. What customers need to understand is the model of Active Directory. Active Directory is a database. As such, it has properties, values, keys, and so on. When a new service is released, or, in database design terms, a new table or field is to be applied, you have to update the database. Because this is the case with Active Directory and LCS in that you want to enable this new set of features, services, and functionality, you must update the schema. The problem that most consultants face in this area is dealing with the customer IT security teams, which in some cases are a completely different organization to work with than the deployment team. I have had experiences where the time frame to obtain approval to update the schema for LCS extended out to seven months. Fortunately, after reviewing every single itemized change, questioning every motive, spending hours in conference calls to discuss specific changes, and then finally deploying the LCS schema update using the command line, we were finished and ready for a manual deployment of LCS. Whew! Once you experience this frustration and navigate through it, you can devise ways to make your deployment smoother.

Active Directory Multi-Forest Organizations

LCS can be deployed on a forest even if it has multiple domains. Unfortunately, some enterprise organizations manage multiple companies or subsidiaries even though they are considered one company. In this case, the solution is to deploy multiple LCS environments and enable LCS federation between Active Directory forests.

This is a major concern that many organizations face. In my experience, a political decision is made regarding the appropriate approach to reduce the amount of servers required to run a federated model. One solution that I have had success with is allowing the holding company or top-level organization to maintain a centrally deployed LCS environment. All subsidiaries will still be able to log in using their SMTP or e-mail alias as their sign-in account name. For example, if `user@company.com` logs into LCS using Communicator, and he or she is a domain user of the entity that is hosting the LCS service, there are no issues. When `user@company2.com` logs into the same environment, a specific property setting within the LCS management console must be set to allow company2 users to log in to the service.

Note that client automatic configuration will not be available for user@company2.com

The following steps are required to enable alternative SIP URIs to log in to an LCS forest:

1. Open the LCS Management console by choosing Start↪All Programs↪Administrative Tools, and then click on Live Communications Server 2005 (see Figure 8-1).

    The LCS Management console will open.

2. In the left task pane, right-click the LCS Forest node and click Properties (see Figure 8-2).

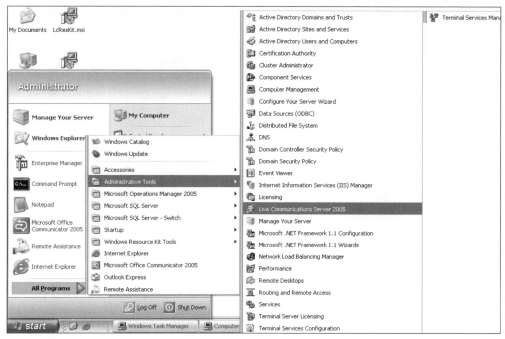

Figure 8-1

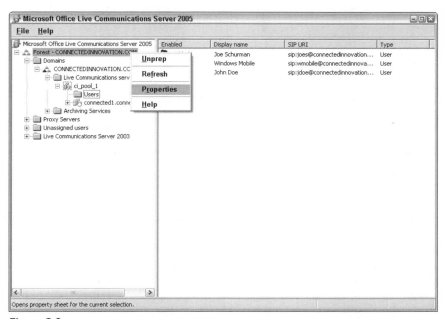

Figure 8-2

3. The Live Communications Server Global Properties window will open, as shown in Figure 8-3.

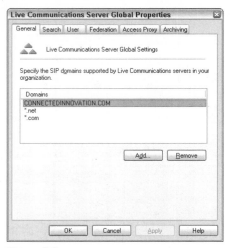

Figure 8-3

4. In the Domains section, the default LCS domain is automatically listed. To support multiple domains or alternate SIP URIs, such as in the example used earlier for `user@company2.com`, you must enter the alias into this list.

5. To add additional aliases, click the Add button. The Add SIP Domain dialog will open.

6. Enter the alias and click the OK button (see Figure 8-4).

Figure 8-4

7. The alias will be added to the SIP Domains list (refer to Figure 8-3). Click the OK button to finish.

Deploying LCS in a Multi-Operating System Environment

Deploying LCS within a 100 percent Windows Operating System environment simply rocks! Unfortunately, in every enterprise environment in which my colleagues and I have deployed LCS, there is a mix of Linux, Unix, Windows, and custom operating systems. Additionally, when DNS records need to be deployed, large organizations and military companies run Unix to manage DNS records. In these circumstances, engaging team members can be difficult, and documentation to connect all the moving pieces is scarce. Lessons learned here include identifying the complete network architecture that will support or interface with your LCS deployment. Make a list of every component and the details of each component to build the necessary team of individuals and resources to engage in the deployment process. If you don't, you will lose a lot of time. In addition, your customer may lack confidence in your inability to correctly scope your deployment.

To help you get started, I have created an LCS Architecture Guide and Design Guide template so that you can merely fill in the blanks. Both guides are available on my blog site at http://jschurman.mvps.org.

If you are working with an organization in which the top-level DNS servers are running Unix, you need to supply the team with a set of instructions for creating the required DNS SRV records to support clients logging in with automatic configuration.

The following table outlines which SRV records are required in your external-facing DNS servers running on Unix to allow Communicator 2005 to connect to the LCS environment:

LCS Use	Protocol Type	Example of DNS SRV Record	Client Application
External	TLS	_SIP._TLS.COMPANY.COM	Both
Federation	TLS	_SIPFEDERATIONTLS._TCP.COMPANY.COM	Communicator

Usually within an enterprise environment, a mix of operating systems also resides on the desktop. With the recent popularity of Linux, many customers raise concerns that they cannot reach every desktop. Linux is out there and running as well as Apple OS X. To provide LCS access to the rebels in each enterprise, Microsoft Office Communicator 2005 Web Access (CWA) is the solution. CWA is a web-based and lightweight version of Communicator that is platform independent. The only requirement on the desktop is that a client has access to a web browser.

IT Security

Like the Capital One credit card commercials with David Spade, the automatic answer provided by any enterprise IT security administrator is no! When deploying LCS within an enterprise environment, it is important to supply the appropriate security administrators with all of the nuts and bolts of LCS from a client and server perspective. The most common concern of security administrators regarding LCS is related to the opening of ports that enable communication between LCS clients, and between clients and servers.

The following table outlines the ports that are used by Communicator for specific features of the product:

Service	UDP Port Use	TCP Port Use	TLS Port Use
LCS Client to Server		5060	5061
LCS Server to Server			5061 (MTLS)
Audio/Video	5004-65535		
Application Sharing, Whiteboard, T.120 Protocol		1503	
Voice (PC to PC)	6901	6901	
Remote Assistance		3389	
File Transfer		6891-6900	

Database Administrators

When working with database administrators (DBAs) of enterprise organizations, in my experience the only request concerns security or ownership to determine who runs the create database operations. LCS setup is modularized enough to run this procedure separately, giving control to the DBA to execute this required step.

For the DBA to run the LCS Create Pool procedure, the user who runs the Create Pool process from the setup CD must be a Local Administrator on the SQL Server itself and must also be a member of the RTCDomainServerAdmins group in Active Directory.

The following table outlines the permissions required per LCS group, which are created during the Prep Domain process of the LCS setup:

Active Directory Group	RTC Database Role	RTCConfig Database Role
RTCDomainServerAdmins	Public and Admin	Public and Read/Write
RTCDomainUser Admins		Public and Read Only
RTCDomainServices	Public and Server	Public and Read Only

Provide this table to the DBA team before running the Create Pool step, which is also part of the LCS setup, and you will be able to smoothly install LCS.

Remote Access Best Practices

Most businesses require some form of remote access to resources at the main office. The criticality and type of remote access required likely varies for different organizations. Many methods are available for providing remote access to resources. Each method has its own advantages and disadvantages, and may or may not be suitable to a particular remote access scenario. Typically, organizations require implementing multiple remote access methods for different remote access scenarios existing in their environment.

There are two ways in which an LCS user can access an LCS environment: by using a virtual private network (VPN) and by using direct remote access. Both of these solutions are covered in the following sections.

Using a Virtual Private Network

Virtual private network (VPN) is the most common scenario for accessing a corporate network nowadays. Accessing your applications and data by using a VPN tunnel is like being connected to a network when you're in the office.

Especially in European countries, using VPN connections to access the corporate network is a popular option because of security considerations companies have. Thankfully, there is no need to configure Microsoft Office Communicator differently. If auto configuration is used, you merely add the necessary DNS host entries on your DNS servers and configure the Group Policy settings according to company policies.

Using Direct Access

As it's used here, the term *direct access* refers to situations in which you can directly access a certain function hosted on the corporate network-for example, from a published website to Outlook's RPC over HTTP, where the application is using standard ways to do its tasks.

This is the same with Microsoft Office Communicator, using a default port such as 5061 or 443 to access the Microsoft Office Live Communications Server Access Proxy.

Microsoft Office Communicator has two configuration options for finding its server: automatic configuration and manual configuration. More information related to DNS setup for automatic configuration of the Microsoft Office Communicator 2005 client can be found in Chapter 4.

Additional Recommendations

You should have one LCS Access Proxy for federation, and one LCS Access Proxy for remote user access. Even though it is possible to have the Microsoft Office Live Communications Server Access Proxy act as a remote access server and federation partner, it is not recommended. A best practice is to separate the two roles. You should use two different DNS names for the two IP addresses of the Access Proxy. If you plan to have remote user access and federation, divide those two roles between two Access Proxies, although it is possible to have these two roles on one server as well.

International Deployments

Currently, Microsoft Office Live Communications Server 2005 SP1 is available in nine different languages: Spanish, Korean, Japanese, Italian, German, French, Chinese Traditional, Chinese Simplified, and English. Trial versions of the different languages can be found and downloaded from `microsoft.com/livecomm`.

From a purely managerial point of view, we strongly recommend you install Microsoft Office Live Communications Server 2005 SP1 in English, and retain the program in English. International clients can seamlessly connect to the English version of LCS.

The full version of Microsoft Office Communicator is in English. With the installation of the MUI Pack (Multi User Interface), a user can switch between the languages, as shown in the following table:

Language	LCID Hex.	LCID Dec.
Spanish	0C0A	3082
Korean	0412	1042
Japanese	0411	1041
Italian	0410	1040
German	0407	1031
French	040C	1036
Chinese Traditional	0404	1028
Chinese Simplified	0804	2052

Before installing the MUI pack, install the Office Communicator 2005 Hotfix KB 903928, which is available by searching for the KB number provided via the `microsoft.com/downloads` website.

To change the language of Communicator, sign out from Live Communications Server and close Communicator completely. If you close Communicator by using the Close button or by clicking File➪Close, it is not really closed; the application is still running. Check for the Communicator icon in the notification area and exit Communicator from there. Open Windows Explorer and select Program Files➪Microsoft Office Communicator. Rename the files `lcc_help.chm`, `lclang.dll`, and `lcres.dll` to something different. Then go to the MUI directory and search for your language, copy the three renamed files to the Microsoft Office Communicator directory, and restart Communicator. During our tests it took some time before the UI showed up after replacing the `dlls`.

Figure 8-5 and Figure 8-6 illustrate the UI in Spanish and German, respectively.

Figure 8-5

Figure 8-6

IBM Sametime Migration

As mentioned in Chapter 2, LCS has entered the enterprise domain in which existing technologies such as IBM Sametime have dominated. This section demonstrates some of the tasks that are required for an enterprise customer who has decided to migrate from the IBM Sametime messaging environment to Microsoft Live Communications Server 2005. Within this scenario, we identify a customer who is currently using Microsoft Exchange as the enterprise e-mail solution and is decommissioning IBM Domino servers to migrate to Live Communications Server. The ability to migrate existing Sametime users as well as their respective Instant Messaging buddies/contacts is a critical requirement for this deployment.

Requirements

The following table outlines the requirements set forth by the customer within the provided scenario described in the overview of this section:

Features	Required Software
IBM Sametime to LCS Migration	Live Communications Server 2005 with Service Pack1 Enterprise or Standard Edition.
	Live Communications Server 2005 with Service Pack1 Resource Kit

Schedule

Based upon the requirements outlined in the previous section, the following table lists the schedule of tasks, with estimated hours required to support the deployment scenario. The estimated schedule numbers have been derived based on customer experience:

Tasks	Timeline Estimate	Consulting Hours
Identify existing IBM Sametime users and enable users within Active Directory for Live Communications Server service.	80 hours	80 hours
Export existing IBM Sametime users' buddy/contact lists.	40 hours	40 hours
Import IBM Sametime users' buddy/contact lists using Live Communications Server 2005 with Service Pack 1 Resource Kit (Sametime Migration Utility).	40 hours	40 hours
Verify matching buddy/contact lists within each system (Sametime/LCS)	40 hours	40 hours
Testing	40 hours	40 hours
Total Estimated Hours	**240 hours**	**240 hours**

Exchange IM Migration

Exchange Instant Messaging, or Exchange IM, is one of the two predecessors to Microsoft Office Live Communications Server 2005 with SP1. Exchange IM is a unique solution within Microsoft Exchange Server 2000 and served as the original enterprise Instant Messaging platform with its client, Windows Messenger. The migration path is straightforward and you do not have to migrate users to LCS 2003 and from there to LCS 2005 with SP1.

As there is no upgrade of Exchange IM to LCS 2005 SP1, you can deploy the new environment in parallel with the old one. We will assume that this has been done and tested prior to moving users from Exchange IM to LCS. Furthermore, we recommend you retain the Exchange IM infrastructure for a while after all users have been moved to the new server. The Exchange IM Service should be stopped to prevent "islands" of Exchange IM users without access to Live Communications Server users and vice versa.

The entire Exchange IM migration is mostly a server-side solution using a set of scripts provided by Microsoft in the resource kit. Because we are talking about Exchange IM migration, we have to talk about different possible scenarios and their effect on the user.

First, however, let's start by comparing the differences between Microsoft Office Communicator as the preferred client for Live Communications Server and Windows Messenger as the client for Exchange IM. Both clients can "talk" SIP, and both can talk to an LCS environment. Windows Messenger is a so-called "multi-stack client" that is able to talk to MSN/Hotmail contacts as well, provided that the firewall is configured to allow that. Communicator can't do that unless you configure your LCS to allow Public Internet Cloud (PIC) federation, which would enable communication with MSN, AOL, and Yahoo. Communicator saves all your contacts in a central database either on the Standard Edition Server (MSDE) or the Enterprise Edition Server (SQL). The Allow and Block lists reside there along with a few other settings. Windows Messenger uses the local registry to save this information.

Keeping these differences in mind, we will split the migration into four scenarios:

❑ The section "Immediate Migration without Importing Users' Contacts and Permissions" explains how to migrate all users in a single phase without migrating users' contacts and permissions.

❑ The section "Immediate Migration with Importing Users' Contacts and Permissions" explains how to migrate all users in a single phase along with migrating users' contacts and permissions

❑ The section "Gradual Migration Importing Users' Contacts and Permissions" explains how to gradually migrate users with their contacts and permissions.

❑ The section "Gradual Migration without Importing Users' Contacts and Permissions" explains how to gradually migrate users without their contacts and permissions until all users are deployed on LCS.

Generally, small organizations make use of an immediate migration strategy over the weekend. Mid-size and large organizations will probably use a gradual migration strategy.

Immediate Migration without Importing Users' Contacts and Permissions

An immediate migration has the advantage of moving all users to LCS at once. It is an aggressive path and has a minimal risk because the Exchange IM service is kept operational for a certain amount of time to allow users to switch back in case of unforeseen issues.

With this approach, users have to migrate their contacts themselves. The period of time during which you have two IM environments could be very short.

This approach consists of four steps:

1. Capacity planning
2. Deploying the Live Communications Server Client Microsoft Office Communicator
3. Homing users
4. Removing Exchange IM after a transition period

Immediate Migration with Importing Users' Contacts and Permissions

This migration path is most achievable in small or mid-size organizations, and as noted earlier it can typically be done during a weekend or overnight. Although it is an aggressive migration path, it presents minimal risk because the Exchange IM service can, and should, be kept operational for a short period of time to resolve unforeseen issues.

System administrators must help users automate the transfer of contact lists from Exchange IM to Live Communications Server.

This approach consists of eight steps:

1. Capacity planning
2. Deploying the Live Communications Server Client Microsoft Office Communicator
3. Generating a list of Exchange IM users
4. Gathering and exporting user contact lists
5. Homing users
6. Importing user contact lists and permissions to Live Communications Server
7. Using dual contacts
8. Removing Exchange IM after a transition period

Gradual Migration Importing Users' Contacts and Permissions

This migration path is mostly designed for large organizations with a significant number of IM users. The idea is to migrate users in batches over a period of time (days, weeks, or even longer). The intention is to make the migration seamless for users and enable them to use IM regardless of whether they or their contacts have been migrated.

There are many reasons for doing it this way, including deployment of a pilot population, the time involved to install client computers, and the learning curve needed for help desk and support teams as they are trained on the new software.

The migration process is more or less identical to that described earlier in the two immediate migration scenarios. Organizations just carry out the process over a longer period of time.

Gradual Migration without Importing Users' Contacts and Permissions

As with the previous example, medium and large organizations with a significant base of Exchange IM users may find that a gradual migration is a more prudent and realistic path. The transition should be, as in the previous example, seamless and with nearly no user interaction.

This approach provides two main benefits. One, users won't see dual contact entries, as they would when both Exchange IM and Live Communications Server services are enabled during the transition period. Two, IT administrators can confirm that everyone can log on to Live Communications Server services before actually needing to do so.

The concept behind this migration path is similar to the previous one; however, the contact lists are migrated after all users are enabled and migrated to Live Communications Server.

After all the users are enabled for Live Communications Server, you need to verify that they can log on, and that their contact lists and permissions have been migrated and the Exchange IM services disabled. In cases where a user's contacts list is not properly migrated, the administrator can migrate it again, because a copy of the user's contact list is stored in the file server that was stored during the export process.

Scripts Provided by Microsoft

Microsoft provides four scripts to help the administrator perform certain steps described in the previous sections. Space not does permit a detailed description here, but it does offer a rough overview of how the scripts are used.

lcsish.wsf

`lcsish.wsf` has two uses. One is to generate a list of Exchange IM users in a specified Active Directory container. This script must be run from the command line with the following parameters:

    /eimdn and /genuserfile

As the name indicates, this script goes to the specified Active Directory container and writes those users out to a specified file. The specified file is created in Unicode format. The output is written directly to the command console and you can redirect that to a file by using redirection.

You can also use `lcsish.wsf` with these parameters:

    /userfile and /eimdn

This initializes the file share and creates the user files, including permissions on the file so that only the user is able to open his or her own text file.

lcsmon.wsf

This script must be placed in the share created with `lcsish.wsf` and can only run from there. This script is used by every user, either by sending a link to the script or by using a login script. The script exports the user's contacts from the registry to the file created earlier for the user. It uses the user's login credentials to run the script and to validate the user against the Exchange IM server. If the user is not logged on to the domain, the script can be used with the `/user` switch with the user's name and FQDN, in the form `user@fqdn`.

lcssipen.wsf

The next script performs the steps to acquire a list of users to be enabled. It uses the `/homeserverdn` switch to determine which Enterprise Pool or Standard Edition Server should be used for the user, as well as a SIP mapping switch to determine and change the mapping of Exchange IM SIP domains to Live Communications Server SIP domains. If `/force` is not specified, the user will be skipped. The `/onlysipenable` switch can be used to only set the value in the `msRTCSIP-UserEnabled` attribute to `TRUE`. Another switch, `/sipenable`, is used to set the attribute `msRTCSIP-UserEnabled` to `TRUE` if provided, or `FALSE` if not. As with all the other scripts, everything is logged to the screen; to redirect the output, use the normal redirection option `lcssipen.wsf param1 param2 paramx > logfile.txt`.

lcsimpac.wsf

Last but not least, this script is used to convert the users' Exchange IM permissions to their equivalent Live Communications Server presence permissions. It migrates the contacts to their respective LCS server. The Exchange IM access control lists (ACLs) are retrieved from Active Directory, and the users' contacts from the files generated earlier by lcsmon.wsf. To run the script you must be logged on with Domain Administrator rights or be in the RTCDomainUserAdmins group. The script must run on a Standard Edition Server or on the Enterprise Edition pool back-end database.

Further Information

For further details on how to migrate users from Exchange IM to Live Communications Server, and for a more detailed view of the scripts that can be used, refer to the Microsoft Office Live Communications Server 2005 SP1 Resource Kit in the subfolder called Migration. The Live Communications Server 2005 SP1 Resource Kit can be found on the Microsoft LCS web site, at www.microsoft.com/lcs.

Implementing LCS for Military and Private Sector Environments

The purpose of this section is to provide guidance for the implementation of Live Communications Server for military and private sector use. The following topics are covered:

- ❑ Satellite connectivity
- ❑ Locate and communicate-Mapping Solutions
- ❑ Protecting communications
- ❑ Archiving communications
- ❑ Deploying LCS for a limited duration
- ❑ Mobile communications
- ❑ Mobile clients
- ❑ LCS within military transport
- ❑ LCS for covert operations

While policy will determine the ability to deploy LCS in the manner discussed in this section, this material provides an overview of how secured Instant Messaging can be a preferred communication tool for military and private sector operations. Deploying the appropriate devices and secured protocols will enable special forces and individual operations to be completed without compromising the security of the operation.

Satellite Connectivity

Live Communications Server 2005 communications and IM communications carry minimal communication weight on the network. LCS 2005 enables an even more structured and secure messaging platform that can run on speeds as low as 28KBD.

Most bases require inbound and outbound satellite communications for external communications. LCS runs consistently on these networks with no collusion. LCS can also be modified so that the inbound and outbound LCS transport, standard at 5061, can be customized to your organization's required port number.

Figure 8-7 shows the communication architecture of an LCS environment utilizing satellite inbound and outbound communications.

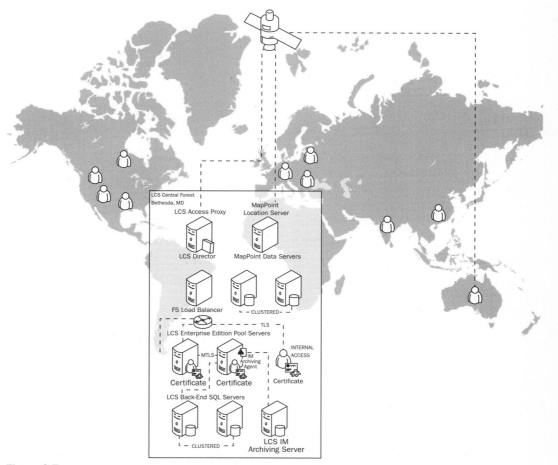

Figure 8-7

Locate and Communicate-Mapping Solutions

In my professional opinion, a contact locator combined with the ability to provide IM and Voice over Internet Protocol (VoIP) is one of the most vital and utilized solutions for U.S. military and private sector agency use. Having the ability to track an asset or ops team located in a remote part of the world or only a few blocks away using a myriad of connections including GSM, GPRS, and GPS communications is simply awesome.

This solution may sound complex, but combining the power of Microsoft Live Communications Server 2005 and Microsoft MapPoint 2005 provides a supported and moderately configurable solution to this scenario.

Using the integration capability of LCS and MapPoint or Microsoft Virtual Earth, tracking an asset using location-based services and then communicating to the user via Live Communications Server 2005 SP1 using either secured VoIP or IM, while providing monitored and archived service, can be accomplished with ease.

Protecting Communications

Live Communications Server provides a secure Instant Messaging platform by utilizing Transport Layer Security (TLS) and Session Initiation Protocol (SIP). SIP is the structured message itself, while TLS is the transport in which the communication is carried. For U.S. military and private sector agencies, this level of security is desperately needed, as tapped communications are common. TLS provides the latest in secured communications since its predecessor, SSL, and provides a layer of encryption over the communication wire itself. For military and private sector agencies that require communication transmissions to be run on customized ports, LCS offers the functionality to modify the port used between LCS clients and servers.

Logging of Instant Messaging Conversations

Live Communications Server provides the ability to monitor and report Instant Messaging conversations through the LCS IM Archiving Service. The IM Archiving Service requires an additional server to support it, and the actual IM messages are stored in a SQL Server database. The LCS IM Archiving Service works by implementing an MSMQ (Microsoft Message Queue) service within the environment to capture Instant Messaging communications and then store them in a SQL Server database for recording and reporting purposes. This is a feature that can be turned on or off based on the required use of the service.

Enabling the Live Communications Server 2005 IM Archiving Service will enable all LCS client communications to be stored in a back-end SQL Server database or SAN environment for reporting and recording purposes. This service is critical when communicating secret-level information, as the IM Archiving Service provides accountability and control.

Deploying LCS for a Limited Duration

Live Communications Server 2005 deployments can be accomplished in limited implantation time frames. The ability to deploy quickly for special operations is critical, as is the ability to tear down an LCS environment.

Microsoft has provided a Live Communications Server 2005 Enterprise and Standard Edition Quick Start Guide that provides comprehensive information to enable a timely install. In our experience, an LCS environment can be set up, assuming that all software, hardware, network, and security components are enabled, in several hours if provided with an account with autonomous control. Such an installation would encompass only 20,000 users or less.

Mobile Communications

Communicator Mobile, known by its nickname "CoMo," enables mobile operatives and vehicle transports with the power of unified communications on the go. As Microsoft has entered into automotive technology solutions, LCS client applications can be easily implemented within a mobile transport. This solution would coincide with the development of a mobile client, but would also include an integrated display panel to provide a user interface and input devices.

Enabling LCS within a mobile transport provides secure Instant Messaging, audio, telephony, and video communications that are both monitored and archived. This solution provides a definitive solution for mobile and covert operations. Scenarios that include military raids, searches and rescues, target identifications, and other covert operations are greatly enhanced using Live Communications Server 2005. Enabling secured Instant Messaging, and audio and video communications, provides a better communications capability to both the base and field operators.

Summary

This chapter described several enterprise deployment lessons that have been learned from real-world scenarios. It also covered new ideas and concepts for implementing Live Communications Server 2005 SP1 in different environments, and various solutions were offered for challenging deployments. It also examined migrating from existing enterprise Instant Messaging platforms. In the next chapter, you will look at troubleshooting tasks within Live Communications Server 2005 SP1.

9

Troubleshooting

This chapter provides useful troubleshooting information related to Microsoft Office Live Communications Server 2005 SP1 and Communicator 2005. It includes a series of commonly asked questions and material that I and my co-authors believe is necessary to understand in order to deploy LCS and Communicator in a real-world environment, rather than a lab. Additional resource material is provided toward the end of this chapter, including a list of website links for obtaining support for LCS and Communicator online.

General Troubleshooting (FAQs)

Following are a few commonly asked questions specifically related to the configuration of Live Communications Server and Microsoft Office Communicator:

❑ **The Create Pool process fails when I try to complete the command. Why?**

This is usually due to SQL Server connectivity. You should run Create Pool on the SQL Server itself or on an LCS server that has the SQL Server DMO files installed on it. Also make sure that you have appropriate permissions to create these databases on the SQL Server itself.

❑ **Why can't I complete Prep Schema?**

This is usually due to Active Directory permissions. Prep Schema requires a user to have write permissions on the Active Directory schema to complete the task. Ensure that you have either Enterprise Administrator rights or write permissions to the schema. These are not commonly given out lightly in enterprise environments.

❑ **How can users with alternate login IDs/SIP URIs connect to my LCS environment?**

You can allow users who have alternate SIP URIs to connect to an LCS environment in a couple of different ways. If they are users within the same Active Directory domain and they have an e-mail alias that they want to use as their SIP URI that differs from the SIP namespace that LCS is deployed within, you can create a listing of this alternate namespace within the LCS Forest Global Settings. If these are users from another domain altogether and they are trying to connect into a centrally deployed LCS environment, you can either use an LCS director to route these users and/or deploy a new certificate on each LCS server and modify this new certificate's subject alternative name (SAN) to include the additional domains you are supporting. More information on the SAN field of a certificate can be found in Chapter 4.

❑ **Why are users unable to communicate with their contacts that are hosted on another LCS server?**

This problem is usually related to TLS configuration. When you deploy more than one LCS server within an environment, you must enable an MTLS connection entry so that these servers can communicate with one another. MTLS, as described in Chapter 4, provides mutual authentication between servers. Please ensure that you have created an MTLS connection, as described in Chapter 4, on each LCS server in your environment.

❑ **Why can't I see the presence of my contacts when everyone is signed in?**

Usually this is attributed to network connectivity issues. Make sure that your Active Directory domain controller is functioning properly, that you can connect to your LCS servers without delayed responses, and that you have configured DNS correctly, as described in Chapter 4. If each of these settings has been correctly configured and you are using LCS Enterprise Edition with a hardware load balancer, ensure that the load balancer has been configured properly. Sometimes the load balancer is not set up correctly between LCS EE pool servers, which can cause SIP messages to disconnect, such as the BENOTIFY method, which is used for presence awareness.

❑ **What should I do when the LCS service does not start after activation?**

First, verify that the LCS service is running. Then, start looking for errors in activation logs and the Windows Server Application event log. Try connecting to the DB using the service account credentials and make sure no one has altered any of the permissions.

❑ **I don't seem to have enough privileges in Active Directory.**

Make sure that your account is a member of RTCDomainServerAdmins; and if you just ran DomainPrep, log off and log on again. This is required in order for Domain Prep granted permissions to take effect.

❑ **I am trying to deploy in a multi-forest environment and the trusts do not seem to work using Kerberos.**

In order for a Kerberos trust between forests to work correctly, both forests must be in Windows Server 2003 native mode. If one or both forests are running in Windows 2000 Server mixed mode, you must use NTLM as the authentication protocol.

❑ **I can't sign in with Microsoft Office Communicator 2005 with automatic configuration.**

This is usually related to a missing DNS host A record for the LCS server or pool; a missing DNS SRV record, as mentioned in Chapter 4; or a misconfigured TLS certificate. Please check DNS to ensure that you have a valid DNS host A record and SRV records matching what we outlined in Chapter 4, as well as a properly configured certificate infrastructure, also covered in Chapter 4.

❑ **Remote users are unable to connect even though everything seems to be set up correctly with LCS.**

Make sure the right ports are open on the firewall. The default port for TLS is 5061; for TCP it is 5060. Try to run the Diagnostic Client simulation test within the LCS Diagnostic tool, described later in this chapter. The test will provide you with a good snapshot of what is causing the connectivity issues.

❑ **I am trying to troubleshoot the connection between MOC and LCS. Where do I start?**

Enable client-side logging via regedit—HKEY_Current_User\Software\Microsoft\Tracing\ RTCDLL. Use Network Monitor or "Siplogger" (LCS 2003 Resource Kit) on the server to follow the traffic and see what is happening.

❑ **Why can't I send files, use audio/video, or enable data collaboration within Communicator when I am connected remotely?**

Audio/video communication, data collaboration with whiteboard, and file transfer are all peer-to-peer sessions that do not run through an LCS server environment. When you are connecting remotely, your client is sending instant messages through your LCS environment remotely, but all of these additional sessions are run over the TCP stack. You need to use a virtual private network (VPN) to enable these features when on the road.

❑ **Why can't I use Group Instant Messaging as I could with IBM Sametime?**

Group IM did not make it into the current version of Live Communications Server 2005 SP1. This feature is scheduled for the next version. In the meantime, you can create groups in your Communicator client and then IM the entire group by clicking on the group name.

❑ **What is the difference between remote call control (RCC) and Voice over IP (VoIP)?**

RCC is used for Communicator control over a PBX system line (dial-tone). Using RCC, you can control your PBX phone as you would on the phone itself. With VoIP, you are connecting over the Internet using a PSTN service to establish an RTP media session.

❑ **Why can't I initiate an outbound call using Communicator?**

This is probably due to a bad configuration of your LCS environment's connection to a PSTN or PBX service. LCS requires a gateway between any PSTN or PBX system that is non–SIP-compliant. Check with your LCS administrator to ensure that your LCS environment is configured appropriately.

❑ **I am unable to send hyperlinks through MOC. What could be the problem?**

Hyperlinks are not always recommended within a Live Communications Server environment. If you need to enable hyperlinks to be sent to each client, use the following steps:

1. Set the policy for Communicator to allow URLs to be clickable.

2. In the Windows registry editor, edit the following key to match the following settings:

HKEY_LOCAL_MACHINE\SOFTWARE\Policies\Microsoft\Communicator\EnableUrl

3. Make sure that the IMFilter.am on the server is not configured to block URLs in messages. If you use the GPO, Undefined is the same as Disabled, so you must explicitly allow URLs in Communicator.

Enabling LCS When AD Permissions Inheritance Is Blocked

Companies often lock down their environment to control who can do what on a forest and/or domain level. Lockdown means an administrator does not rely on the settings and options that Microsoft specified during the forest and domain preparation steps, for security reasons. The administrator deletes a set of entries and stops the OU structure from "self-replicating" its settings from the top down.

Active Directory permission inheritance can also be blocked when you are using tools that set the Active Directory permissions, such as NetIQ's Directory and Resource Administrator or bv-Control for Microsoft Active Directory. Both tools hold their information in a central database and just apply it to the Active Directory. The tools do that from the top down, so there is no need to have that inherited automatically from the Active Directory.

The following sections cover deployment issues you may face and how to overcome them.

Authenticated Users ACE Removed

The authenticated users ACE is removed from a domain's default container, such as System, Users, Computer, or Domain Controllers.

Microsoft Office Live Communications Server 2005 Prep Domain adds direct ACEs on relevant default containers on that domain to remove the reliance of Live Communications Server 2005 on these "authenticated users ACEs." However, note that removing authenticated users "Read" ACEs on the forest root main containers blocks the deployment of Live Communications Server 2005 in a child domain. This scenario cannot be addressed by LCS in its default configuration. The workaround is to add Read ACEs on these root domain containers for the Domain Admins from the child domains that will be activating the Live Communications Server.

Custom Organizational Unit

Custom organizational unit (OU) containers are created to hold user and computer objects with permission inheritance disabled.

Live Communications Server provides an optional CreateLcsOuPermissions procedure, available from the LcsCmd.exe command-line deployment tool. This procedure enables an administrator to add the remaining Live Communications Server ACEs to objects in specified OU containers to which the inheritance is blocked. In order to successfully accomplish this, you must specify the type of objects in the OU container (e.g., computer, user, InetOrgPerson) so that the procedure adds only the relevant ACEs for that object type. There is also an option for selecting OU type of contacts for supporting the central forest topology scenario. You have to run this procedure, CreateLcsOuPermissions, on every OU with users enabled for Live Communications Server 2005, and every OU with computers hosting Live Communications Server 2005. This is required for the successful deployment, operation, and administration of Live Communications Server 2005.

Figure 9-1 shows the Security tab of the Computers Properties dialog, which indicates the default permission set on that OU. To access the Security tab in Active Directory Users and Computers, select Advanced Settings from the View menu.

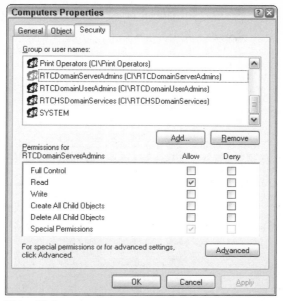

Figure 9-1

Figure 9-2 shows the inheritance settings and from where they are inherited. If permission inheritance is disabled by a lockdown, the Inherited From column is empty, or says <not inherited>.

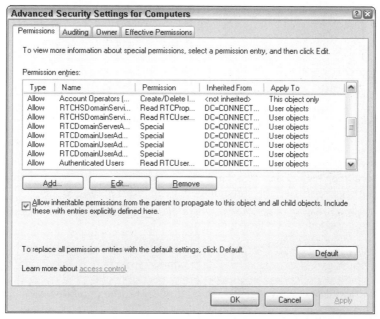

Figure 9-2

Using LcsCmd.exe with CreateLcsOuPermissions

In a locked down environment, one of the options for creating the necessary rights on an organizational unit level is to use LcsCmd.exe with the CreateLcsOuPermissions switch. The following paragraphs demonstrate how to do that. If you are unsure whether the permissions are set correctly or not, you can use the CheckLcsOuPermissions switch to check that. Following is the syntax for the CreateLcsOuPermissions switch:

```
LcsCmd.exe /domain [:{FQDN}] /action:CreateLcsOuPermissions /ou:<CN=name>
/objectType:<name> [/refdomain: <domain FQDN>]
```

The following table describes the parameters used with the CreateLcsOuPermissions action:

Parameters	Required?	Usage
/ou:{distinguishedname}	Yes	Indicates the container for which permissions should be created. This is the container in which inheritance is disabled or authenticated user permission is removed — the so-called "locked down container."
/objectType:{User | InetOrgPerson | Computer | Contact}	Yes	Indicates the type of objects stored in the container and for which you want to create permissions
/refdomain:{FQDN}	Optional	This action gives permissions on the container to that same domain's Live Communications Server groups. If you specify /refdomain:<domain FQDN>, then this action overrides the default by giving permissions on the container to the specified domain's Live Communications Server groups instead of the domain where the container is located.

Example:

```
LcsCmd.exe /domain /action:CreateLcsOuPermissions /ou:"OU=Dept1Users,OU=UsersOU
/objectType:user
```

The following guidelines describe some prerequisites and notes:

❑ You have to be logged on to the computer using Domain Admins credentials for the domain with the organizational unit containers that will receive permissions.

❑ Verify that this task was successful by running the CheckLcsOuPermissions command-line switch.

❑ Alternatively, you could verify that this task was successful by checking the HTML log files that were created by LcsCmd.exe; the final result has to be Success.

This part of Chapter 9 should have helped you to find the right tools and ways to implement Microsoft Live Communications Server in a locked-down environment. You should have all the information you need to set permissions correctly and continue with your installation.

LCS Certificate Troubleshooting

This section will help you troubleshoot LCS certificate problems.

There was a problem verifying the certificate from the server.

This error message is usually shown when there is a conflict with a certificate on a specific LCS server. To resolve this problem, ensure that the following settings are correctly configured:

❑ **Friendly Name/Common Name of the Certificate:** If you are deploying an LCS Standard Edition server, make sure that the certificate applied to the TLS connection in the LCS properties of the server has the following settings:

  ❑ The name of the certificate should match the FQDN (fully qualified domain name) of the server. For example, if the server name is `Server1.Domain.Company.com`, the certificate name should be the same. If the name does not match, the connection will not work.

If you are deploying an LCS Enterprise Edition server and it is the only server in the pool, make sure that the certificate applied to the TLS connection in the LCS properties of the server has the following settings:

  ❑ The name of the certificate must match the FQDN (fully qualified domain name) of the server. For example, if the server name is `Server1.Domain.Company.com`, the certificate name should be the same. If the name does not match, the connection will not work. It is best practice, however, to use the FQDN of the pool in preparation for the addition of other pool servers in the environment. For example, if the pool name is `Pool1.Domain.Company.com`, the certificate name should be the same. If the name does not match, the connection will not work.

If you are deploying an LCS Enterprise Edition pool, make sure that the certificate applied to the TLS connection in the LCS properties of each pool server has the following settings:

  ❑ The name of the certificate should match the FQDN (fully qualified domain name) of the pool. For example, if the pool name is `Pool1.Domain.Company.com`, the certificate name should be the same. If the name does not match, the connection will not work.

❑ **EKU (Enhanced Key Usage):** The EKU requirement for an LCS server or pool server certificate is a Server Authentication EKU. You can use a Server and Client Authentication EKU type as well, but this is not required. If your certificate EKU type is not a Server Authentication EKU type or a Server and Client Authentication EKU type, the certificate will be unusable.

❑ **Validity Period:** Ensure that your certificate has not expired. If it is expired, follow the steps provided in Chapter 4 to request and configure a new certificate for your LCS server or pool server.

❑ **Certificate Chain:** Another reason why you would not be able to connect is because your client machine does not trust against the root certificate authority. If your client machine and LCS server or pool server certificate do not all match the same CA chain, the certificates used are invalid and the connection will not work.

Error Message: The certificate you selected is issued for a subject that differs from the fully qualified domain name (FQDN) of this pool. If you continue, clients and other servers may not be able to connect to this server. Do you wish to proceed with this certificate?

This error message occurs when you are applying a certificate to an LCS server connection entry and it does not match the name of the pool. Try these fixes:

❑ Some organizations have a pool name that consists of the full domain or subdomain of a network, but have DNS host A records that are flat. For example, if an LCS pool's actual FQDN is `Pool1.SubDomain.Company.com`, but the DNS host A record and SRV records point to `Pool1.Company.com`, then the certificate name should be `Pool1.Company.com` to match the record, which does not match the FQDN of the pool. In this case, ignore the error message by clicking the Yes button.

❑ If the previous scenario does not apply and the name of your certificate is invalid, click the No button, request a new certificate as described in the steps listed in Chapter 4, and then re-apply the certificate to the connection entry.

IM Archiving FAQs

Many new LCS customers have questions about how the LCS IM Archiving Service works, including both technical and scenario-based inquiries. This section provides responses to some of these frequently asked questions

❑ **Which LCS pool server kicks off the archiving process during a one-to-one conversation?**

LCS uses Session Initiation Protocol (SIP) as its communication protocol. SIP has two methods that are of significant use to the LCS IM Archiving Service: INVITE and BYE. If User 1 fires up their client (Communicator or Windows Messenger) and begins a conversation with User 2, User 1 initiates the SIP INVITE method. The INVITE method, if both users are set to be archived, kicks off the entry into the LCS IM Archiving database by CALLER ID. All subsequent messages during this session are grouped under this CALLER ID and TIME STAMP record. User 2's pool server—again, if the user is set to be archived—will also archive User 2's messages, but will not duplicate the insert of User 1's message. User 2's pool server is intelligent in that it notices the CALLER ID entry, posting its messages under that record. This is a major difference from that of IM Logic's solution, whereby duplicates are stored and then eventually removed. The LCS IM Archiving Service's solution enables you to appropriately follow the conversation in the IM Archiving database.

❑ **What if the initiating user (User 1 in the previous scenario) closes their conversation window and User 2 is still hanging there, and then User 1 comes back online?**

When a user closes their conversation window, and only the conversation window, it initiates a SIP BYE method. The BYE method closes the CALLER ID record, so even if User 2 is hanging there with all of the previous messages and User 1 signs back in and starts messaging again, this is considered a new conversation.

❑ **What if User 1 and User 2 both have their clients open for days?**

Only closing the conversation window sends the SIP BYE method, so even if User 1 and User 2 have their conversation windows open from a day ago, it will still be lumped under the original CALLER ID record, but you will also see the difference in time stamps. In addition, note that by design, every eight hours the client will re-sign in. This does not initiate a SIP BYE method either.

❑ **What if my client hibernates during this period?**

In this case, hibernation equals a SIP BYE method and the conversation ends. Any new messages are stored under a new CALLER ID record.

❑ **What happens if User 1 is set to be archived and User 2 is set to not be archived because of reasons such as international privacy laws?**

In the current version of the LCS IM Archiving Service, if User 1 is messaging with User 2, then the message is not archived even if User 1 is set to be archived. A proposed change in the next version of LCS would change that behavior, and User 1's side of the conversation would be logged.

❑ **What reports can I use to show archived IM messages?**

With LCS, there is not a solution to provide a search or reporting of archived instant messages from the IM Archiving database. To remedy this, my team at Connected Innovation, www .connectedinnovation.com, has developed a solution called *LCSpy*. This tool will enable you to query the IM Archiving database based on keywords, dates, or sign-in names, and it includes capabilities for exporting to Adobe PDF, Microsoft Word, and Microsoft Excel document formats.

Figure 9-3 shows the IM Archiving query page.

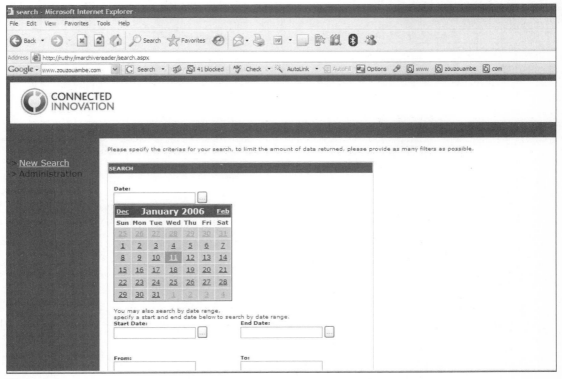

Figure 9-3

Figure 9-4 shows the IM Archiving results (raw data).

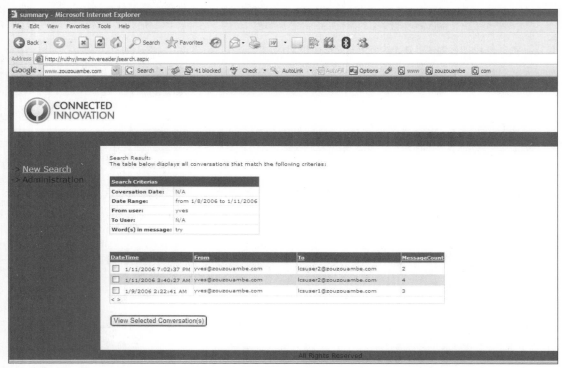

Figure 9-4

Figure 9-5 shows the IM Archiving results (IM Conversation).

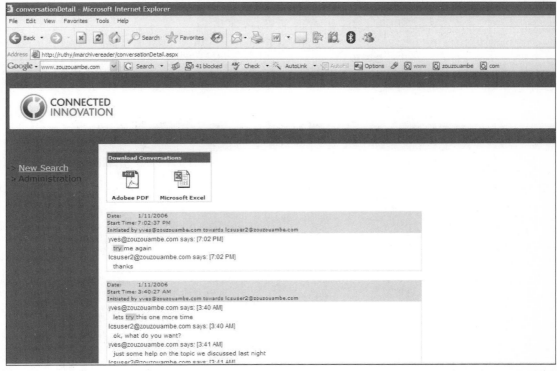

Figure 9-5

Live Communications Server 2005 Support Resources

The LCS 2005 SP1 Resource Kit can be downloaded from the Microsoft Office Live Communications Server website at microsoft.com/lcs.

Live Communications Server Resource Kit

The resource kit contains valuable tools for testing and verifying the validity of your LCS deployment within a lab, test, or production environment. The following utilities are a few of the many utilities available in the kit.

LCS Diagnostics Tool

The LCS Diagnostics tool (LCSDiag.exe) is probably the best utility in the resource kit. I use this tool on a regular basis for testing a configuration of an LCS infrastructure, as well as to simulate client connectivity tests before I add any users to the environment. This tool is also useful when debugging an LCS deployment for common occurrences such as users not being able to log in. Figure 9-6 shows the Live Communications Diagnostics Console.

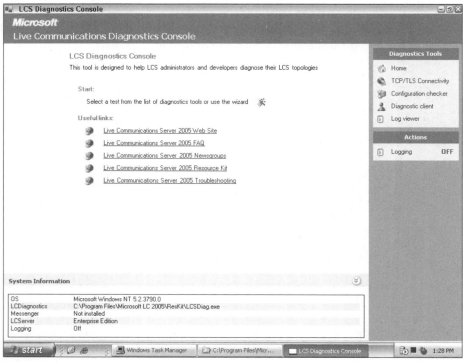

Figure 9-6

Certificate Request Tool

If you still do not understand how to request and configure certificates for LCS servers after reading this book, do not fear! The LCS Resource Kit includes a nifty utility called the Certificate Request tool. This utility eases the pain of requesting a certificate for an LCS server by naming the certificate correctly and embedding the required properties of the certificate for its use. Figure 9-7 shows a snapshot of the Certificate Request tool.

LCS Ping Utility

The LCS Ping utility is useful for checking the connectivity of an LCS server. With simple commands, you can confirm that the LCS server you have deployed can be accessed through the network.

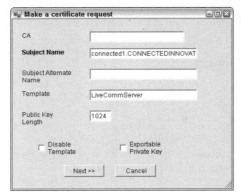

Figure 9-7

Flat File Logging Tool

The Flat File Logging utility is useful if you need more verbose logging details about each of your LCS servers. Server logs are extremely useful when debugging an LCS server. The log files show client connections from start to finish and include all of the SIP methods that are used during the session. The Flat File Log utility also enables you to customize the server log file to your liking by updating WMI (Windows Management Instrumentation) settings on an LCS server.

Resources

The purpose of this book was to provide a real-world guide based on our experience in the field deploying Live Communications Server and Communicator. Microsoft has provided a great deal of documentation for these products, which can be found via the resource links provided at the end of this section. Because of this available information, we did not want to duplicate installation documents or other existing guides available online. Covered in this book was information that we noticed was missing, or additional material that presented itself based on installations that we have worked on in the field.

A consultant is only as successful as the tool belt he or she carries. While this book covers many facets of LCS based on the experience of field consultants, many available resources can provide additional details. The following is a list of websites and blogs that provide a great source of information covering LCS and RTC material:

❑ **Microsoft Live Communications Server web site:** `microsoft.com/livecomm`

❑ **Microsoft Real Time Collaboration TechNet Events web site:** `microsoft.com/events/ series/rtccollaboration.mspx`

❑ **Microsoft Real Time Collaboration TechNet web site:** `microsoft.com/technet/community/ en-us/livecomm/`

❑ **Microsoft Live Communications Server TechNet discussion groups** — `microsoft.com/ communities/newsgroups/en-us/default.aspx?dg=microsoft.public.livecomm .general`

❑ **My personal blog site:** `http://jschurman.mvps.org`

Summary

This chapter addressed some of the common issues that require troubleshooting a Live Communications Server and Communicator deployment. It is important that you fully test your LCS environment before adding users, as debugging a live environment can be costly and embarrassing to your clients. Using some of the methods described in this chapter will help you configure your environment properly and guide you to locations where additional help can be found.

Thank you for investing your time and money in this book. It is our hope that we have covered material that could not be found online or in existing documentation related to Live Communications Server 2005 SP1 or Communicator 2005. Please continue to work with these products and join upcoming beta programs available this year for the next version of LCS and Communicator to see what is new and exciting with Microsoft unified communications. As you have seen, Microsoft has invested a great deal in these products as true, unified communications in the enterprise are coming into fruition. Catch you on IM!

Live Communications Server 2005 Test Plan

The purpose of the Live Communications Server Test Plan is to provide a template test plan for testing an LCS deployment. In my experience, deployment documentation is as important as the deployment itself. My goal was to reduce the amount of duplicated documentation by creating design guides and a test plan to be re-used for each implementation, appropriately editing for the specific customer or engagement I was working on. Please use this test plan as a guide for your deployment. A digital copy of the test plan is provided on the CD included with this book.

Test Objectives

This test plan specifies detailed testing scenarios to ensure a properly configured Live Communications Server 2005 environment.

The testing objectives are as follows:

- ❑ Verify that the Live Communications Server infrastructure has been configured to specification.
- ❑ Ensure that the Microsoft Office Communicator client can connect to the Live Communications Server service.
- ❑ Verify that the proper security measures have been implemented to protect Instant Messaging communications.
- ❑ Verify that the infrastructure supporting the Live Communications Server environment is functioning and is configured properly.
- ❑ Test the performance and load of the Live Communications Server environment.
- ❑ Verify that the enabled features of the Microsoft Office Communicator client function as expected.

Test Strategy

The overall approach to the Company Name LCS environment testing is to carry out the tests described here.

Testing will be performed with the following completed tasks:

- ❑ Verify that the Live Communications Server environment has been configured to specification.
- ❑ Assign a specified number of Company Name users to the Live Communications Server environment.
- ❑ Enable the created user accounts for Live Communications Server service.
- ❑ Assign each user to the available Live Communications Server pool.
- ❑ Set up and configure each user for Microsoft Office Communicator, including automatic configuration into the LCS environment.
- ❑ Add a contact to the Office Communicator contact list.
- ❑ Verify that the enabled features of Office Communicator perform as expected.

Responsibilities

Participants in the test program have the following responsibilities:

Person/Group	Responsibility
Vendor Name	Administer and document each testing procedure meeting the objectives stated in this document.
	Provide completed testing documentation results to Company Name project management teams.
	Immediately notify team members of any issues concerning performance, or objectives falling short of expectations, and address or assign a team to remedy the issue within a 24-hour turnaround period.
Company Name	Participate as test users of the environment, following the test plan identified within this document, and meeting objectives stated in this document.
	Immediately inform the testing team about any requested changes or modifications that need to be made to the environment.
Testing participants from outside the development group	Participate in testing and provide timely feedback.

Test Environment

The required hardware has already been implemented within the Company Name respective environments (test, pre-production, and production). Client test machines will be provided if remote access/VPN is not provided.

The following sections include system architecture diagrams and locations for each testing environment.

LCS Architecture: Production Environment

The production implementation for Live Communications Server will involve the following components, with all equipment located in [enter physical location].

LCS Required Servers

The following servers will be utilized for this implementation:

- LCS Enterprise Edition pool servers — 7 (6 active, 1 passive)
- LCS Back-End Database servers — 2 (utilizing log shipping)
- LCS load balancer — 1 (F5/BIG-IP)
- LCS Admin server — 1
- Microsoft Operations Manager server — 1

LCS Required Hardware and Software Configurations

Following are the LCS Enterprise Edition pool server requirements:

- Quad Intel Xeon 3.06 GHz, 1MB cache, 533 MHz FSB
- 4GB DDR, 266 MHz RAM
- 2 × 18GB hard disks
- 1GB network adapter
- Windows Server 2003 Standard Edition

Following are the Live Communications Server 2005 back-end database requirements:

- Quad Intel Xeon 2.8 GHz, 2MB cache
- 8GB DDR RAM
- 1-gigabit network adapter
- Windows Server 2003 Enterprise Edition
- SQL Server 2000 SP3a Enterprise Edition

Figure A-1 shows an architecture diagram that depicts the technical architecture for production.

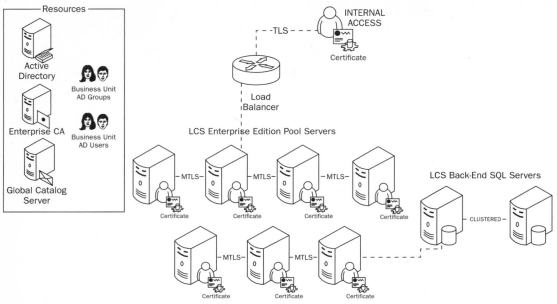

Figure A-1

LCS Architecture: Pre-Production Environment

The pre-production implementation for Live Communications Server involves the following components, with all equipment located in [enter physical location].

LCS Required Servers

The following servers will be utilized for this implementation:

- ❑ LCS Enterprise Edition pool servers — 3
- ❑ LCS Back-End Database servers — 2 (utilizing log shipping)
- ❑ LCS load balancer — 1 (F5/BIG-IP)
- ❑ Microsoft Operations Manager server — 1

LCS Required Hardware and Software Configurations

Following are the LCS Enterprise Edition pool server requirements:

- ❑ Quad Intel Xeon 3.06 GHz, 1MB cache, 533 MHz FSB
- ❑ 4GB DDR, 266 MHz RAM
- ❑ 2 × 18GB hard disks
- ❑ 1-gigabit network adapter
- ❑ Windows Server 2003 Standard Edition

The Live Communications Server 2005 Back-End Database requirements are as follows:

- ❏ Quad Intel Xeon 2.8 GHz, 2MB cache
- ❏ 8GB DDR RAM
- ❏ 1-gigabit network adapter
- ❏ Windows Server 2003 Enterprise Edition
- ❏ SQL Server 2000 SP3a Enterprise Edition

Figure A-2 shows an architecture diagram depicting the technical architecture for pre-production.

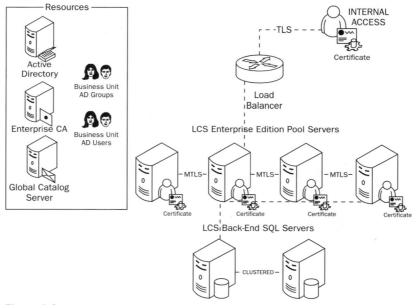

Figure A-2

LCS Architecture: Test Environment

The test implementation for Live Communications Server will involve the following components, with all equipment located in [enter physical location].

LCS Required Servers

The following servers will be utilized for this implementation:

- ❏ LCS Enterprise Edition pool servers — 2
- ❏ LCS Back-End Database servers — 1
- ❏ Microsoft Operations Manager server — 1

LCS Required Hardware and Software Configurations

Following are the LCS Enterprise Edition pool server requirements:

- ❑ Quad Intel Xeon 3.06 GHz, 1MB cache, 533 MHz FSB
- ❑ 4GB DDR, 266 MHz RAM
- ❑ 2 × 18GB hard disks
- ❑ 1-gigabit network adapter
- ❑ Windows Server 2003 Standard Edition

Following are the LCS 2005 Back-End database requirements:

- ❑ Quad Intel Xeon 2.8 GHz, 2MB cache
- ❑ 8GB DDR RAM
- ❑ 1-gigabit network adapter
- ❑ Windows Server 2003 Enterprise Edition
- ❑ SQL Server 2000 SP3a Enterprise Edition

Figure A-3 depicts the technical architecture for testing.

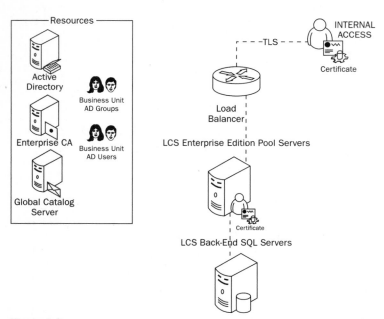

Figure A-3

Test Procedures

The following testing procedures describe the objectives stated in this document in greater detail, including results, and how to plan for alternative results.

Verifying Active Directory Configuration

The following test procedures will verify the configuration of Active Directory to ensure proper configuration to host the Live Communications Server service. These testing procedures include the following components:

- ❑ Validate Active Directory schema changes
- ❑ Verify that Active Directory User objects contain the Live Communications Server tab
- ❑ Validate DNS configuration (automatic configuration)
  - ❑ LCS pool host record
  - ❑ SIP Service records (TCP, TLS)
- ❑ Validate GPO (Group Policy object) configuration
  - ❑ LCS Server policies
  - ❑ Office Communicator client policies

Validating Active Directory Changes

The following operations will be validated during this testing procedure.

Dependencies:

- ❑ LCS Prep Schema command has been executed
- ❑ LCS Prep Forest command has been executed
- ❑ LCS Prep Domain command has been executed
- ❑ LCS CreateLCSOUPermissions has been executed
- ❑ Active Directory team is engaged

Perform the following tasks:

1. Using the command-line operators, open the LCSCmd.exe file from DOS by clicking Start⇨Run, type **cmd,** and then press Enter.

2. Change the current location to the location where the LCSCmd.exe file is stored using the DOS CD switch.

3. Verify that Prep Schema has been successfully executed by typing the command, the path of your file, followed by **\Setup\I386\LCSCmd.exe /forest /action:CheckSchemaPrepState** (see Figure A-4).

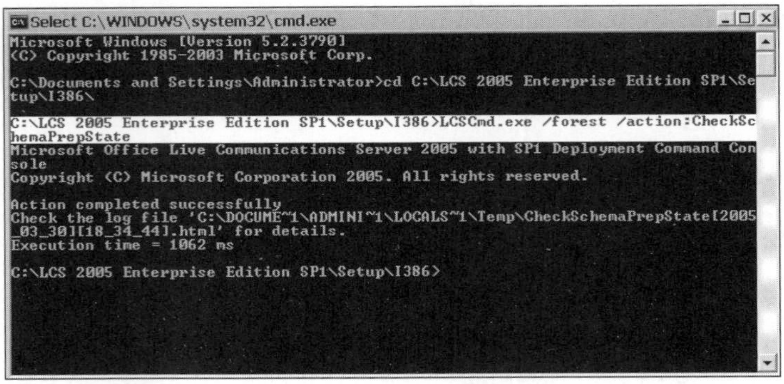

Figure A-4

4. Verify that Prep Forest has been successfully executed by typing the path of your file, followed by **I386\LCSCmd.exe /forest /action:CheckForestPrepState,** as shown in Figure A-5.

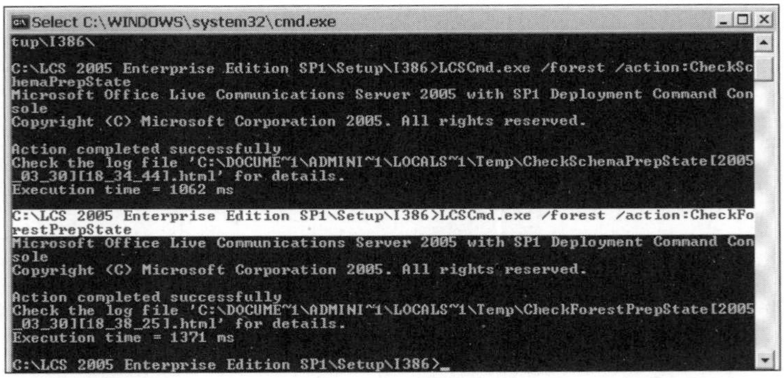

Figure A-5

5. Verify that Prep Domain has been successfully executed by typing the path of your file, followed by **\LCSCmd.exe /domain:corp.company.com /action: CheckDomainPrepState**.

6. Verify that Domain Add has been successfully executed by typing the path of your file, followed by **\LCSCmd.exe /domain:company.com /action:CheckDomainAddState /refdomain:corp.company.com**.

7. Verify that CreateLCSOUPermissions has been successfully executed by typing the path of your file, followed by **\LCSCmd.exe /domain:corp.company.com /action:CheckLCSOUPermissions /ou:"OU=AccountsOU" /objectType:computer**.

Insert the installation CD and after each Prep command has completed, view the log that is created after each sequential step when the installation wizard prompts you. Figure A-6 shows the checked tasks.

Results:

[Populate results.]

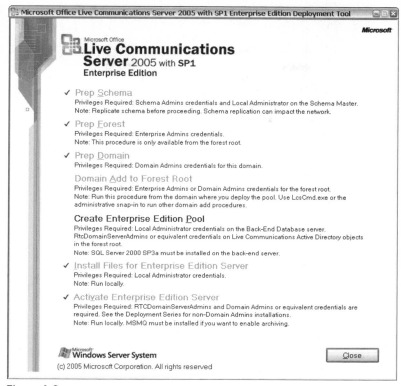

Figure A-6

Verifying That AD User Objects Contain the LCS Tab

The following operations will be performed during this testing procedure.

Dependencies:

❑   LCS 2005 Prep commands have been executed successfully.

❑   The Active Directory team is engaged.

Perform the following tasks:

1.   Log on to an Active Directory domain controller with Schema Admin permissions.

2.   Either open Active Directory Users and Computers by selecting Start⇨Programs⇨ Administrative Tools⇨Active Directory Users and Computers, or from the Start⇨Run command, type **dsa.msc** and press Enter.

3.   After the Active Directory Users and Computers console opens, open the Users folder, shown in Figure A-7.

4.   Open one of the user names/user objects.

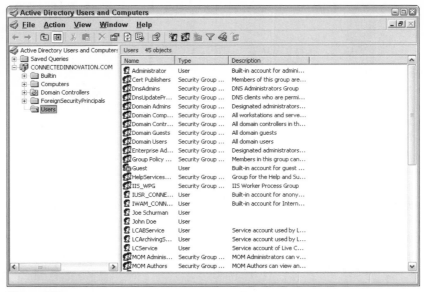

Figure A-7

5. Check whether there is a Live Communications tab within the User Object console, as shown in Figure A-8.

Figure A-8

6. Click the Live Communications tab to see whether the LCS properties are present, as shown in Figure A-9.

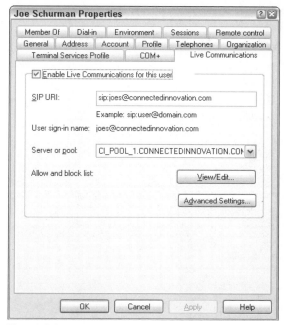

Figure A-9

Results:

[Populate results.]

Validating DNS Configuration (Automatic Configuration)

The following operations will be performed during this testing procedure.

Dependencies:

❑ Engage the appropriate administrator with DNS Admin permissions.

Perform the following tasks:

1. Access a workstation, server, or virtual image with DNS Admin rights.

2. Open the DNS management console by selecting Start⇨Programs⇨Administrative Tools⇨DNS.

3. In order for automatic configuration to work within LCS, the following DNS entries must exist:

   ❏ DNS host A record for the LCS pool

   ❏ DNS SRV records for both TLS and TCP for SIP

4. To determine whether the required DNS host A record exists for the LCS pool, open the DNS management console and expand the DNS Forward Lookup Zones folder, and then the folder for your domain (i.e., corp.company.com). Figure A-10 shows the `ConnectedInnovation.com` folder in the left pane.

5. In the right pane, verify that there is a DNS host A record entry for the LCS pool (i.e., pool_1). Figure A-10 shows CI_pool_1 in the right pane.

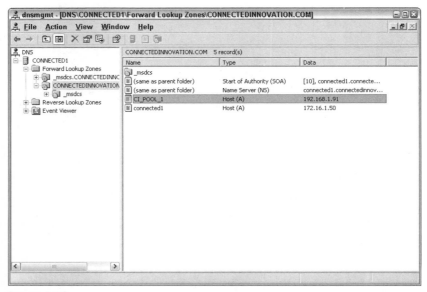

Figure A-10

6. Open the record to verify that the correct FQDN and IP address have been entered to point the record to, i.e., pool_1 maps to IP address 192.168.1.80 (see Figure A-11).

7. To verify that a SIP entry has been applied to each DNS SRV record, ensure that the TLS and TCP SRV record have been created as shown by expanding the domain node and then selecting the `_tcp` folder in the left pane, viewing the DNS SRV record _sipinternal in the right pane, as depicted in Figure A-12.

Figure A-11

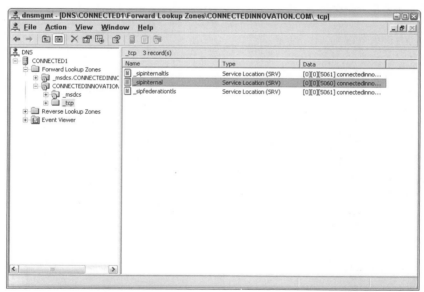

Figure A-12

8. To verify that a SIP entry has been applied to each DNS SRV record, ensure that the TLS SRV record has been created as shown by expanding the domain node and then selecting the `_tcp` folder in the left pane, viewing the DNS SRV record _sipinternaltls in the right pane. Figure A-13 shows the `_tcp` folder in the left pane.

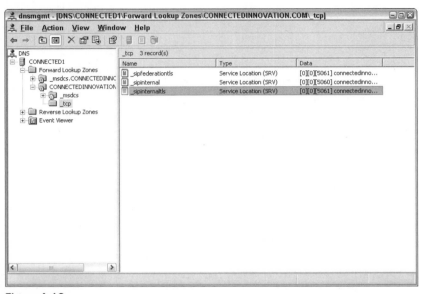

Figure A-13

9. Open the `_sip` record to ensure that the correct port has been configured. The default port in Live Communications Server for SIP running on TCP is port 5060. Also verify that the SIP record points to the FQDN of the domain hosting the LCS service, i.e., corp.domain.com (see Figure A-14).

10. Using the same procedure, open the `_sip` record under the TLS DNS SRV record to ensure that the correct port has been configured. The default port in Live Communications Server for SIP running on TLS is port 5061. Also verify that the SIP record points to the FQDN of the domain hosting the LCS service, i.e., corp.domain.com (see Figure A-15).

Results:

[Populate results.]

_sip Properties
Service Location (SRV)
Security
Domain:
CONNECTEDINNOVATION.COM
Service:
_sip
Protocol:
_tcp
Priority:
0
Weight:
0
Port number:
5060
Host offering this service:
connected1.connectedinnovation.com.
OK
Cancel
Apply

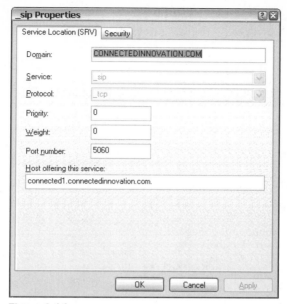

Figure A-14

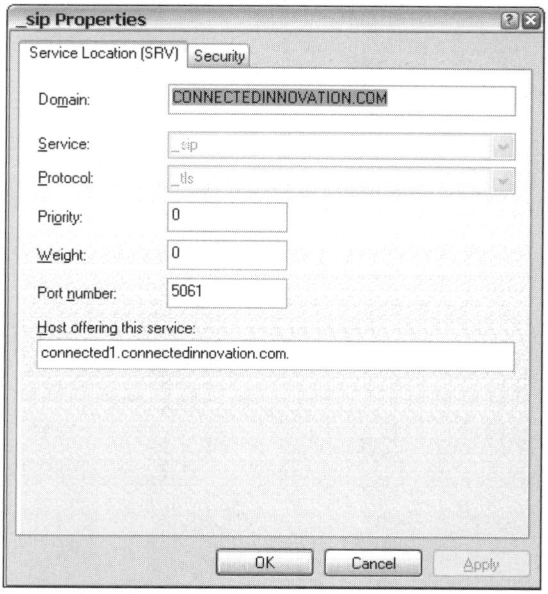
_sip Properties
Service Location (SRV)
Security
Domain:
CONNECTEDINNOVATION.COM
Service:
_sip
Protocol:
_tls
Priority:
0
Weight:
0
Port number:
5061
Host offering this service:
connected1.connectedinnovation.com.
OK
Cancel
Apply

Figure A-15

Appendix A

Validating Group Policy Object Configuration

The following operations will be performed during this testing procedure.

Dependencies:

❏ The Live Communications Server 2005 SP1 Administration template (`lcclient.inf`) has been applied to the Group Policy Editor.

❏ The appropriate resource with Domain Admin rights to the domain has been engaged.

Perform the following tasks:

1. Log on to an Active Directory domain controller with Domain Admin rights.

2. Open Active Directory Users and Computers either by selecting Start➪Programs➪ Administrative Tools➪Active Directory Users and Computers or by selecting Start➪ Run, typing **dsa.msc,** and pressing Enter.

3. After the Active Directory Users and Computers console opens, right-click on the domain (i.e., corp.company.com), and then choose Properties.

4. In the Domain Properties menu, choose the Group Policy tab, shown in Figure A-16.

Figure A-16

5. Click the Edit button to edit the default domain policy.

6. Once in the Group Policy Editor console, drill down through the console tree under both Computer and User Configuration and open the Administrative Templates folder.

7. Under Administrative Templates, choose the Microsoft Office Communicator Policy Settings folder to expose the Microsoft Office Communicator Feature Policies and the SIP Microsoft Office Communicator Service Policies folders, as shown in Figure A-17.

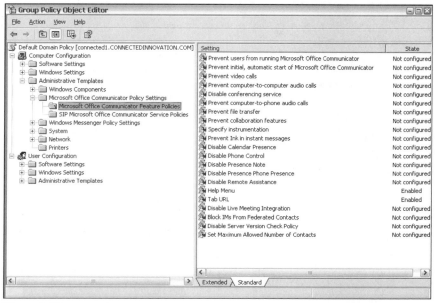

Figure A-17

8. Verify that each policy is set to the requirements identified in the Live Communications Server Architecture Guide and Live Communications Server Clients Feature Guide.

Results:

[Populate results.]

Verifying Configuration of Live Communications Server Environment

The following test procedures will verify the configuration of the Live Communications Server environment. These testing procedures include all of the following components:

- ❏ Validate LCS forest configuration
    - ❏ Supported LCS domains
- ❏ Validate LCS pool configuration
    - ❏ Authentication (NTLM, Kerberos, or both)
    - ❏ Enable users
- ❏ Validate LCS pool server configuration
    - ❏ Connection entries (TCP, TLS)
    - ❏ Certificate configuration

Appendix A

Validating LCS Forest Configuration

The following operations will be performed during this testing procedure.

Dependencies:

❑ Live Communications Server Active Directory preparations must have been executed successfully.

❑ Live Communications Server 2005 SP1 must be installed.

❑ Live Communications Server 2005 administration tools must be installed.

Perform the following tasks:

1. To validate the LCS forest configuration, access a workstation, server, or virtual PC that has access to run the Live Communications Server MMC management console with RTCDomainServerAdmins or RTCDomainUserAdmins permissions.

2. When the active LCS forest is selected, the summarized status of the LCS forest is displayed in the right pane of the management console, as shown in Figure A-18.

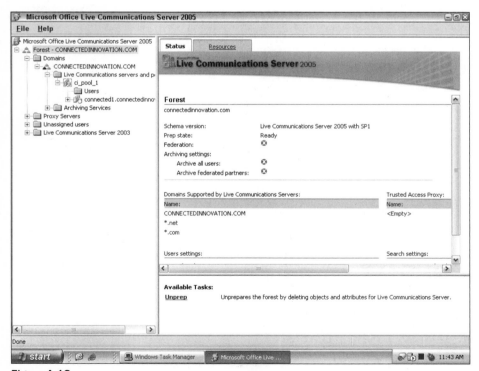

Figure A-18

3.   To view additional properties and to edit the LCS forest properties, right-click on the Forest icon within the topology pane and choose Properties. The Global Properties dialog box for the LCS forest will appear (see Figure A-19).

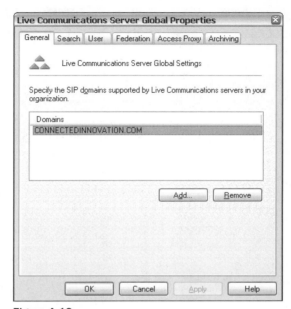

Figure A-19

4.   Within the Live Communications Server Global Properties menu, verify that the settings are configured correctly. In the General tab, ensure that the correct domains are entered for supporting LCS users.

Results:

[Populate results.]

Validating LCS Pool Configuration

The following operations will be performed during this testing procedure.

Dependencies:

❑   Live Communications Server Active Directory preparations must have been executed successfully.

❑   Live Communications Server 2005 SP1 must be installed.

❑   Live Communications Server 2005 administration tools have been installed.

Perform the following tasks:

1. To validate the LCS pool configuration, access a workstation, server, or virtual PC that has access to run the Live Communications Server MMC management console with RTCDomainServerAdmins or RTCDomainUserAdmins permissions.

2. When the active LCS pool is selected, its summarized status is displayed in the right pane of the management console (see Figure A-20).

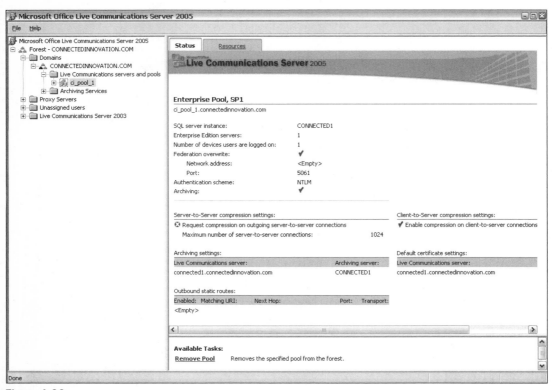

Figure A-20

3. To view additional properties and to edit the LCS pool properties, right-click on the Pool icon within the topology pane and choose Properties. The Properties window will appear, as shown in Figure A-21

4. Verify that the settings configured within the pool Properties menu are configured correctly.

5. Verify that the appropriate authentication scheme has been selected based on your network requirements (NTLM, Kerberos, or both) by choosing the Authentication tab (see Figure A-22).

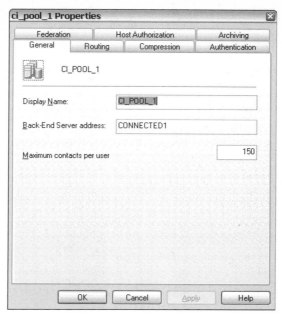

Figure A-21

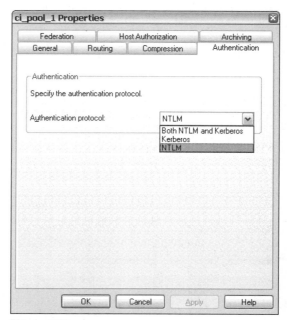

Figure A-22

6. To view users that have been enabled within a specific LCS pool, click the Cancel button in the Properties menu and expand the LCS Pool icon to expose the Users folder in the topology pane on the left (see Figure A-23).

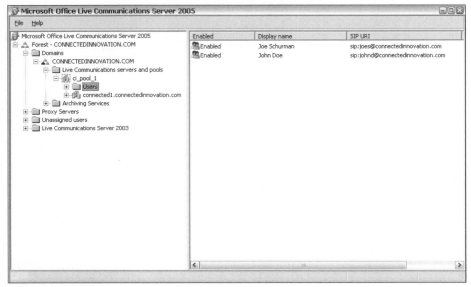

Figure A-23

7. Verify that the correct users are located within each LCS pool.

Results:

[Populate results.]

Validating LCS Pool Server Configuration

The following operations will be performed during this testing procedure.

Dependencies:

❑ Live Communications Server Active Directory preparations must have been executed successfully.

❑ Live Communications Server 2005 SP1 must be installed.

❑ The Live Communication Server pool server(s) must be activated.

❑ Live Communications Server 2005 administration tools have been installed.

Perform the following tasks:

1. To validate the LCS pool server configuration, access a workstation, server, or virtual PC that has access to run the Live Communications Server MMC management console with RTCDomainServerAdmins or RTCDomainUserAdmins permissions.

2. When the active LCS pool server is selected, its summarized status is displayed in the data pane on the right of the management console (see Figure A-24).

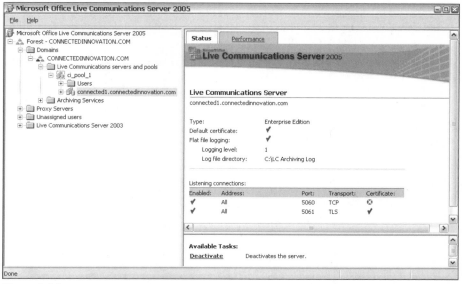

Figure A-24

3. To view additional properties and to edit the LCS pool server properties, right-click on the Pool Server icon(s) within the topology pane on the left and choose Properties. The Properties dialog will appear (see Figure A-25).

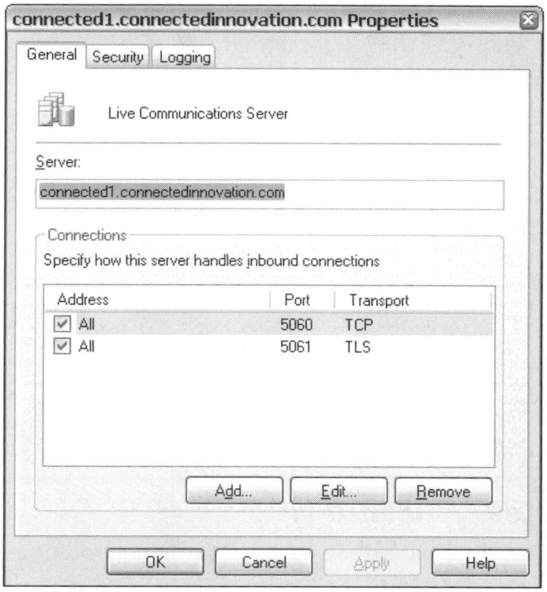

Figure A-25

4. Within the pool server Properties menu, ensure that the correct connections entries have been added, and validate that these settings match the settings identified in the Live Communications Server Architecture Guide.

5. If a TLS entry has been entered, verify that the correct certificate has been applied to the connection entry. To verify that, highlight the TLS connection and then click the Edit button.

6. Within the Edit Connection dialog box, verify that the correct settings are configured and that the correct certificate has been applied. For TLS connectivity, ensure that the certificate contains a certificate EKU of Server and Client Authentication. For an MTLS connection, ensure that the certificate contains a certificate EKU of either a Server and Client Authentication or Server Authentication (see Figure A-26).

Figure A-26

Results:

[Populate results.]

Verifying Live Communications Server Security

The following test procedures will verify the configuration of the Live Communications Server security configuration. These testing procedures include all of the following components:

❑ Validate certificate configuration

    ❑ Verify certificate chain (client and server certificate trust)

    ❑ Verify appropriate certificates have been applied (LCS server and client)

Validating Certificate Configuration

The following operations will be performed during this testing procedure.

Dependencies:

- ❑ Live Communications Server SP1 has been installed, configured, and activated.
- ❑ Live Communications Server 2005 administration tools have been installed.
- ❑ Certificate or PKI resource has been engaged.

Live Communications Server uses certificates to enable TLS (Transport Layer Security). When configured, TLS carries LCS SIP (Session Initiation Protocol) messages between contacts within the LCS messaging environment.

To understand how certificates work within Live Communications Server, you must understand the different certificate types. Certificates work by authenticating against a valid chain of security. Most organizations will deploy an internal enterprise certificate authority (CA). This enterprise CA establishes a trusted root. Using this trusted root CA, the CA can create client and server certificates that enable a trust throughout the environment in which the CA is applied. Each user requires a client certificate to validate that the user has the appropriate access to the LCS system. This client certificate is validated against a certificate that resides on the LCS pool server, a certificate that is enabled with client and server authentication. The LCS pool server also communicates with other LCS pool servers using MTLS (Mutual TLS). This communication, or connection, requires either a Server Authentication certificate or a Server and Client Authentication certificate.

Perform the following tasks:

1. To verify that the correct certificates have been applied within the Live Communications Server environment, you must access the Live Communications Server management console.

2. With the LCS management console open, expand the left-hand topology pane to expose the LCS pool server(s). (Refer to Figure A-24.)

3. Right-click on a given LCS pool server and choose Properties.

4. Within the pool server Properties menu, highlight the TLS connection entry and click the Edit button (refer to Figure A-25).

5. With the Edit Connection window open, click the Select Certificate button (refer to Figure A-26).

6. Select the certificate that has the Server Authentication EKU for a TLS Connection. For an MTLS connection, you can use the same certificate or a certificate with a Server Authentication EKU (see Figure A-27).

Figure A-27

Results:

[Populate results.]

Assessing the Live Communications Server Management Environment

The following test procedures will verify the configuration of the Live Communications Server management and operations configuration. These testing procedures include all of the following components:

❏ Verify that LCS management console (MMC console) features perform as expected.

❏ Verify that forest, pool, pool server(s), and user(s) settings can be modified.

❏ Microsoft Operations Management (LCS 2005 package)

❏ Verify that MOM functionality performs as expected.

Verifying the LCS Management Console Features Perform as Expected

The following operations will be performed during this testing procedure.

Dependencies:

❏ Live Communications Server 2005 SP1 has been installed, configured, and activated.

❏ Live Communications Server 2005 administration tools have been installed.

Perform the following tasks:

1. Access a workstation, server, or virtual PC that has access to run the Live Communications Server management console with RTCDomainServerAdmins or RTCDomainUserAdmins permissions.

2. With the LCS management console open, verify that the following steps can be completed,

3. Verify that the topology pane on the left can be fully expanded.

4. Verify that an admin can view and edit the properties of an LCS forest by right-clicking on the LCS Forest icon in the topology Pane and choosing Properties (refer to Figure A-18).

5. Verify that an admin can view and edit the properties of an LCS pool by right-clicking on the LCS Pool icon in the topology pane and choosing Properties (refer to Figure A-20).

6. Verify that an admin can view and edit the properties of an LCS pool server by right-clicking on the LCS Pool Server icon in the topology pane and choosing Properties (refer to Figure A-24).

7. Verify that an admin can view properties, move users, configure users, and delete user options within a pool (see Figure A-28).

Results:

[Populate results.]

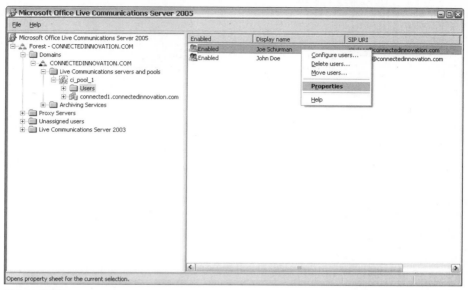

Figure A-28

Validating Microsoft Operations Management (LCS 2005 Package) Configuration

The following operations will be performed during this testing procedure.

Dependencies:

❑ Microsoft Operations Manager 2005 with the Live Communications Server 2005 Management Pack must be installed and configured.

❑ A Live Communications Server 2005 pool and pool server must exist.

Perform the following tasks:

1. Open Microsoft Operations Manager 2005 (MOM) by selecting Start⇨Programs⇨Microsoft Operations Manager, and choose the Administrator Console.

2. Within the MOM topology pane, expand the Management Packs node to expose the Live Communications Server folders.

3. Expand the Microsoft Office Live Communications Server 2005 Enterprise Edition folder to expose all of the MOM management tasks (see Figure A-29).

4. Verify that each component under the Microsoft Office Live Communications Server 2005 Enterprise Edition node is operational.

Results:

[Populate results.]

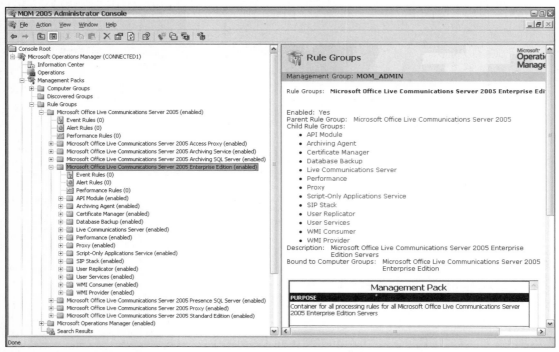

Figure A-29

Microsoft Office Communicator 2005 Client Testing

The following test procedures will verify the configuration and features of the Microsoft Office Communicator 2005 client. These testing procedures include all of the following components:

❑ Connectivity

    ❑ Verify that clients can connect to the LCS service using TCP.

❑ Verify that DOMAIN 1, DOMAIN 2, and DOMAIN 3 clients can connect to the LCS service using TLS.

❑ Verify that clients residing in subdomains can connect to the LCS service.

    ❑ Verify that clients using alternate SIP URIs can connect to the LCS service.

    ❑ Verify that clients with specially configured user objects can connect to the LCS service.

    ❑ Verify that clients can connect to the LCS service using automatic configuration.

    ❑ Verify that GPO (Group Policy Object) settings are enforced upon the client when connected to the LCS service.

❑ Features and functionality

    ❑ Verify the ability to search for a contact.

    ❑ Verify the ability to add a contact.

    ❑ Verify the ability to block contacts.

- ❑ Verify the ability to remove contacts.
- ❑ Verify the ability to create groups.
- ❑ Verify that IM (Instant Messaging) between contacts is operational.
- ❑ Verify that multi-party or n-way IM is operational.
- ❑ Verify the ability to tag a contact.
- ❑ Verify that presence is operational (online and other status settings).
- ❑ Verify that the DND (do not disturb) feature is operational.
- ❑ Verify that the Set Note feature is operational.

Testing Connectivity

Verify that clients can connect to the LCS service using TCP.

The following operations will be performed during this testing procedure.

Dependencies:

- ❑ Live Communications Server 2005 SP1 must be installed, configured, and activated.
- ❑ Microsoft Office Communicator 2005 must be installed and configured with connectivity to the LCS environment using TCP.

Perform the following tasks:

1. Open Microsoft Office Communicator (MOC) 2005 by selecting Start⇨Programs⇨Microsoft Office Communicator 2005.

2. With the MOC client open, click on the Actions menu, and then choose Options (see Figure A-30).

Figure A-30

3. In the Options dialog box, click on the Accounts tab, and then click the Advanced button (see Figure A-31).

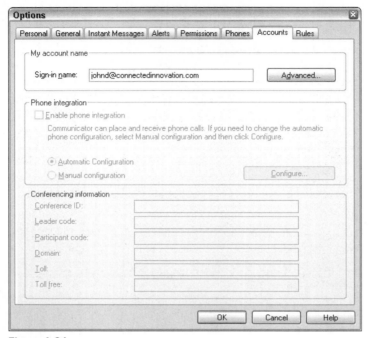

Figure A-31

4. Within the Advanced Connection Settings window, shown in Figure A-32, choose the Configure Settings option and enter the following information:

❑ Enter the correct server name or IP address of the server or pool hosting the Live Communications Server service.

❑ Choose the TCP option under the Connect Using section.

❑ Click the OK button.

5. Click OK in the Options dialog box.

6. From the main MOC screen, click the sign-in link, shown in Figure A-33.

Figure A-32

Figure A-33

7. If the client successfully signs into the service, you will see a screen like the one shown in Figure A-34 and the test is complete.

Figure A-34

Results:

[Populate results.]

Verifying That Clients Can Connect to the LCS Service Using TLS

The following operations will be performed during this testing procedure.

Dependencies:

❑ Live Communications Server 2005 SP1 must be installed, configured, and activated.

❑ Microsoft Office Communicator 2005 must be installed and configured with connectivity to the LCS environment using TLS.

Perform the following tasks:

1. Open Microsoft Office Communicator (MOC) 2005 by selecting Start⇨Programs⇨Microsoft Office Communicator 2005.

2. With the MOC client open, click on the Actions menu and choose Options (refer to Figure A-30).

3. In the Options window, click on the Accounts tab and then click the Advanced button (refer to Figure A-31).

4. Within the Advanced Connection Settings window, choose the Configure Settings option and enter the following information:

❑ Enter the correct server name of the server or pool hosting the Live Communications Server service. The server name in this entry must match the name of the Pool Server certificate the user/client signs into.

❑ Choose the TLS option under the Connect Using section.

❑ Click the OK button (refer to Figure A-32).

5. Click OK on the Options menu.

6. From the main MOC screen, click the sign-in link (refer to Figure A-33). If the client successfully signs into the service, the test is complete.

Results:

[Populate results.]

Verifying That Clients Residing in Subdomains Can Connect to the LCS Service

While verifying DOMAIN 1, the following operations will be performed during this testing procedure.

Dependencies:

❑ Live Communications Server 2005 SP1 must be installed, configured, and activated.

❑ Microsoft Office Communicator 2005 must be installed and configured with connectivity to the LCS environment.

❑ User must be a user of the DOMAIN 1 domain.

Perform the following tasks:

1. Open Microsoft Office Communicator (MOC) 2005 by selecting Start⇨Programs⇨Microsoft Office Communicator 2005.

2. From the main MOC screen, sign in (refer to Figure A-33).

3. If the client successfully signs into the service, the test is complete (refer to Figure A-34).

Results:

[Populate results.]

While testing DOMAIN 2, the following operations will be performed.

Dependencies:

❑ Live Communications Server 2005 SP1 must be installed, configured, and activated.

❑ Microsoft Office Communicator 2005 must be installed and configured with connectivity to the LCS environment.

❑ User must be a user of the DOMAIN 2 domain.

Perform the following tasks:

1. Open Microsoft Office Communicator (MOC) 2005 by selecting Start⇨Programs⇨Microsoft Office Communicator 2005.

2. From the main MOC screen, sign in (refer to Figure A-33).

3. If the client successfully signs into the service, the test is complete (refer to Figure A-34).

Results:

[Populate results.]

Verifying That Clients Using Alternate SIP URIs Can Connect to the LCS Service

The following operations will be performed during this testing procedure.

Dependencies:

❑ Live Communications Server 2005 SP1 must be installed, configured, and activated.

❑ Microsoft Office Communicator 2005 must be installed and configured with connectivity to the LCS environment.

❑ The alternate SIP domain has been entered in the LCS forest properties within the LCS management console (see Figure A-35).

Figure A-35

Perform the following tasks:

1. Open Microsoft Office Communicator (MOC) 2005 by selecting Start⇨Programs⇨Microsoft Office Communicator 2005.

2. From the main MOC screen, sign in (refer to Figure A-33).

3. If the client successfully signs into the service, the test is complete (refer to Figure A-34).

Results:

[Populate results.]

Verifying That Clients with Specially Configured User Objects Can Connect to the LCS Service

The following operations will be performed during this testing procedure.

Dependencies:

❑ Live Communications Server 2005 SP1 must be installed, configured, and activated.

❑ Microsoft Office Communicator 2005 must be installed and configured with connectivity to the LCS environment.

❑ The user within the alternate forest must have a user object within the forest and domain hosting the LCS service. If the user has only a contact object representation, then the user must have a contact object with the correct SID mapping enabled within the forest and domain hosting the LCS Service. If the user is connecting to LCS within a resource forest, the user must have a disabled user object within the resource forest hosting the LCS Service.

❑ User must be a user of the alternate forest.

Perform the following tasks:

1. Open Microsoft Office Communicator (MOC) 2005 by selecting Start⇨Programs⇨Microsoft Office Communicator 2005.

2. From the main MOC screen, sign in (refer to Figure A-33).

3. If the client successfully signs into the service, the test is complete (refer to Figure A-34).

Results:

[Populate results.]

Verifying That Clients Can Connect to the LCS Service Using Automatic Configuration

The following operations will be performed during this testing procedure.

Dependencies:

❑ Live Communications Server 2005 SP1 must be installed, configured, and activated.

❑ Microsoft Office Communicator 2005 must be installed and configured with connectivity to the LCS environment.

❑ The correct DNS entries must be configured for LCS automatic configuration to work. These entries include the following:

❑ A DNS host A record for the LCS pool or LCS pool server

❑ A DNS SRV record for SIP communications using TCP or TLS

Refer to Figure A-10 to view the DNS host A record and SRV record created in DNS.

Perform the following tasks:

1. Open Microsoft Office Communicator (MOC) 2005 by selecting Start⇨Program⇨Microsoft Office Communicator 2005.

2. With the MOC client open, click on the Actions menu and then choose Options (refer to Figure A-30).

3. In the Options dialog box, click on the Accounts tab, and then click the Advanced button (refer to Figure A-31).

4. Within the Advanced Connection Settings dialog box, choose the Automatic Configuration option (see Figure A-36).

Figure A-36

5. Click the OK button.

6. Click OK on the Options menu.

7. From the main MOC screen, sign in (refer to Figure A-33).

8. If the client successfully connects, this procedure is complete (refer to Figure A-34).

Results:

[Populate results.]

Verifying That Group Policy Object Settings Are Enforced

The following operations will be performed during this testing procedure.

Dependencies:

❏ Live Communications Server 2005 SP1 is installed, configured, and activated.

❏ Microsoft Office Communicator 2005 is installed, configured, and is being utilized within a domain issuing Group Policy.

❏ The Microsoft Office Communicator Administrative template (lcclient.inf) has been added and configured to the domain Group Policy with applied settings that match the requirements outlined in the LCS Architecture Guide and LCS Client Feature Guide.

❏ A network resource with DNS Admin permissions must be engaged.

Perform the following tasks:

1. Log on to an Active Directory domain controller with Domain Admin rights.

2. Open Active Directory Users and Computers by selecting Start⇨Programs⇨Administrative Tools⇨Active Directory Users and Computers, or select Start⇨Run, type **dsa.msc,** and press Enter.

3. After the Active Directory Users and Computers console opens, right-click on the domain (i.e., corp.company.com) and choose Properties.

4. In the domain Properties menu, choose the Group Policy tab.

5. Click the Edit button to edit the Default Domain Policy (refer to Figure A-16).

6. From the Group Policy Object Editor console, drill down through the console tree under both Computer and User Configuration and the Administrative Templates folders (refer to Figure A-17).

7. Under Administrative Templates, choose the Microsoft Office Communicator Policy Settings folder to expose the Microsoft Office Communicator Feature Policies and the SIP Microsoft Office Communicator Service Policies folders.

8. Choose the Microsoft Office Communicator Feature Policies folder (refer to Figure A-17).

9. Double-click on the Help Menu setting to edit its properties.

10. In the Settings tab, configure the following:

❑ Select the Enabled option.

❑ Enter the Help Menu Text information (e.g., CI LCS Help)

❑ Enter a URL associated with the Help Menu text (e.g., `www.microsoft.com/technet/community/en-us/livecomm/default.mspx`), as shown in Figure A-37.

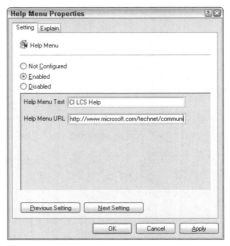

Figure A-37

11. Click the OK button.

12. Exit out of the GPO Editor and the Active Directory Users and Computers console.

13. Open Microsoft Office Communicator (MOC) 2005 by selecting Start⇨Programs⇨Microsoft Office Communicator 2005.

14. From the main MOC screen, sign in (refer to Figure A-33).

15. Once signed in, click on the Help menu, as shown in Figure A-38.

16. If the Help menu text that was entered in Step 10 is displayed, the GPO Policies for your domain and within the LCS service are enforced, successfully completing this test procedure.

17. Test to confirm whether Help menu text, when selected, sends the user to the URL that was specified in Step 10 (see Figure A-39).

Results:

[Populate results.]

Figure A-38

Figure A-39

Testing Features and Functionality

In the section, you verify the capability to search for a contact. The following operations will be performed during this testing procedure.

Dependencies:

- ❑ Live Communications Server 2005 SP1 has been installed, configured, and activated.
- ❑ Microsoft Office Communicator 2005 has been installed and configured.

Perform the following tasks:

1. Open Microsoft Office Communicator (MOC) 2005 by selecting Start⇨Programs⇨Microsoft Office Communicator 2005.

2. From the main MOC screen, sign in (refer to Figure A-33).

3. Once signed into MOC, in the Find field, enter text to search for a contact, as shown in Figure A-40.

Figure A-40

4. If the Search service is working, then a list of matches to the entered text will appear, along with the contact's current presence.

Results:

[Populate results.]

Verifying the Capability to Add a Contact

The following operations will be performed during this testing procedure.

Dependencies:

❑   Live Communications Server 2005 SP1 has been installed, configured, and activated.

❑   Microsoft Office Communicator 2005 has been installed and configured.

Perform the following tasks:

1.   Open Microsoft Office Communicator (MOC) 2005 by selecting Start⇨Programs⇨Microsoft Office Communicator 2005.

2.   From the main MOC screen, sign in (refer to Figure A-33).

3.   Once signed into MOC, select Contacts⇨Add a Contact, as shown in Figure A-41.

Figure A-41

4. In the Add a Contact dialog box, shown in Figure A-42, either option will work. For this test, use the e-mail address option.

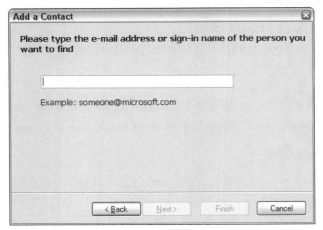

Figure A-42

This option requires the user to know the contact's e-mail address or SIP URI address. Enter the address of the contact that is to be added, and then click the Next button.

If the contact is found, the next screen will display a success message, as shown in Figure A-43.

Figure A-43

5. Click the Finish button to close the Add a Contact dialog box. The added contact should appear in the main MOC screen (refer to Figure A-34). If the contact has been successfully added, this test procedure is complete.

Results:

[Populate results.]

Verifying the Capability to Block Contacts

The following operations will be performed during this testing procedure.

Dependencies:

❑ Live Communications Server 2005 SP1 has been installed, configured, and activated.

❑ Microsoft Office Communicator 2005 has been installed and configured.

Perform the following tasks:

1. Open Microsoft Office Communicator (MOC) 2005 by selecting Start⇨Programs⇨Microsoft Office Communicator 2005.

2. From the main MOC screen, sign in (refer to Figure A-33).

3. Once signed into MOC, a list of added contacts will appear in the main screen (refer to Figure A-34).

4. To block a contact, right-click on a contact and choose Block, as shown in Figure A-44.

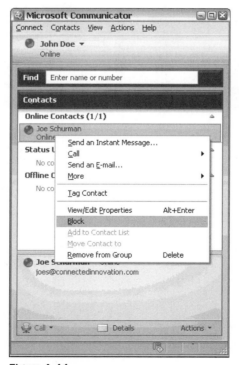

Figure A-44

5. If this is the first time the client has used the Block feature, a message box will appear to confirm the action, as shown in Figure A-45.

Figure A-45

6. To block the contact, click the OK button. To disable the message box from reappearing, select the "Don't show me this message again" checkbox.

Note that the contact is not removed, but the status indicator displays the contact as blocked, as shown in Figure A-46.

Figure A-46

Results:

[Populate results.]

Verifying the Capability to Remove Contacts

The following operations will be performed during this testing procedure.

Dependencies:

❑ Live Communications Server 2005 SP1 has been installed, configured, and activated.

❑ Microsoft Office Communicator 2005 has been installed and configured.

Perform the following tasks:

1. Open Microsoft Office Communicator (MOC) 2005 by selecting Start⇨Programs⇨Microsoft Office Communicator 2005.

2. From the main MOC screen, sign in (refer to Figure A-33).

3. Once signed into MOC, a list of added contacts will appear in the main screen (refer to Figure A-34).

4. To remove a contact, right-click on a contact and choose Remove from Group, as shown in Figure A-47.

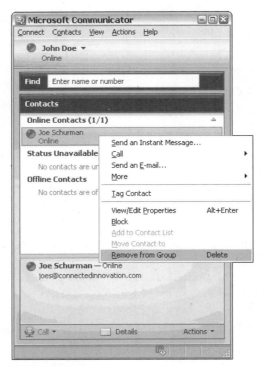

Figure A-47

5. A message box will appear to confirm the action, as shown in Figure A-48. To remove the contact, click the Yes button.

Figure A-48

6. The contact should be removed and will no longer appear in the client's contact list, as shown in Figure A-49.

Figure A-49

Results:

[Populate results.]

Verifying the Capability to Create Groups

The following operations will be performed during this testing procedure.

Dependencies:

❑ Live Communications Server 2005 SP1 is installed, configured, and activated.

❑ Microsoft Office Communicator 2005 is installed and configured.

Perform the following tasks:

1. Open Microsoft Office Communicator (MOC) 2005 by selecting Start⇨Programs⇨ Microsoft Office Communicator 2005.

2. From the main MOC screen, sign in (refer to Figure A-33).

3. Once signed into MOC, the main screen will appear (refer to Figure A-34).

4. To add a group to MOC, choose Contacts⇨Create New Group, as shown in Figure A-50.

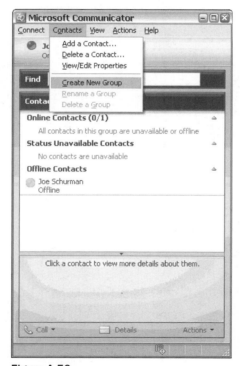

Figure A-50

A new group is created, with the cursor waiting for you to enter the new group name, as shown in Figure A-51.

Figure A-51

5.   Enter the name of the new group (e.g., LCS Team), as shown in Figure A-52. Once the new group has been entered, this test is complete.

Results:

[Populate results.]

Verifying That IM Between Contacts Is Operational

The following operations will be performed during this testing procedure.

Dependencies:

- ❑   Live Communications Server 2005 SP1 has been installed, configured, and activated.
- ❑   Microsoft Office Communicator 2005 has been installed and configured.

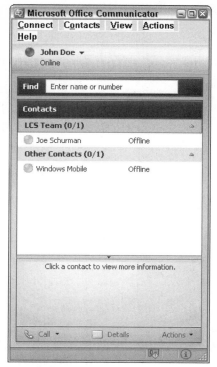

Figure A-52

Perform the following tasks:

1. Open Microsoft Office Communicator (MOC) 2005 by selecting Start⇨Programs⇨Microsoft Office Communicator 2005.

2. From the main MOC screen, sign in (refer to Figure A-33). Once signed into MOC, the main screen will appear.

3. To instant message another contact, right-click on a contact's name and choose Send an Instant Message, as shown in Figure A-53. This opens the Conversation window.

4. Type a message to send to the contact.

5. If the instant message is successful, the contact will receive the message and respond with another instant message (see Figure A-54).

6. If the Instant Messaging session is successful, this test is complete.

Results:

[Populate results.]

Figure A-53

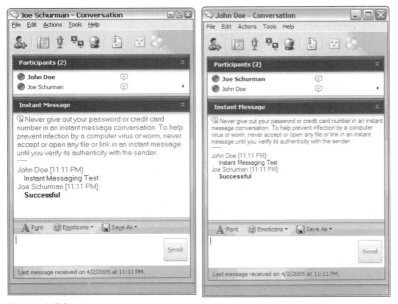

Figure A-54

Verifying That Multi-Party or N-Way Instant Messaging Is Operational

The following operations will be performed during this testing procedure.

Dependencies:

❑ Live Communications Server 2005 SP1 has been installed, configured, and activated.

❑ Microsoft Office Communicator 2005 has been installed and configured.

❑ At least three contacts are signed into Live Communications Server with Microsoft Office Communicator.

Perform the following tasks:

1. Open Microsoft Office Communicator (MOC) 2005 by selecting Start⇨Programs⇨Microsoft Office Communicator 2005.

2. From the main MOC screen, sign in (refer to Figure A-33). The main screen will appear.

3. Select a contact to begin an IM session by clicking on the name. In the Actions menu, select Send an Instant Message (refer to Figure A-53).

4. The Conversation window will open. Within the Conversation window, click on the icon to invite someone to join a conversation, as shown in Figure A-55, or from the Actions menu, select Invite Someone to Join This Conversation.

Figure A-55

5. Select the contact you wish to add to the conversation and then click the OK button.

The selected contact will be added to the conversation and a message will appear within the Conversation window indicating that the contact has been added to the conversation,

6. Send an instant message to each member of the conversation.

7. If each participant in the conversation can see the instant message and respond, then this test is complete.

Results:

[Populate results.]

Verifying the Capability to Tag a Contact

The following operations will be performed during this testing procedure.

Dependencies:

❑ Live Communications Server 2005 SP1 has been installed, configured, and activated.

❑ Microsoft Office Communicator 2005 has been installed and configured.

Perform the following tasks:

1. Open Microsoft Office Communicator (MOC) 2005 by selecting Start⇨Programs⇨Microsoft Office Communicator 2005.

2. From the main MOC screen, sign in (refer to Figure A-33). Once signed into MOC, the main screen will appear.

3. To tag another contact, right-click on a contact's name and choose Tag Contact, as shown in Figure A-56.

4. When a contact is tagged, a message box will continue to appear, indicating the status changes of the contact until the contact has been untagged, as shown in Figure A-57.

5. To untag a contact, right-click on the contact and select Tag again.

Results:

[Populate results.]

Verifying That Presence Is Operational (Online and other Status Settings)

The following operations will be performed during this testing procedure.

Dependencies:

❑ Live Communications Server 2005 SP1 has been installed, configured, and activated.

❑ Microsoft Office Communicator 2005 has been installed and configured.

Figure A-56

Figure A-57

Perform the following tasks:

1. Open Microsoft Office Communicator (MOC) 2005 by selecting Start⇨Programs⇨Microsoft Office Communicator 2005.

2. From the main MOC screen, sign in (refer to Figure A-33).

3. Once signed into MOC, the main screen will appear. Status is displayed by color, with the text of a contact's status adjacent.

4. To verify that status changes function properly, from the main screen, select the arrow button adjacent to your name and change your status to one of the options listed. For this test, choose a different status setting, as shown in Figure A-58.

Figure A-58

5. If your status changes, then this test has completed successfully.

6. To further test presence and status changes, have one of your offline contacts sign in and verify that their status changes from Online to Busy.

Results:

[Populate results.]

Verifying That the Do Not Disturb Feature Is Operational

The following operations will be performed during this testing procedure.

Dependencies:

❑ Live Communications Server 2005 SP1 has been installed, configured, and activated.

❑ Microsoft Office Communicator 2005 has been installed and configured.

Perform the following tasks:

1. Open Microsoft Office Communicator (MOC) 2005 by selecting Start⇨Programs⇨Microsoft Office Communicator 2005.

2. From the main MOC screen, sign in (refer to Figure A-33). Once signed into MOC, the main screen will appear (refer to Figure A-34).

3. The Do Not Disturb feature should automatically turn on if a contact has a window open in full-screen mode. To test this feature, have a contact set their presence status to Do Not Disturb using the menu displayed in Figure A-58 previously. Verify that their status changes to Do Not Disturb, as shown in Figure A-59.

Figure A-59

If the contact status changes to Do Not Disturb without setting the status manually, this test has completed successfully.

Results:

[Populate results.]

Live Communications Server Back-End Testing

The following procedures will test the Live Communications Server Back-End SQL Server(s). These testing procedures include all of the following components:

❑ Verify that the SQL Server databases are populated with data from the LCS Service

    ❑ RTC database

    ❑ Pool table

    ❑ RTCCONFIG database

    ❑ MSFT_SIPEsEmSetting

Verifying That the SQL Server Databases Are Populated with Data from the LCS Service

First, test the RTC database. The following operations will be performed during this testing procedure.

Dependencies:

❑ Live Communications Server 2005 has been installed, configured, and activated.

❑ LCS users have been enabled and have configured their contact lists and personal settings within Microsoft Office Communicator 2005.

❑ The back-end LCS SQL Server 2000 database is online.

❑ A resource with permissions of at least read-only to the RTC database is engaged.

Perform the following tasks:

1. Log on to the primary LCS back-end SQL Server or to a workstation, server, or virtual PC image that has the SQL Server administration tools installed to connect to the server that contains the RTC database.

2. Open the SQL Server Enterprise Manager by selecting Start⇨Programs⇨Microsoft SQL Server, and then select Enterprise Manager.

3. The SQL Server Enterprise Manager management console will appear, as shown in Figure A-60.

4. Expand the Microsoft SQL Servers tree to expose the RTC database, as shown in Figure A-61.

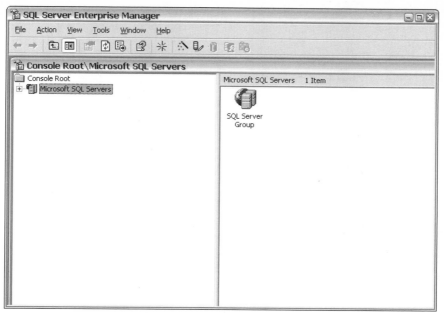

Figure A-60

Figure A-61

5. Expand the RTC node to view the tables for the RTC database. Select the Tables node to view the tables within the RTC database in the right pane of the management console, as shown in Figure A-62.

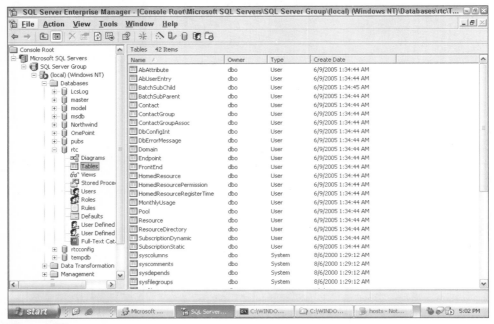

Figure A-62

6. Open the Pool table to see whether the correct pool entries have been made. To view the data within the Pool table, right-click on the Pool table and select Open Table⇨Return All Rows, as shown in Figure A-63.

7. The query result should display a list of LCS pools that are supported by this LCS back-end database server, as shown in Figure A-64.

If the list is correct, this test has completed successfully.

Results:

[Populate results.]

Now you test the RTCCONFIG database. The following operations will be performed during this testing procedure.

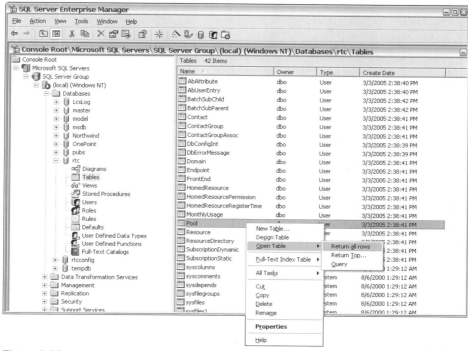

Figure A-63

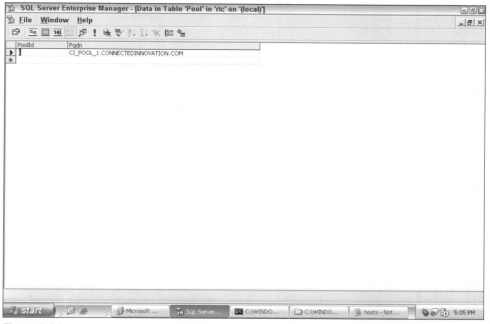

Figure A-64

Dependencies:

- ❑ Live Communications Server 2005 has been installed, configured, and activated.
- ❑ LCS users have been enabled and have configured their contact lists and personal settings within Microsoft Office Communicator 2005.
- ❑ The back-end LCS SQL Server 2000 database is online.
- ❑ A resource with permissions of at least read-only to the RTCConfig database is engaged.
- ❑ Live Communications Server 2005 administration tools have been installed.

Perform the following tasks:

1. Log on to the primary LCS back-end SQL Server or to a workstation, server, or virtual PC image that has the SQL Server administration tools installed to connect to the server that contains the RTCConfig database.

2. Open the SQL Server Enterprise Manager by selecting Start➪Programs➪Microsoft SQL Server, and then select Enterprise Manager. The SQL Server Enterprise Manager management console will appear (refer to Figure A-60).

3. Expand the Microsoft SQL Servers tree to expose the RTCConfig database, as shown in Figure A-65.

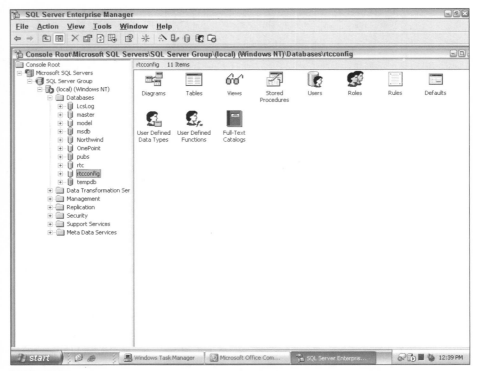

Figure A-65

4. Expand the RTCConfig node to view the tables for the `RTCConfig` database, as shown in Figure A-66.

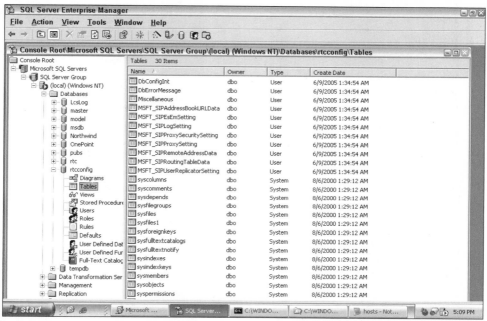

Figure A-66

5. Open the `MSFT_SIPEsEmSetting` table to see whether the maximum number of contacts per user number matches what is listed in the LCS pool properties of the LCS Management console. To view the data within the `MSFT_SIPEsEmSetting` table, right-click on the `MSFT_SIPEsEmSetting` table and select Open Table⮕ Return All Rows, as shown in Figure A-67.

The query result should display the maximum contacts per user that has been set in the LCS pool properties within the LCS Management console, as shown in Figure A-68.

6. Match this number to the number set in the LCS pool properties within the LCS Management console.

To validate the LCS pool configuration, access a workstation, server, or virtual PC that has access to run the Live Communications Server MMC management console with RTCDomainServerAdmins or RTCDomainUserAdmins permissions.

When the active LCS pool is selected, its summarized status is displayed in the data pane of the management console.

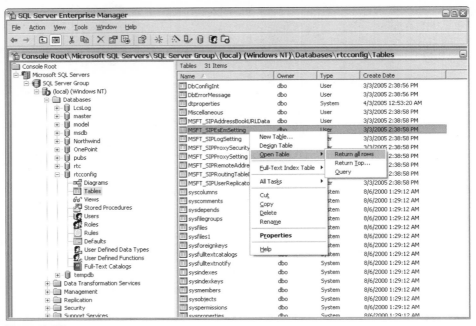

Figure A-67

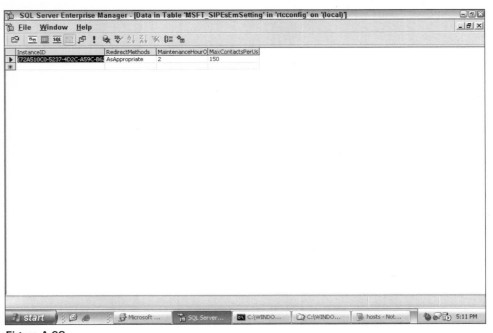

Figure A-68

7. To verify that the maximum number of contacts per user listed in the MSFT_SIPEsEmSetting table matches the number listed in the LCS pool properties, right-click on the Pool icon within the topology pane and choose Properties, as shown in Figure A-69. The numbers should match those shown in Figure A-68.

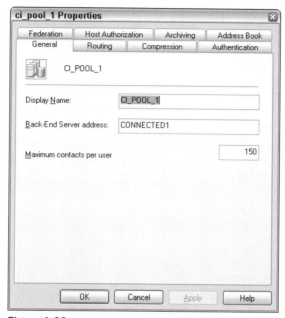

Figure A-69

8. If these numbers match, this test has completed successfully.

Results:

[Populate results.]

B

Live Communications Server and Communicator Design

The Live Communications Server and Communicator Design Guide serves as a template for your use when deploying Live Communications Server. The purpose of this design guide is to give you an understanding of what should be delivered in terms of documentation for the deployment record. When deploying a technical application or infrastructure, it is important to make a record of the overall design and configuration of the environment. This is good practice for every deployment you take part in, teaching you professionalism and completeness, as I have learned over the years. This design guide should be updated from testing through production phases of a project and should be given as a deliverable for each engagement. The digital version of this document can be found on the companion CD included with the book. Please use this template to your liking. It is sure to impress your project team, as well as save a tremendous amount of time.

Test Domain Environment

The design documented within this section represents the Live Communications Server deployment within the Test Domain environment.

Live Communications Server Active Directory Design

Assuming that Live Communications Server has been deployed in Test Domain at the root level and is configured as a central forest, the following table outlines the Active Directory schema changes and Live Communications Server preparation tasks that have been completed:

Tasks	Forest/Domain	Software Version
LCS Prep Schema	TEST DOMAIN.COM	Live Communications Server 2005 SP1 Beta
LCS Prep Forest	TEST DOMAIN.COM	Live Communications Server 2005 SP1 Beta
LCS Prep Domain	CORP.TEST DOMAIN.COM	Live Communications Server 2005 SP1 Beta
LCS Domain Add	CORP.TEST DOMAIN.COM	Live Communications Server 2005 SP1 Beta

Figure B-1 depicts the Live Communications Server Active Directory architecture in Test Domain.

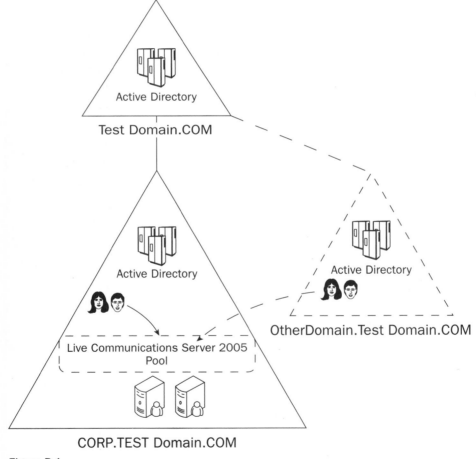

Figure B-1

Live Communications Server Environment

The following information details the design of the LCS deployment in the Test Domain environment.

Live Communications Server Forest

The following table details the configuration settings for the LCS forest settings within the TEST DOMAIN.COM forest:

LCS Forest	Configuration
TEST DOMAIN.COM	**Supported SIP Domains** (allows all SIP URIs): TEST DOMAIN.COM **User Settings:** Maximum subscribers per user = 200 Maximum devices per user = 1

Live Communications Server Pools

The following table details the configuration settings for the LCS pool settings within the CORP.TEST DOMAIN.COM domain:

LCS Pool FQDN	Configuration
LCS.CORP.TEST DOMAIN.COM	Server-to-server compression (1024) Client-to-server compression NTLM authentication Address book URL: HTTP://SERVERNAME/LCSABS 150 contacts per user No archiving
LCS2.CORP.TEST DOMAIN.COM	Server-to-server compression (1024) Client-to-server compression NTLM authentication Address book URL: HTTP://SERVERNAME/LCSABS 150 contacts per user Archiving enabled

Live Communications Server Pool Servers

Within the Test Domain LCS environment are two LCS pool servers. The following table outlines each pool server and its configuration:

Pool FQDN/Server FQDN/IP Address	Configuration
LCS.CORP.TEST DOMAIN.COM SERVERNAME.TEST DOMAIN.COM Enter IP address here	Microsoft Live Communications Server 2005 Service Pack 1 MTLS port 5061 TCP port 5060 Server Auth EKU Certificate (CN=POOL1 FQDN) Flat file logging–level 2 Windows Server 2003, Enterprise Edition GAP Build LCS Address Book Service running IM URL Filter turned off Remote Registry Service running Service Account = LCSSAPPSVC
LCS2.CORP.TEST DOMAIN.COM SERVERNAME.TEST DOMAIN.COM Enter IP address here	Microsoft Live Communications Server 2005 Service Pack 1 MTLS port 5061 TCP port 5060 Server Auth EKU Certificate (CN=POOL2 FQDN) Flat file logging–level 2 Windows Server 2003, Enterprise Edition GAP Build MSMQ enabled (Archiving) IM URL Filter turned off Remote Registry Service running Service account = LCSSAPPSVC

Live Communications Server Back-End Server

The Test Domain LCS environment consists of one back-end LCS server supporting both LCS pools. The following table outlines the LCS back-end server and its configuration:

LCS Back-End Server FQDN/IP Address	Configuration
SERVERNAME.TEST DOMAIN.COM Enter IP address here	Microsoft SQL Server 2000 with Service Pack 4 SQL Server 2000 Build Default instance supports LCS Instance ID: LCS2, supports LCS2 Service account: LCSSQLSVC

Live Communications Server Address Book Service

The LCS Address Book Service has been deployed via HTTP for Test Domain client access, and the service is running on the primary LCS pool server. The following tables outline the LCS Address Book Service and its configuration:

LCS Address Book Service FQDN/IP	Configuration
SERVERNAME.TEST DOMAIN.COM Enter IP address here	LCS ABS HTTP URL: `HTTP://SERVERNAME/LCSABS` Service account: `LCSABSSVC`
LCS Address Book IIS Server FQDN/IP	**Configuration**
SERVERNAME.TEST DOMAIN.COM Enter IP address here	IIS virtual directory: `HTTP://SERVERNAME/LCSABS` ABS file server location: `D:\LCSABS` Service account: `LCSABSSVC`

Test Domain DNS

DNS host records have been applied to resolve the addresses of the LCS pools and to enable client connectivity for Microsoft Office Communicator clients. The following table outlines the DNS entries and their configuration:

DNS Host A Records	IP Address/Function
LCS.CORP.TEST DOMAIN.COM	Enter IP address here/POOL 1 server
LCS2.CORP.TEST DOMAIN.COM	Enter IP address here/POOL 2 server

Microsoft Office Communicator Clients

The following information describes the Test Domain LCS client configuration. All Test Domain clients are connecting to LCS using Microsoft Office Communicator 2005. The following table depicts the Communicator client configuration:

Communicator Client Version	Configuration
Microsoft Office Communicator 2005 RTM	Manual configuration Enabled both TLS and TCP for various TOA users TLS uses Test Domain.com root CA Pool server: `LCS.CORP.TEST DOMAIN.COM` Pool2 users connect through LCS address URL entry accepted (LCS IM URL Filter turned off) Enabled Features: Instant Messaging File transfer Application sharing/whiteboard Remote assistance

Live Communications Server Detailed Architecture

Figure B-2 shows the current LCS architecture for the Test Domain environment.

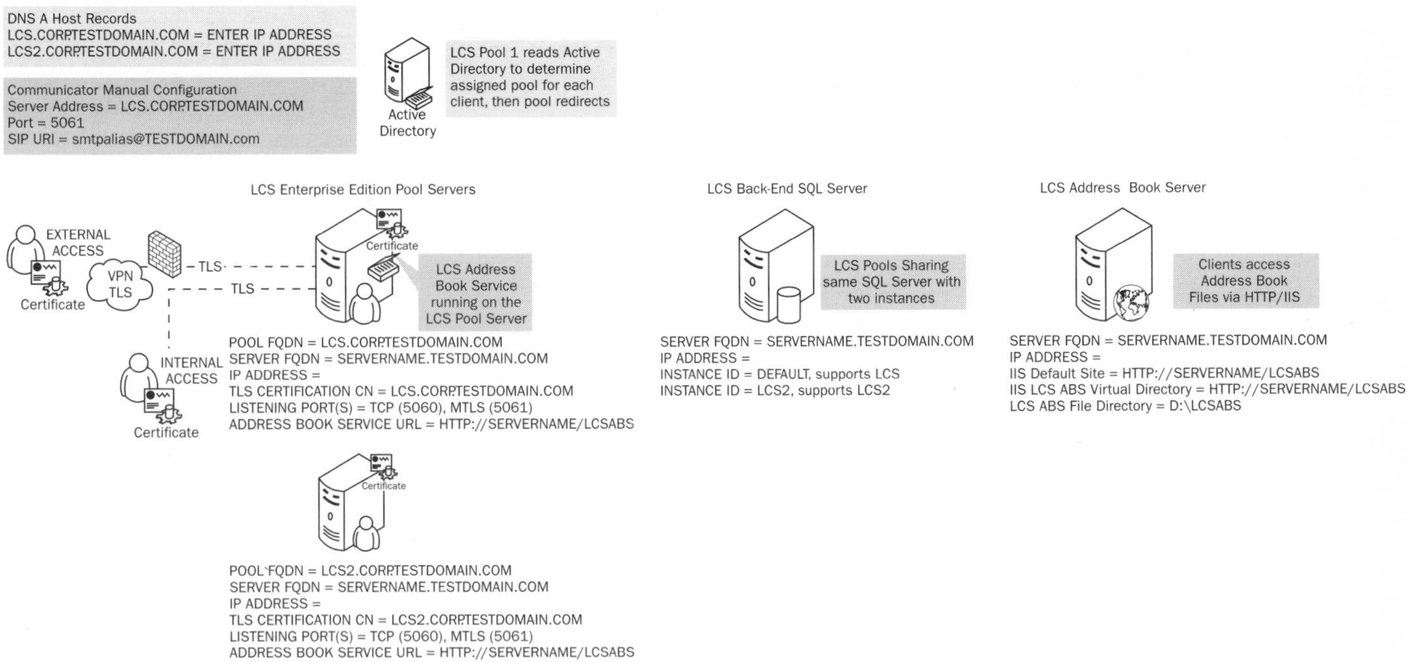

DNS A Host Records
LCS.CORPTESTDOMAIN.COM = ENTER IP ADDRESS
LCS2.CORPTESTDOMAIN.COM = ENTER IP ADDRESS

Communicator Manual Configuration
Server Address = LCS.CORPTESTDOMAIN.COM
Port = 5061
SIP URI = smtpalias@TESTDOMAIN.com

LCS Pool 1 reads Active
Directory to determine
assigned pool for each
client, then pool redirects

Active
Directory

LCS Enterprise Edition Pool Servers

LCS Address
Book Service
running on the
LCS Pool Server

Certificate

EXTERNAL
ACCESS

VPN
TLS

—TLS—

—TLS—

Certificate

INTERNAL
ACCESS

Certificate

POOL FQDN = LCS.CORPTESTDOMAIN.COM
SERVER FQDN = SERVERNAME.TESTDOMAIN.COM
IP ADDRESS =
TLS CERTIFICATION CN = LCS.CORPTESTDOMAIN.COM
LISTENING PORT(S) = TCP (5060), MTLS (5061)
ADDRESS BOOK SERVICE URL = HTTP://SERVERNAME/LCSABS

Certificate

POOL FQDN = LCS2.CORPTESTDOMAIN.COM
SERVER FQDN = SERVERNAME.TESTDOMAIN.COM
IP ADDRESS =
TLS CERTIFICATION CN = LCS2.CORPTESTDOMAIN.COM
LISTENING PORT(S) = TCP (5060), MTLS (5061)
ADDRESS BOOK SERVICE URL = HTTP://SERVERNAME/LCSABS

LCS Back-End SQL Server

LCS Pools Sharing
same SQL Server with
two instances

SERVER FQDN = SERVERNAME.TESTDOMAIN.COM
IP ADDRESS =
INSTANCE ID = DEFAULT, supports LCS
INSTANCE ID = LCS2, supports LCS2

LCS Address Book Server

Clients access
Address Book
Files via HTTP/IIS

SERVER FQDN = SERVERNAME.TESTDOMAIN.COM
IP ADDRESS =
IIS Default Site = HTTP://SERVERNAME/LCSABS
IIS LCS ABS Virtual Directory = HTTP://SERVERNAME/LCSABS
LCS ABS File Directory = D:\LCSABS

Figure B-2

Pre-Production Environment

The design documented within this section represents the Live Communications Server deployment within the pre-production environment.

Live Communications Server Active Directory Design

Live Communications Server has been deployed in pre-production at the root level and is configured as a central forest. The following table outlines the Active Directory schema changes and Live Communications Server preparation tasks that have been completed:

Tasks	Forest/Domain	Software Version
LCS Prep Schema	PRE-PRODUCTION DOMAIN.COM	Live Communications Server 2005 SP1 RTM
LCS Prep Forest	PRE-PRODUCTION DOMAIN.COM	Live Communications Server 2005 SP1 RTM
LCS Prep Domain	CORP2.PRE-PRODUCTION DOMAIN.COM ASIA2.PRE-PRODUCTION DOMAIN.COM EMEA2.PRE-PRODUCTION DOMAIN.COM LATAM2.PRE-PRODUCTION DOMAIN.COM	Live Communications Server 2005 SP1 RTM
LCS Domain Add	CORP2.PRE-PRODUCTION DOMAIN.COM	Live Communications Server 2005 SP1 RTM

Figure B-3 shows the Live Communications Server Active Directory architecture in pre-production.

Live Communications Server Environment

The following information details the design of the LCS deployment in the pre-production environment.

Live Communications Server Forest

The following table outlines the configuration settings for the LCS forest settings within the PRE-PRODUCTION DOMAIN.COM forest:

LCS Forest	Configuration
PRE-PRODUCTION DOMAIN.COM	Supported SIP domains: * (allows all SIP URIs) User Settings: Maximum subscribers per user = 200 Maximum devices per user = 1

Live Communications Server Pools

The following table details the configuration settings for the LCS pool settings within the CORP2 .PRE-PRODUCTION DOMAIN.COM domain:

LCS Pool FQDN	Configuration
LCS.CORP2.PRE-PRODUCTION DOMAIN.COM	Server-to-server compression (1024) Client-to-server compression NTLM authentication Address book URL: `HTTP://SERVERNAME/LCSABS` 150 contacts per user No archiving
LCS2.CORP2.PRE-PRODUCTION DOMAIN.COM	Server-to-server compression (1024) Client-to-server compression NTLM authentication Address book URL: `HTTP://SERVERNAME/LCSABS` 150 contacts per user Archiving enabled

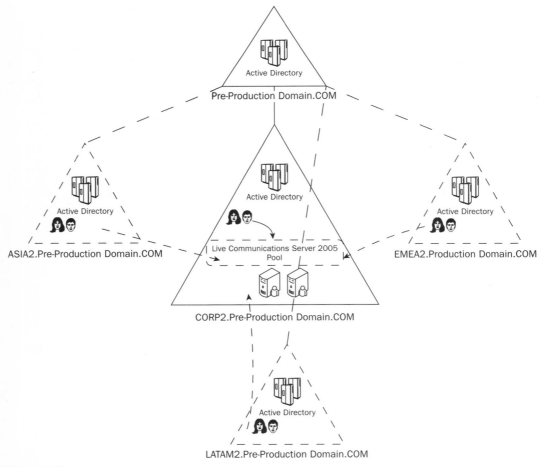

Figure B-3

Live Communications Server Pool Servers

There are three LCS pool servers within the pre-production LCS environment. The following table outlines each pool server and its configuration:

Pool FQDN/Server FQDN/IP Address	Configuration
LCS.CORP2.PRE-PRODUCTION DOMAIN.COM CR2CLTLCS01.PRE-PRODUCTION DOMAIN.COM Enter IP address here	Microsoft Live Communications Server 2005 Service Pack 1 MTLS port 5061 Server Auth EKU Certificate (CN=POOL1 FQDN) Flat file logging–level 2 Windows Server 2003, Enterprise Edition GAP Build LCS Address Book service running IM URL Filter turned off Remote Registry Service running Service account: LCSSAPPSVC
LCS.CORP2.PRE-PRODUCTION DOMAIN.COM CR2CLTLCS02.PRE-PRODUCTION DOMAIN.COM Enter IP address here	Microsoft Live Communications Server 2005 Service Pack 1 MTLS port 5061 Server Auth EKU Certificate (CN=POOL1 FQDN) Flat file logging–level 2 Windows Server 2003, Enterprise Edition GAP Build IM URL Filter turned off Remote Registry Service running Service Account: LCSSAPPSVC
LCS2.CORP2.PRE-PRODUCTION DOMAIN.COM CR2CLTLCS03.PRE-PRODUCTION DOMAIN.COM Enter IP address here	Microsoft Live Communications Server 2005 Service Pack 1 MTLS port 5061 Server Auth EKU Certificate (CN=POOL2 FQDN) Flat file logging–level 2 Windows Server 2003, Enterprise Edition GAP Build LCS Address Book Service running IM URL Filter turned off Service account: LCSSAPPSVCGAP Build Remote Registry Service running Service account: LCSSAPPSVC

Live Communications Server Back-End Server

The pre-production LCS environment consists of one back-end LCS server supporting both LCS pools. The following table outlines the LCS back-end server and its configuration:

LCS Back-End Server FQDN/IP Address	Configuration

SERVERNAME.PRE-PRODUCTION DOMAIN.COM
Enter IP address here
	Microsoft SQL Server 2000 with Service Pack 4
	SQL Server 2000 Build
	Default instance supports LCS
	Instance ID: LCS2, supports LCS2
	Service account: `LCSSQLSVC`
	Default instance data log drive: `E:\MSSQL\DATA\`
	Default instance transaction log drive:
	`E:\MSSQL\DATA\`
	LCSPOOL2 instance data log drive:
	`E:\MSSQL$LCSPOOL2\DATA\`
	LCSPOOL2 instance transaction log drive:
	`E:\MSSQL$LCSPOOL2\DATA\`

Live Communications Server Address Book Service

The LCS Address Book Service has been deployed via HTTP for pre-production client access, and the service is running on the primary LCS pool server. The following table outlines the LCS Address Book Service and its configuration:

LCS Address Book Service FQDN/IP	Configuration
SERVERNAME.PRE-PRODUCTION DOMAIN.COM Enter IP address here	LCS ABS HTTP URL: HTTP://SERVERNAME/LCSABS Service account: `LCSABSSVC`

LCS Address Book IIS Server FQDN/IP	Configuration
SERVERNAME.PRE-PRODUCTION DOMAIN.COM Enter IP address here	IIS virtual directory: `HTTP://SERVERNAME/LCSABS` ABS file server location: `D:\LCSABS` Service account: `LCSABSSVC`

Microsoft Operations Manager Server

Microsoft Operations Manager (MOM) Server 2005 will be monitoring the LCS pool server environment. The following table outlines the LCS MOM server and its configuration:

MOM Server FQDN/IP Address	Configuration
SERVERNAME.PRE-PRODUCTION DOMAIN.COM Enter IP address here	Microsoft Operation Manager 2005 Live Communications Server 2005 Pack Service account: `LCSMOMSVC`

BIG-IP Load Balancer

BIG-IP will be deployed in pre-production as the load-balancing solution for the LCS pool servers in LCS. The following table outlines the BIG-IP load balancer and its configuration:

BIG-IP VIP FQDN/IP	Servers
LCS.CORP2.PRE-PRODUCTION DOMAIN.COM	SERVERNAME: Enter IP address SERVERNAME: Enter IP address

Pre-Production DNS

DNS host records have been applied to resolve the addresses of the LCS pools and the BIG-IP Load Balancer to enable client connectivity for Microsoft Office Communicator clients. The following table outlines the DNS entries and their configuration:

DNS Host A Records	IP Address/Function
LCS.CORP2.PRE-PRODUCTION DOMAIN.COM	IP address of the BIG-IP Load Balancer
LCS2.CORP2.PRE-PRODUCTION DOMAIN.COM	Enter IP address here/Pool 2 Server (single server, no LB)

Microsoft Office Communicator Clients

The following information describes the pre-production LCS client configuration. All pre-production clients are connecting to LCS using Microsoft Office Communicator 2005. The following table depicts the Communicator client configuration:

Communicator Client Version	Configuration
Microsoft Office Communicator 2005 RTM	Manual configuration Pool server: LCS.CORP2.PRE-PRODUCTION DOMAIN.COM TLS Clients use CORP2 root CA Pool2 users connect through LCS address URL entry accepted (LCS IM URL Filter turned off) Enabled Features: Instant Messaging File transfer Application sharing/whiteboard Remote assistance

Live Communications Server Detailed Architecture

The diagram shown in Figure B-4 depicts the current LCS architecture for the pre-production environment.

The architecture displayed in Figure B-4 is an example of a detailed production architecture for an LCS deployment. Please edit these Microsoft Office Visio figures to match the production architecture you are deploying.

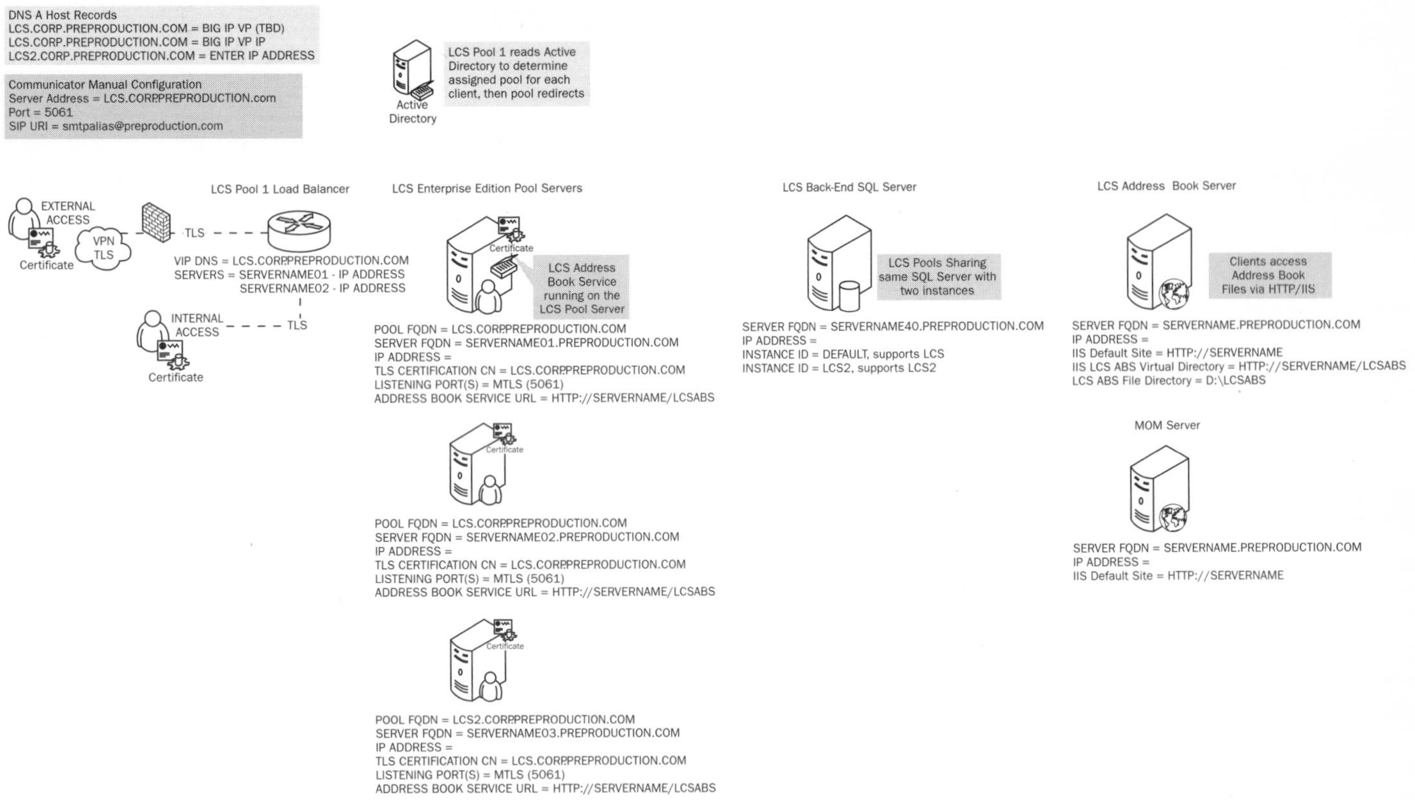

DNS A Host Records
LCS.CORP.PREPRODUCTION.COM = BIG IP VP (TBD)
LCS.CORP.PREPRODUCTION.COM = BIG IP VP IP
LCS2.CORP.PREPRODUCTION.COM = ENTER IP ADDRESS

Communicator Manual Configuration
Server Address = LCS.CORPPREPRODUCTION.com
Port = 5061
SIP URI = smtpalias@preproduction.com

Active Directory
LCS Pool 1 reads Active Directory to determine assigned pool for each client, then pool redirects

LCS Pool 1 Load Balancer

EXTERNAL ACCESS
VPN TLS
Certificate
— TLS —

VIP DNS = LCS.CORPPREPRODUCTION.COM
SERVERS = SERVERNAME01 - IP ADDRESS
SERVERNAME02 - IP ADDRESS

INTERNAL ACCESS
Certificate
— — — TLS

LCS Enterprise Edition Pool Servers

Certificate
LCS Address Book Service running on the LCS Pool Server

POOL FQDN = LCS.CORPPREPRODUCTION.COM
SERVER FQDN = SERVERNAME01.PREPRODUCTION.COM
IP ADDRESS =
TLS CERTIFICATION CN = LCS.CORPPREPRODUCTION.COM
LISTENING PORT(S) = MTLS (5061)
ADDRESS BOOK SERVICE URL = HTTP://SERVERNAME/LCSABS

Certificate
POOL FQDN = LCS.CORPPREPRODUCTION.COM
SERVER FQDN = SERVERNAME02.PREPRODUCTION.COM
IP ADDRESS =
TLS CERTIFICATION CN = LCS.CORPPREPRODUCTION.COM
LISTENING PORT(S) = MTLS (5061)
ADDRESS BOOK SERVICE URL = HTTP://SERVERNAME/LCSABS

Certificate
POOL FQDN = LCS2.CORPPREPRODUCTION.COM
SERVER FQDN = SERVERNAME03.PREPRODUCTION.COM
IP ADDRESS =
TLS CERTIFICATION CN = LCS.CORPPREPRODUCTION.COM
LISTENING PORT(S) = MTLS (5061)
ADDRESS BOOK SERVICE URL = HTTP://SERVERNAME/LCSABS

LCS Back-End SQL Server

LCS Pools Sharing same SQL Server with two instances

SERVER FQDN = SERVERNAME40.PREPRODUCTION.COM
IP ADDRESS =
INSTANCE ID = DEFAULT, supports LCS
INSTANCE ID = LCS2, supports LCS2

LCS Address Book Server

Clients access Address Book Files via HTTP/IIS

SERVER FQDN = SERVERNAME.PREPRODUCTION.COM
IP ADDRESS =
IIS Default Site = HTTP://SERVERNAME
IIS LCS ABS Virtual Directory = HTTP://SERVERNAME/LCSABS
LCS ABS File Directory = D:\LCSABS

MOM Server

SERVER FQDN = SERVERNAME.PREPRODUCTION.COM
IP ADDRESS =
IIS Default Site = HTTP://SERVERNAME

Figure B-4

Index

Index

P